The Frugal CISO

Using Innovation and
Smart Approaches to Maximize
Your Security Posture

OTHER INFORMATION SECURITY BOOKS FROM AUERBACH

Advances in Biometrics for Secure Human Authentication and Recognition
Dakshina Ranjan Kisku, Phalguni Gupta, and Jamuna Kanta Sing (Editors)
ISBN 978-1-4665-8242-2

Anonymous Communication Networks: Protecting Privacy on the Web
Kun Peng
ISBN 978-1-4398-8157-6

Automatic Defense Against Zero-day Polymorphic Worms in Communication Networks
Mohssen Mohammed and Al-Sakib Khan Pathan
ISBN 978-1-4665-5727-7

Conflict and Cooperation in Cyberspace: The Challenge to National Security
Panayotis A. Yannakogeorgos and Adam B. Lowther
ISBN 978-1-4665-9201-8

Conducting Network Penetration and Espionage in a Global Environment
Bruce Middleton
ISBN 978-1-4822-0647-0

Core Software Security: Security at the Source
James Ransome and Anmol Misra
ISBN 978-1-4665-6095-6

Data Governance: Creating Value from Information Assets
Neera Bhansali
ISBN 978-1-4398-7913-9

Developing and Securing the Cloud
Bhavani Thuraisingham
ISBN 978-1-4398-6291-9

Effective Surveillance for Homeland Security: Balancing Technology and Social Issues
Francesco Flammini, Roberto Setola, and Giorgio Franceschetti
ISBN 978-1-4398-8324-2

Enterprise Architecture and Information Assurance: Developing a Secure Foundation
James A. Scholz
ISBN 978-1-4398-4159-4

Information Security Fundamentals, Second Edition
Thomas R. Peltier
ISBN 978-1-4398-1062-0

Intrusion Detection in Wireless Ad-Hoc Networks
Nabendu Chaki and Rituparna Chakiv
ISBN 978-1-4665-1565-9

Intrusion Detection Networks: A Key to Collaborative Security
Carol Fung and Raouf Boutaba
ISBN 978-1-4665-6412-1

Iris Biometric Model for Secured Network Access
Franjieh El Khoury
ISBN 978-1-4665-0213-0

Managing Risk and Security in Outsourcing IT Services: Onshore, Offshore and the Cloud
Frank Siepmann
ISBN 978-1-4398-7909-2

PCI Compliance: The Definitive Guide
Abhay Bhargav
ISBN 978-1-4398-8740-0

Responsive Security: Be Ready to Be Secure
Meng-Chow Kang
ISBN 978-1-4665-8430-3

Security and Privacy in Smart Grids
Yang Xiao
ISBN 978-1-4398-7783-8

Security for Service Oriented Architectures
Walter Williams
ISBN 978-1-4665-8402-0

Security without Obscurity: A Guide to Confidentiality, Authentication, and Integrity
J.J. Stapleton
ISBN 978-1-4665-9214-8

The Complete Book of Data Anonymization: From Planning to Implementation
Balaji Raghunathan
ISBN 978-1-4398-7730-2

The Frugal CISO: Using Innovation and Smart Approaches to Maximize Your Security Posture
Kerry Ann Anderson
ISBN 978-1-4822-2007-0

The State of the Art in Intrusion Prevention and Detection
Al-Sakib Khan Pathan
ISBN 978-1-4822-0351-6

Trade Secret Theft, Industrial Espionage, and the China Threat
Carl Roper
ISBN 978-1-4398-9938-0

AUERBACH PUBLICATIONS
www.auerbach-publications.com • To Order Call: 1-800-272-7737 • E-mail: orders@crcpress.com

The Frugal CISO

Using Innovation and Smart Approaches to Maximize Your Security Posture

Kerry Ann Anderson

CRC Press
Taylor & Francis Group
Boca Raton   London   New York

CRC Press is an imprint of the
Taylor & Francis Group, an **Informa** business

AN AUERBACH BOOK

CRC Press
Taylor & Francis Group
6000 Broken Sound Parkway NW, Suite 300
Boca Raton, FL 33487-2742

© 2014 by Taylor & Francis Group, LLC
CRC Press is an imprint of Taylor & Francis Group, an Informa business

No claim to original U.S. Government works

Printed on acid-free paper
Version Date: 20140324

International Standard Book Number-13: 978-1-4822-2007-0 (Paperback)

Visit the Taylor & Francis Web site at
http://www.taylorandfrancis.com

and the CRC Press Web site at
http://www.crcpress.com

This book is dedicated to my mother, the late Jane W. Anderson. Jane was a mother, grandmother, and educator. She served as an inspiration to her students, especially the women, whom she taught that a dream delayed is not a dream denied, even if you start later in life. My mother used to frequently quote the movie "Flashdance," "When you give up your dream, you die." She always encouraged others to follow their dreams. Her dream was for me to write this book.

Contents

About the Author

Kerry A. Anderson, CISA, CISM, CRISC, CGEIT, CISSP, ISSMP, ISSAP, CSSLP, CFE, CCSK, MBA, MSCIS, MSIA, is an information security and records management consultant with more than fifteen years of experience in information security and IT across a variety of industries. She has worked in information security, application development, financial systems operations, network administration, IT audit, records management, business contingency planning, and graduate-program instruction. She can be reached at *kerry.ann.anderson@verizon.net.*

Introduction

Frugal Information Security Practitioner

Frugality is a hot trend since the economic downturn began in late 2007 and remains equally cool during the long financial recovery. Evidence of this trend is visible in popular television programming, such as *Extreme Couponing*[1] and *Extreme Cheapskates*,[2] and various books and magazine articles. The basic theme of this frugality movement is that with careful spending, an individual or family can live well and still stay within their budget, and perhaps put away some money in a savings account.

Many information security budgets have remained flat or have declined between 2007 and 2012,[3] with occasional boosts in funding to manage specific compliance requirements, such as the Payment Card Industry Data Security Standard (PCI-DSS). While the majority of organizations predicted modest increases of 5% to 10%[4] in 2013, and project an average budget increase of 4.06 percent in 2014,* budgets will likely remain tight for some time to come. The popular mantras will likely remain "do more with less"[5] and "work smarter, not harder."[6]

Since the beginning of my career in information technology, I have experienced a variety of economic downturns and their impact on the

---

* http://www.tripwire.com/state-of-security/featured/security-budget-research-roundup-cios-cisos/

companies for which I worked. The reality is that tight budgets have been generally the rule rather than the exception in business, especially over the last two decades. I have also had experience supporting products in the last few years of their life cycle. The basic reality is that management wants to limit resources devoted to the maintenance and support of applications heading for decommissioning. This experience in the shallow end of the budget pool gave me an opportunity to hone my frugality strategy, which minimized the effect of limiting resources and still provided adequate (and sometimes excellent) operational effectiveness. The frugality techniques I learned in IT have been easily transferable to the information security function because they address some of the same basic issues and resource drains experienced in operational environments. These tactical approaches use a combination of innovation and a long, hard look at core requirements to accomplish specific functions. They will not always make you popular with all involved, but neither will they create a working environment resembling a *Death March*[7] scenario. Often, these techniques will involve making hard choices, tough decisions, and getting real with staff and clients alike.

Reduce Complexity

One of the greatest enemies of security and cost management is complexity. Complexity can occur because of a number of factors, such as personal preferences, technical biases, desire to remain on technology's leading edge, and functional requirements. Every variation in software, operating systems, and hardware incurs a cost in terms of supporting and maintaining a secure environment. The cost of software maintenance has risen to a whopping 90% of the total lifetime cost of software, and each layer of software complexity puts stress on IT budgets.[8] Complexity creates the potential for undesirable or unexpected interactions between technologies. One approach is to reduce the number of technology options. Some areas for technology reduction and simplification include

1. Reduce the overall software inventory.
2. Reduce the number of components used to build applications.
3. Reduce the number of operating systems (OS) and OS versions supported or in use.

4. Standardize configurations based on business, technical, and security requirements.

Reduction in complexity decreases the overall number of things for which we need to manage security. Software portfolios tend to bloat when they are not actively managed. Frequently, the only impetus to retire software is either a termination of a licensing agreement or some other substantial costly penalty, such as Y2K, which required costly modifications for software going forward into the new millennium. While keeping older software is viewed as having no costs associated with it, older software can create hidden costs and insecurities. Older applications, sometimes called *legacy software*, may suffer from *resiliency degradation*,[9] in which the capability of software to resist attacks degrades over time due to changes in technology, threats, and staffing. Older versions of software may not permit upgrading or patching to fix known vulnerabilities. Older hardware and software may be susceptible to even low-velocity denial-of-service (DoS) attacks or cannot resist most attempts at penetration testing without creating production outages.[10] At its worst, legacy software can result in exploitable vulnerabilities or failure to meet compliance requirements. Older versions of software can create costs by requiring additional testing of security patches to certify compatibility with planned upgrades.

Many applications suffer from overdesign resulting from a plethora of rarely used functionality or someone's desire to *build the resume* (BTR)[11] by using a "cool" technology. As an application support manager in the late 1990s, I frequently managed software applications that resembled school projects because they used multiple nonstandard or *bleeding-edge[12]* technology that was not reliable and was expensive to support. These applications often required excessive support and often devolved into kludges to deal with constant production problems and requests for new functionality. Standardizing components and operating environments reduces the burden of testing security patches for compatibility with other applications and operating environments. It also prevents an all-too-common scenario in which critical applications develop an operational dependency on obsolete components without an upgrade path. The day of reckoning generally arrives after failure to pass a compliance audit due to vulnerabilities in underlying obsolete components or the occurrence of an actual breach.

Reduce Data Storage

Data tends to expand to use the amount of storage space available to stow it. In addition to the innate tendency to hoard data because we may need it, trends like Big Data are fueling the requirements to hold on to large amounts of data. Data may hang around because there is no centralized inventory of electronic records. Many official *records hold*[13] requirements occur due to compliance or potential legal actions and are rarely rescinded after the precipitating events are resolved. While storage costs have fallen over the years, the costs of managing data remain high. According to a 2011 survey by the Association for Information and Image Management (AIIM), legal costs are 25% higher than they could be if organizations followed best practices in records management, including the appropriate disposal of electronic records past their scheduled retention date.[14] Due to the 2006 Changes to the Federal Laws of Evidence,[15] excessive data retention can escalate legal costs associated with eDiscovery. One of the most significant risks associated with excessive data retention is protection of sensitive information, especially personally identifiable information (PII). The retention of records containing unnecessary sensitive information, especially PII, can magnify the impact of a data breach to catastrophic proportions, such as the case of the TJX breach in 2007, as well as the Target data breach of 2013.[16] In addition to the structured storage of records containing PII, unstructured storage of PII is a significant threat. The solution to reducing the impact of data breaches is to reduce the overall storage of records, especially records containing PII or similar sensitive information. By collaborating with the records and information management (RIM) area, excessive retention of information can be reduced by enforcement of records disposal schedules and current inventories of electronic records. Data leakage prevention (DLP) tools can identify and inventory unstructured data storage containing PII and facilitate either its disposal or encryption based upon business requirements. The less information an organization stores, the lower the amount of resources required to protect it. A collateral benefit is that a data reduction project can pay for itself in the cost savings generated by freeing up storage space.

Reduce the Number of Security Solutions

Proliferation of security tools and solutions may be a symptom of the early stages of information security that focus primarily on compliance objectives. This is similar to Contagion (Stage 2)[17] in Richard L. Nolan's "The Stages of Growth Model for IT Systems." I utilized Nolan's model to develop my own maturity model for information security maturity. The Contagion stage is characterized by a "Silver Bullet" mindset characterized by rapid tool acquisition, development, and deployment. Much of the tool deployment occurs in separate silos targeting specific business functions or compliance requirements. This can result in the purchases of multiple tools with the same functionality; for example, several secure email solutions for external email. The emphasis is on tools acquisition and rapid deployment. However, there may be limited acceptance and use of tools because of deficient implementation and lack of adequate user training. Rather than trying to correct issues with a security product, the hunt begins for the "next big thing," which is purchased, and the cycle repeats. In addition to the total initial costs of all purchases, there are many hidden costs, such as the costs of supporting and training end users on multiple solution sets.

One way to reduce information security costs while increasing the effectiveness of security tools is to pare down the list of supported products to one or two per functional category. Another way to reduce cost on security solutions is to avoid purchasing components that you will not utilize, such as application programming interface (API) or scripting tools, if you do not plan to use them. By buying more of a tool, for instance more licenses, your organization may qualify for volume pricing or site licenses at a lower unit cost. However, avoid purchasing large numbers of licenses for a product to obtain a favorable volume discount when your organization has limited experience with a technology and no concrete strategy for using it. Many times, I have seen managers negotiate a great price per unit by committing to volume procurement only to utilize a small number of what they purchased.[18] Sometimes, it is more prudent to purchase a small number of units to perform a proof of concept before making a significant monetary commitment to a product.

Another potential area of cost avoidance for a reduced solution set is in the ongoing cost and effectiveness of support. Rather than multiple groups supporting siloed solutions, support and training can be centralized. This offers a collateral benefit of higher user satisfaction because support may be more consistent, available, and less dependent on a single *sole living expert* (SLE).[19] The net result is a lower lifetime cost for a security solution.

When purchasing a new category of security solutions or researching a replacement for an existing solution, vendor-neutral assessment criteria can clarify the features and key success factors that need to be satisfied. This may lower the cost of reviewing potential vendor offerings and avoid purchasing inappropriate solutions that could require premature replacement.

Hire the Right People

There exist a number of hiring strategies. All might work within a specific organization or work environment. We all want to hire the "star" who exhibits both strong technical expertise and superior *soft skills* (people literacy), as is described in many job postings listed on career websites. One of my former coworkers described these types of posting as, "looking for the Lord himself, but willing to take a sinner, when necessary." Some managers use the strategy of trying to get staff *on the cheap*. While occasionally a manager might luck out by getting a diamond in the rough, more often they hire an individual with a limited skill set or underlying problems. I remember a manager bragging about getting a technician for less than the posted salary. He got what he paid for because this individual was an example of the Peter Principle.[20] This limited the manager's flexibility in assigning work. Most of this manager's prior hires were polymaths drawn from the college graduate-student population with keen intellectual curiosity that allowed them to excel at any tasks given. Most of these individuals were drawn to these positions because of access to computing power and viewed their job as a learning environment for future employment opportunities.

The economic downturn allowed some organizations to attract staff with more expertise at lower salaries. However, this has the potential to create turnover as employment opportunities improve. From a value proposition, hiring the right people, regardless of economic environment, may result in better long-term succession planning and the development of sustainable staff competencies. Good hires can "hit the ground running" and often possess hidden proficiencies[21] that management can exploit to increase productivity and reduce overall staffing costs in the end. For example, many experienced IT security practitioners are experienced project managers who can be utilized to avoid hiring staff to perform this function on small projects.

It is important to view staffing costs from a total cost perspective. High turnover and less than optimal hires may result in higher overall staffing costs. In addition, investments in training and developing experience can be lost due to high turnover. In addition, the criticality of hiring strong, credible, and competent management to lead an information security team cannot be overstated. Incompetent or immature management can affect the overall productivity of the information security team and lead to excessive staff turnover. While tight budgets often restrict or eliminate training dollars, this is one area where investment can yield significant return on investment (ROI) by increasing the value of existing staff and allowing them to optimize their activities.

"Is This Necessary?" Do We Need to Do Everything We Are Currently Doing?

When my sister-in-law moved from Mexico to Massachusetts, it was an unusually warm January day (60 degrees). I took her shopping to buy winter clothes. Her response to being inundated with winter gear was, "Is this necessary?" and the next more seasonable day (mid-30s), she got her answer. I do not think we ask the question, "Is this necessary?" enough. We continue to do something because we have always done it and autopilot takes over. One way to reduce costs is to reduce the overall amount of work, if that work yields little security value. This is similar to zero-base budgeting.[22] It starts by reviewing all security tasks, controls, solutions, and procedures to determine their contribution to the overall security posture. Some security processes hang around for a variety of reasons and may have outlasted their original purpose. I remember a complex control that required reconciling three reports against each other. The effort took three weeks in total. There were never any variances between the three reports. After a little research, I determined that all three reports used the same data and were the same report with minor formatting differences. I eliminated this task and regained three weeks of effort to apply to activities that were more beneficial.[23]

One way to avoid the perpetuation of "zombie" controls[24] is to maintain an inventory of all security mechanisms and their objectives. Periodically, this inventory needs to undergo an evaluation to determine the continued effectiveness and efficiency of each control.

My system has three possible fates[25] for each control:

1. Keep (Continue to perform.)
2. Toss (Terminate because it has no real security benefit.)
3. Replace (This is still a control objective, but the current mechanism is insufficient.)

By periodically reviewing controls, we can identify ineffective ones and target those controls for elimination or replacement. Some collateral benefits of this process include maintaining a current inventory of controls and identifying controls with the potential for reuse in other areas.

Maximize the Value of Controls

A way to get the "most bang for the buck"[26] is to focus on a set of strong general IT controls that support most functions and compliance requirements rather than implement security mechanisms in silos for specific compliance or security needs. A potential solution to expensive single-purpose controls might involve implementing broad control categories aimed at securing classes of information based upon an organization's data classification groups, such as highly confidential, personally identifiable (PI), or personal health information. This approach could provide coverage for up to 90% of the organization's data. The remaining controls inventory could target specific regulatory requirements that exist beyond these general IT controls, such as two-factor authentication required for remote access of some PCI environments. Some potential candidates for IT general controls include vulnerability management applications, encryption tools suites, and data-loss prevention applications. By buying multiple-purpose security controls that service multiple environments, it may be possible to purchase licenses using a volume discount pricing agreement or share costs across multiple business areas.

Use the Goldilocks Principle

Size and scope your information security management program to fit *just right* by using the *Goldilocks Principle.*[27] This avoids the common mistake of underbuilding or overbuilding your security program. The Goldilocks Principle says that something must fall within certain margins rather than going to opposite ends of the spectrum of options. To build a long-term sustainable program, the best place to be is *just right*, where the amount of resources devoted to efforts is commensurate with the risk landscape of the organization it serves. One common error occurs when a practitioner attempts to re-create the program at their prior employer rather than develop a program based upon their new organization's risk profile. I call this approach "If it doesn't fit, I will make it fit."[28] The primary issue is that the former employer's risk landscape may differ considerably from that of the current employer, creating a mismatch between risks and control costs. A common symptom of this desire to re-create a prior employer's information security program is the purchasing of the same security products used at the new employee's former company, even when this security function already exists in the new work environment. Not every organization needs a world-class risk management program. The risk management program needs to support compliance and identified risks for the organization it services. Overarchitecting a security program can waste resources by implementing unnecessary or inappropriate controls. The scope and resource intensity of a specific organization's information security management activities should reflect the risks identified in the current IT risk assessments and audit reports. Controls should be added as required based on newly identified risk issues and threats associated with emerging technology trends.

The question that the information security practitioner needs to be able to answer is "How much security is enough?" to reasonably secure assets from potential threat agents. The response is often to meet all identified compliance requirements plus best practices. *Best practices* represent the most efficient or effective way to accomplish an objective[29] based upon the opinions or recommendations of a subject matter expert or other authority, such as a governing body. While best practices generally dictate the recommended course of action, they are predicated upon specific circumstances. Best practices are situational in nature and therefore their implementation is not always prudent. One key concept that I learned during my MBA studies[30] is that the amount of resources are finite. In the last couple of years, resources have become increasingly scarce, especially for activities that are perceived as having no direct contribution to revenue generation. Therefore, from a cost and risk management perspective, it becomes important to devote available resources to the most significant areas of risk. Frederick the Great said, "In trying to defend everything he defended nothing.[31] Implementing controls around best practices is often an attempt to protect *everything* rather than taking a bespoke approach, which evaluates the specific risks and targets the preponderance of controls around these threats. The effective implementation of best practices is dependent upon the maturity stage of the organization's information security program. Certain best practices are dependent upon an organization's information security (IS) program maturity stage for effective implantation. Some practices require a very high level of maturity to be effective.

For instance, noncompulsory information security certifications, such as ISO 27001,[32] have a strategic focus and are best adopted by an IS organization that has achieved at least the midpoint stage of maturity, equivalent to Nolan's Control stage,[33] in which security evolves from a project to a program approach. The best reason for not adopting ISO 27001 at an earlier maturity stage is that this certification evaluation is targeted at the program level and the process itself requires significant resources to manage successfully. Some IS practitioners substitute the *recommended practice* for the best practice to reduce the perspective that "best" is appropriate for all organizations. In reality, "best practices" seek to offer the most security possible for information assets balanced against responsibility budget management and information access.[34] They are meant to provide *guidelines* and not dictate particular methods, materials, or practices. They are discretionary and can be modified or customized to meet a specific organization's needs.[35]

Frugality as a Continuing Strategy for Information Security Management

Unfortunately, economies will likely continue to trend in boom and bust cycles. There is nothing that we can do to prevent this. However, we can choose not to mirror economic cycles in our fiscal strategy. We all love a budget flush with cash, but this situation rarely lasts more than a few years at best, as cycles of bubbles and busts in the economy repeat,[36] and then dread the fallout of severe budget reductions. Extreme budgetary shifts can affect both the effectiveness and motivation of the team in the long term. We should approach information security budgeting by looking at the cost of providing essential services first and then plan for adding additional functionality to support one of five objectives:

1. Achieve compliance with external or internal requirements.
2. Support controls for emerging threats in the risk landscape.
3. Update, extend, or enhance security to grow with business plans (alignment).
4. Invest in training to expand the value of staff.
5. Fund initiatives designed to help the overall maturity level of the information security organization evolve.

Depending upon the available funding for a specific budget cycle, not all of these five objectives may receive support, but they should exist on a "wish list" for when or if financial support becomes available. While most of us have heard at some point in our careers to approach budget management as if the money was our own, this sage advice sometimes is ignored during a generous budget cycle. Spending tends to expand to consume funds available. If other groups spend lavishly on nonessential items, we might feel compelled to follow suit to motivate our teams. However, the flip side of the scenario can get ugly when budgets are reduced. Rather than spending extra funds on nice-to-have expenditures, invest in areas such as training, security tool upgrades, or risk assessments that will provide lasting value and assist in maintaining a strong security posture during restrictive budgeting cycles. Most of us are familiar with the Aesop fable, "The Ant and Grasshopper."[37] The Ant works away all summer storing food for the winter and the Grasshopper plays away because he does not believe that the salad days will end. In the winter, the Ant has food, while the Grasshopper dies from starvation. The moral of the story is, "It is best to prepare for the days of necessity." The frugal information security practitioner manages budgetary resources so that expenditures during strong economic cycles continue to pay benefits during leaner times and maintain continuity in security posture. A collateral benefit of this approach is that it avoids the creation of excessive stress and frustration of information security staff attempting to maintain the security program with inadequate resources and tools.

Endnotes

1. *Extreme Couponing* (TLC television network) follows savvy shoppers as they plan and plot their way to unbelievable saving; http://tlc.how-stuffworks.com/tv/extreme-couponing.
2. *Extreme Cheapskates* is an American reality television series that airs on the TLC network, documenting the lives of frugal people. It premiered on October 16, 2012; http://www.tlc.com/tv-shows/extreme-cheapskates.
3. "How to Maintain Security during a Recession," *Information Security*, February 2009, http://media.techtarget.com/searchSecurity/downloads/0209_ISM_F_sm.pdf.
4. "Information Security Budgets to Increase in 2013," 451 Research, October 29, 2012, http://theinfopro.blogs.451research.com/index.php/2012/10/information-security-budgets-to-increase-in-2013/.
5. "The phrase 'do more with less' had its origins in the Reagan administration. The underlying premise was that there was a lot of waste, and that budgets could be cut dramatically while services were simultaneously improved and increased." Frank Schneiger, "Source Manager's Journal: Doing More with Less," St. Croix Source, July 22, 2012, http://stcroixsource.com/content/commentary/op-ed/2012/07/22/source-manager-s-journal-doing-more-less-vi-budget.
6. The phrase "work smarter, not harder ever" was coined by Allan F. Mogensen, the creator of Work Simplification, in the 1930s. The 1990s equivalent term is probably *business process reengineering*. Useless Facts Website, http://www.angelfire.com/ca6/uselessfacts/other/008.html.
7. *Death March* (Prentice Hall, 2003) by Edward Yourdon is an iconic project management book. Yourdon's definition: "Quite simply, a death march project is one whose 'project parameters' exceed the norm by at least 50 percent"; http://www.amazon.com/Death-March-2nd-Edward-Yourdon/dp/013143635X.
8. "How to Save on Software Maintenance Costs," Omnext white paper, March 2010, http://www.omnext.net/downloads/Whitepaper_Omnext.pdf.
9. Paul Mano, *The 7 Qualities of Highly Secure Software*, Boca Raton, FL: CRC Press, 2012.
10. The author has experienced pen-testing efforts by an external firm that resulted in server halt from even low-level scanning due to older hardware and software.
11. The author's first manager during her cooperative work assignment frequently used the acronym "BTR" to describe opportunities to enhance his resume to impress recruiters (headhunters) in the future.

12. *Bleeding-edge technology* is so new that it has not been widely adopted and therefore carries a higher degree of risk as to how it will fit in or work within the current environment. It is more advanced than something considered cutting edge. See Investopedia, http://www.investopedia.com/terms/b/bleeding-edge.asp.

13. A records hold is a Records and Information Management procedure that prohibits the spoliation of records due to legal or regulatory requirements.

14. Association for Information and Image Management (AIIM), "Records Management Strategies: Plotting the Changes," November 21, 2010, http://www.aiim.org/Research-and-Publications/Research/Industry-Watch/RM-Strategies-2011.

15. The 2006 amendments to the Federal Rules of Civil Procedure concerning the discovery of "electronically stored information" covered procedures concerning the discovery of electronic evidence. The package includes revisions and additions to Rules 16, 26, 33, 34, 37, and 45, as well as Form 35. The goal was to clarify the definition of discoverable electronic evidence, formats for such evidence, reasonableness of requests for electronic evidence, and provide protections for electronic evidence that might be comingled with requested information. K&L Gates, "E-Discovery Amendments to the Federal Rules of Civil Procedure Go into Effect Today, December 1, 2006," http://www.ediscoverylaw.com/2006/12/articles/news-updates/ediscovery-amendments-to-the-federal-rules-of-civil-procedure-go-into-effect-today/.

16. Gary G. Berg, Michelle S. Freeman, and Kent N. Schneider, "Analyzing the TJ Maxx Data Security Fiasco: Lessons for Auditors," *CPA Journal Online*, August 2008, http://www.nysscpa.org/cpajournal/2008/808/essentials/p34.htm.

17. Richard L. Nolan, "Managing the Crises in Data Processing," originally published in the *Harvard Business Review* in March 1979, known as The Stages of Growth Model for IT systems, http://www.comp.dit.ie/rfitzpatrick/Business%20Perspectives%20slides/Conceptual%20Business%20Models/Managing%20the%20crises%20in%20data%20processing%20-%20Nolan.pdf.

18. The actually per-unit cost of some volume contracts can be high if the product is adopted by a small number of users. In one instance, a complex and prolonged negotiation requiring a million-unit purchase agreement ended with only a few thousand being deployed across the enterprise.

19. A single individual controls all pertinent information regarding a specific domain or area. This knowledge is rarely documented or available to others. This often results in a single point of failure (SPOF) in accomplishing objectives for others requiring assistance.

20. Every employee will rise or get promoted to his or her level of incompetence. This phenomenon was first described in a book by the same name written by Dr. Laurence J. Peter in 1968. Investopedia, http://www.investopedia.com/terms/p/peter-principle.asp.

21. Patrick Gray, "Find the Hidden Talent in Your Organization," Tech Decision Maker, April 2, 2013, http://www.techrepublic.com/blog/tech-manager/find-the-hidden-talent-in-your-organization/8233?tag=nl.e106&s_cid=e106&ttag=e106.

22. Zero-based budgeting (ZBB) is a method of budgeting in which all expenses must be justified for each new budget. Zero-based budgeting starts from a zero base and every function within an organization is analyzed for its needs and costs. Investopedia, http://www.investopedia.com/terms/z/zbb.asp.

23. This did not make everyone happy. The team member who worked on this project was very angry because he liked the power involved in managing this intradepartmental project. Doing the right thing does not always make you popular with all team members.

24. Zombie controls is the author's term for security controls that have no useful purpose, but continue to be performed.

25. My mother's approach to managing everything.

26. *Bang for the buck* is an idiom that means to get the most value for the money spent. The earliest confirmed mention of bang for the buck is found in 1968 in the first edition of William Safire's *New Language of Politics*. Mr. Safire claims that the phrase was coined in 1954 by Charles E. Wilson, the Secretary of Defense, in reference to the "massive retaliation" policy of John Foster Dulles; http://answers.yahoo.com/question/index?qid=20080417111050AAe6d7M.

27. Chris Dixon, "Business Development: The Goldilocks Principle," November 28, 2011, http://cdixon.org/2011/11/28/business-development-the-goldilocks-principle/.

28. This is an expression my brother uses when he assembles an item and gets frustrated because he has a number of extra parts left over after he completes the task or uses a "kluge" to finish the project.

29. "Best Practices," Investopedia, http://www.investopedia.com/terms/b/best_practices.asp.

30. Master's degree in business administration.

31. Quotations Book, http://quotationsbook.com/quote/15198/.

32. The objective of ISO 27001, an international information security standard, is to "provide a model for establishing, implementing, operating, monitoring, reviewing, maintaining, and improving an Information Security Management System." "An Introduction to ISO 27001," ISO 27000 Directory, http://www.27000.org/iso-27001.htm.

33. Richard L. Nolan, "Managing the Crises in Data Processing," originally published in the *Harvard Business Review* in March 1979, known as The Stages of Growth Model for IT systems, http://www.comp.dit.ie/rfitzpatrick/Business%20Perspectives%20slides/Conceptual%20Business%20Models/Managing%20the%20crises%20in%20data%20processing%20-%20Nolan.pdf.

34. "Management of Security," Chapter 6 in *Security Management Models and Practices*, http://www.sis.pitt.edu/~jjoshi/IS2820/Spring06/chapter06.doc.

35. National Information Standards Organization (NISO) "Recommended Practices," http://www.niso.org/publications/rp/.
36. Robert J. Shiller, *Irrational Exuberance* (Princeton University Press) is a classic book, first released in 2000 and in its second edition in 2005, that documents cycles of boom and bust in the economy starting in 1990.
37. "The Ant and the Grasshopper," *Aesop's Fables*, http://www.umass.edu/aesop/content.php?n=0&i=1.

1

"NEW NORMAL"

When Can We Get Back to Normal?

"It was the best of times; it was the worst of times."[*] Most of us recognize this as the first line of the literary classic, *A Tale of Two Cities*. For many information security executives, it is also a metaphor for budget cycles. While most budgets have ridden the wave of constantly changing economic conditions, we recall best budgets that allowed InfoSec to thrive and innovate, while hoping that restricted budget years would pass quickly and not affect the program's progress in the long term. Most strategies for managing tight budgets look at adverse financial conditions as a temporary situation that will improve as the economy recovers. For the past several decades, economic cycles have followed a predictable pattern of recession followed by a recovery within a year or two, so short-term tactics for managing budget shortfalls work to minimize the lasting impact on the information security posture of the organization. This approach may work in the short term. However, their fundamental flaw is the assumption that the same results can be achieved with decreased resources indefinitely. Employees are often amenable to working hard, putting in long hours, and assuming additional responsibilities for periods. This is often the norm in information technology (IT)-related areas that frequently involve projects with aggressive delivery dates.

Many IT and information security projects in which I have participated have required mandatory six-day work weeks during "crunch" periods to facilitate meeting a delivery date. While this creates some grumbling initially, most team members will "buck up," roll up their collective sleeves, and do what needs to be done regardless of the need for personal sacrifice to some degree. The successful delivery of many of these

---

[*] A Tale of Two Cities by Charles Dickens

projects requires the herculean efforts of a few good men (and women) to achieve. Employees are willing to put forth the effort and make personal sacrifices to support the greater good of the team or organization. Some individuals may even thrive in these stressful environments.

In the mid-1990s, I worked for a software company where a number of senior software professionals regularly tried to beat each other on the number of hours worked in a week by noting their current tally on their whiteboards. Most individuals are only willing to expend extra effort for a specific duration or event, such as the end of the project or the achievement of compliance deliverables. There is a maximum time that individuals will tolerate difficult conditions. The amount of time is often dependent upon the criticality of goal requiring achievement.

A good example of this is the rationing and other hardships that people were willing to endure during World War II. The United Kingdom used the slogan "Make Do and Mend" to promote resource conversation in light of rationing of food, fabric, and other commodities to support war efforts. Because the goal was vital to survival of many nations, the populations of many allied nations were willing to endure hardships for periods of years. It was supported by patriotic fervor. For less lofty goals, individuals are willing to tolerate adversity for shorter durations.

In the last couple of milder economic slumps, such as 2001, the recoveries followed a more predictable and shorter resurgence than the "Great Recession" of 2008, whose effect is still being felt more than five years later. The long-term consequences of "do more with less" and "working smarter" can be frustration, fatigue, and decreasing levels of motivation. While some improvement has occurred, many information security professionals have not experienced significant improvements in their workloads or stress levels.

Frugal versus Cheap

Many individuals see the words *frugal* and *cheap* as synonymous. Both words express a strategy for management of money or resources. *Frugal* is defined in the different online dictionaries as "being characterized by or reflecting economy in the use of resources" and "economical in use or expenditure; not wasteful." Frugal implies making prudent choices to optimize the value of resources spent to obtain a result. There is a stark distinction between being frugal and being cheap.

Dictionary.com defines the word *cheap* as "of little account; of small value; mean; shoddy." Cheap is often analogous to poor quality. Cheap carries a negative connotation when used in some expressions, such as "What do you expect? It was dirt cheap" or "He took a cheap shot at her." Using cheap as a strategy can actually end up costing more money in the end. Cheap is not really about the best value. Cheap is about spending the least resources or cash in the moment.

Frugality can bring admiration or teasing. Cheap behavior may create disdain. Sometimes, it is possible to cross the line between frugal and cheap. Often, this occurs without the individual knowing. This is a human version of "boiled frog syndrome." The "boiled frog" is a popular business analogy that I first saw mentioned in Peter Senge's book, *The Fifth Discipline: The Art & Practice of the Learning Organization* (Doubleday, 2006).

The gist of the story is based on the frog's biology as a cold-blooded animal. If you put a frog in boiling water, it will react and jump out to save itself. However, if you place the frog in a pot of cold water and gradually turn up the heat, the frog will remain in the pot and boil to death. The concept that the story tries to express is that we need to adapt to current circumstances rather than just continue with one course of action.

Frugal turns to cheap when we have progressed past thrifty into cheapness, regardless of other decision-making criteria. Some managers progress into cheap territory without their conscious awareness or recognition that others view their behavior as cheap. Most people do not like others, especially management, that they perceive as cheap. Cheapness recalls negative stereotypes of famous misers in literature, such as Charles Dickens' Ebenezer Scrooge and George Eliot's Silas Marner. In my experience, one of the attributes many individuals find objectionable in management is cheapness.

Using cheapness as a financial strategy can result in more problems than it is worth. Being frugal is having good-quality office furnishings cleaned and repaired rather than purchasing new equipment. Being cheap means using old laptops until the hardware fails, despite a serious drop in productivity and increased frustration in employees.

Cheapness may work successfully as a near-term tactic. However, in the end, the results may range from bad to disastrous. I have had experience resolving issues created by managers who prided themselves on cheapness. Often, fixing issues costs more than doing them right in the first place. Cheapness can result in security risks, productivity declines, insufficient quality, poor service levels, and diminished team morale.

Time, Cost, and Quality Paradox

At some point, many information security professionals have read of or experienced the *three-legged stool* as analogy to describe the interrelationship between the three dimensions of a project or deliverable: time, cost, and quality. Experienced professionals describe this situation as, "you can have it cheap, good, or quick, pick two." The underlying concept is balancing the three dimensions to achieve the optimal result in face of any constraints, such as limited resources. The proficiency to manage the three dimensions without sacrificing essential business and technical requirements is the mark of true project wizardry. The key is to know when a dimension, such as cost, cannot be manipulated any further without resulting in a less than optimal outcome.

The information security function is often characterized by a series of projects, some iterative, such as achieving compliance with the internal or external regulations, while others may be unique one-time events, such as ISO 27001 certification. Sometimes, at least for a while, it can appear that one or more of the three dimensions can be manipulated beyond what appears possible. For example, dramatic reductions in resources, such as staff (cost) or time, can occur without what appears to be any significant impact on outcome.

Some type of magic allows the practitioner to buck the "laws" of project management and still come out a "winner." It is the equivalent to beating the house in a Las Vegas casino. Many managers have experienced the phenomenon, especially after major budget reductions or retrenchments. If this happens more than once, managers often can become emboldened to cut more and see what happens. For some managers, these initial successes that appear to validate the axiom of "doing more with less" without any compromises in quality can be exhilarating, like being *king* (or queen).

There is a common explanation for the initial successes of these scenarios, which can be summed up by the presence of a few strong team members. These highly motivated players can use a combination of innovation and willingness to work an extraordinary number of hours to make the team and its efforts successful. While a strong supportive manager helps, this phenomenon is largely attributable to team composition and their *esprit de corps*. To quote the great baseball coach, Tommy Lasorda, "The difference between the impossible and the possible lies in a man's determination." The snag in using this strategy exclusively on a long-term basis is that even the most motivated team member can lose motivation, if no other tactic is used to mitigate the stress, frustration, and exhaustion that are often the by-product of "death march" environments.

One instance of overuse of this strategy remains etched in my mind, even after almost twenty years. During a governmental budget period, a middle manager was pressured to work long hours and assume extra assignments to avoid paying overtime to union employees. Pushed to his physical and mental breaking point, he pleaded for some measure of relief from the crushing workload, to which the department head stated, "Everything is *your* job." The middle manager shortly thereafter suffered a complete mental collapse, which resulted in his leaving his position. There has to be another and better way.

We Are Special?

From my "probie" days in information security in the late 1990s to just prior to the economic meltdown in 2008, many corporate information security organizations seemed obsessed with comparing the percentage of the IT budget (or overall technology budget) that their group received against some theoretical industry "average."

This obsession had two purposes. The first was determining how their share of the budget pie stacked up against the "average" of their peers' financial allocations. If they beat the "average" percentage, they could feel appreciated for their excellent program. It made them "special." If they received less than the "average," they were underappreciated or worse (like being put in the slow readers group in grade school). When we are children, we might experience some competition with our siblings. We might drive our mothers crazy by peppering them with questions in regard to which of their kids are superior to the others in some attribute, such as "Who is smarter?," "Who is prettier?," or the perennial favorite, "Who is your favorite child?" Kids look for affirmation of their importance in the sibling hierarchy. While this is okay for kids, trying to make comparisons between organizations on budgets based upon some theoretical average may be meaningless.

It is difficult to make head-to-head comparisons because it is difficult to find organizations that are perfectly matched in terms of critical attributes such as:

A. Industry or sector
B. Ownership model, such as public, partnership, or privately owned
C. Overall stage of organizational maturation
D. Stage of maturation of the information security function
E. Centralized, distributed, or hybrid information security function
F. Number of employees
G. Technical infrastructure
H. Budgeting techniques
I. Organizational culture
J. Risk tolerance/risk appetite of the organization
K. Past information security problem
L. Current and past audit reports (internal and external)
M. Current regulatory sanctions
N. Inherent business risks
O. Current threat landscape
P. Profit or nonprofit
Q. Compliance and regulatory environment

The appropriate budget percentage (and budget itself) is often unique to the circumstances of a specific organization. It is situational in nature. There is no "best" budgetary percentage. A budget must be appropriate to support the amount of security required by a specific organization based upon an assessment of its threat environment, regulatory requirements, and management's current level of risk tolerance.

Unfortunately, the industry itself promotes this type of "magical thinking" through its many annual surveys to determine averages in a number of information security areas, such as average budget, average practitioner's salary, and so on. The closer an information security program is to reflecting these norms, the more it symbolizes a "best in breed" information security program. But, like most things, *the devil is in the details.*

You have to be knowledgeable about the specifics of a survey to determine its relevance to your particular organization. This is true of most research studies and surveys because you need to understand who and what is being analyzed before drawing any conclusions. There have been numerous news stories in which long-held truths have been uncovered as false or questionable due to flaws in the research techniques. This is not to completely underestimate the value of industry surveys, but to put them in perspective. All surveys, even the leading industry variety using a variety of controls to account for margins of error, depend on the accuracy of information from respondents, as well as getting a broad sample of participants. Some annual surveys utilize a pool of potential participants, often those belonging to an industry group or members of a professional association. These survey pools may not reflect smaller information security programs and industry segments. The information gleaned from these studies may best be thought of as indicators of trends rather than benchmarks against which a specific organization is measured.

At the end of the day, information security managers need to utilize the skills at which they excel, which is making a solid assessment of their organization to determine if their budget can provide "enough security" to protect their collective assets. Use "average" budget amounts in the same way that fashion makeover shows suggest that participants use clothing sizes, as guides rather than absolutes.

Over the years, research studies have reported that companies spend 3% to 5% of their total IT budget on information security, depending on the industry sector, according to a 2010 Gartner study. This breaks down to around $525 per employee in 2009. One interesting trend revealed in this study was that the security spending on a per-employee basis had declined from $636 since the 2008 economic downturn.

What is enough security remains a calculated decision between identified risk and cost based upon each organization's circumstances. Devoting more or less than the average security budget should not necessarily concern organizations. As TV ads say, "actual results may vary," so the overall effectiveness of any information security program may not have a direct correlation to its budget. Information security managers need to make their own evaluations of the adequacy of their budget amount.

It is possible to have a generous security budget and still have ineffective security. This is similar to an IT endeavor. Most of us with years of technology experience have encountered this common scenario. An organization announces a large technology project with a lofty goal, such as transformation of business, and receives substantial funding and visibility. The project may miss deliverable deadlines, often accompanied by frequent shifts in management. Management may attempt multiple changes in direction to steer the project back on course.

A well-known example is the Internal Revenue Service (IRS) system modernization effort in the late 1990s that ultimately resulted in an expenditure of more than $4 billion and did not work. Over time, the project's visibility decreases and attempts are made to salvage some parts of the effort so it will not appear to be a total loss. Even these efforts may fail. The project slips off quietly into the night, but its name lives in infamy to be used to denote bad decisions in the future. For those involved, it may become an RGE (resume-generating event).

The opposite can also be true in some situations where budget and resources are scarce. A good example is documented in the classic business book, *Soul of a New Machine*. After its primary well-financed design team failed to bring a new minicomputer to market to compete with a rival computer manufacturer, the Data General Corporation succeeded in using a machine developed through a "skunk works" effort using an inexperienced team of engineers with minimal resources. Budget alone does not determine the effectiveness and outcome of initiative or function.

"It's the Economy, Stupid," or Is Something Impacting Security Budgets?

Many information security managers look back on the deep-pocket budget days of the late 1990s/early 2000s created by a booming economy fueled by irrational exuberance and use this period as a measuring stick for funding of security budgets. This was a transitional period for many organizations as they evolved from a closed system environment characterized by internal applications encased by a firewall to a more open e-commerce infrastructure susceptible to new types of attacks.

In some organizations, the information security function was limited to only security administration tasks. The role of the information security officer was not taken seriously. The old joke at one company was, the way to be appointed the information security officer was to miss the staff meeting. Many of these newly minted information security officers had limited experience in cyber security and some did not possess a significant amount of knowledge of IT issues.

Changes in business strategy, revenue models, and significant transformation of IT infrastructure introduced new categories of risk and created new twists on risks. To manage this evolving threat landscape, organizations invested heavily in new cyber security technology and accompanying increases in staff levels that increased information security budgets significantly. Many of the new risks, such as email infections, remote access Trojans (RATs), and phishing attacks, also necessitated the creation of awareness programs to educate end users about new dangers.

This decade could also be labeled the *compliance years* because of the need to implement major regulatory requirements, including the Health Insurance Portability and Accountability Act (HIPAA), the Payment Card Industry Data Security Standard (PCI-DSS), and numerous state data-privacy laws designed to contain the emerging problem of data breaches. Achieving compliance with these regulations and laws required additional funding to manage the specifics of each compliance requirement.

Compliance initiatives often took place in isolation from other regulatory projects, as well as its internal risk management efforts. Little effort was made to implement common security solutions, despite similar or overlapping compliance requirements. The consequence was the implementation of many security solutions performing the same basic functions, such as secure email. This redundancy was missed because different groups managed compliance projects within isolated silos with limited opportunities for communication.

While the Great Recession is the major culprit for decreased or flat information security budgets, there are a number of contributing factors that can have an influence on C-level executives' decisions to curb any significant boosts in security spending, at least through the end of 2013 and likely beyond.

Slowing of Compliance

For the last couple of years, the numbers of new compliance regulations have slowed down, at least for the time being. While most risk professionals welcome a breather from implementing new regulations, for many information security organizations, funding for these projects offered a justification for additional funding that could be used for projects that achieved the necessary compliance targets and offered the opportunity to strengthen the overall posture of the organization.

After achieving initial compliance with regulations, the line items, as well as the cost centers associated with them, vanished from later budgets. This can create a funding crisis for information security managers because the costs associated with maintaining compliance with these regulatory requirements, such as the annual PCI-DSS attestation process, and any changes to manage revisions in requirements, must be absorbed by the annual budget.

By seeking additional funding with a focus on the initial achievement of compliance with a regulatory requirement rather than presenting it as a new iterative activity, some chief information security officers (CISOs) may have failed to communicate the true nature of the compliance process. Compliance entails continuing maintenance and adjustments, sometimes on an annual basis. A good example is the PCI-DSS regulation, which released its third revision in late 2013. Each revision has, to some degree, increased mandatory controls. Some controls that were optional in prior revisions or requisite only at higher risk levels become included in the compliance criteria for most covered organizations.

If an organization's strategy involves only obtaining compliance with the specific mandatory controls for their risk level, this may present a problem during subsequent regulation revisions. If the CISO fails to communicate this to management during the budgeting cycle, this often necessitates diverting funds away from current projects or other core activities to achieve compliance with the revised compliance standards. There exists a major security and budget management risk in only aiming for the bottom bar (just compliant) when achieving regulatory compliance.

If the CISO now goes back to the budget well for additional funding in subsequent years, a C-level executive may very well conclude that the company already funded this item in prior budgets.

Security Technology Fatigue

In some cases, the C-level has funded the acquisition of numerous security solutions, such as secure email and antimalware products, but have yet to see a significant increase in overall security posture. This is a symptom of an information security organization in the early stages of its maturity. This is similar to Contagion (Stage 2) in Richard L. Nolan's Stages of Growth Model for IT systems.[1]

Nolan's original model for IT maturity is easily adapted to information security because it is a subset of the IT discipline. The Contagion stage is characterized by a silver bullet mind-set characterized by rapid tool acquisition, development, and deployment. The net result is the proliferation of multiple similar solutions, often in different organizational silos, that serve the same security objective, such as the protection of personally identifiable information (PII) in transit.

These security tools may not integrate well with others, or in some cases create technical conflicts when deployed in the same environment, such as user desktops. A good example of this type of technology incompatibility occurs with client antimalware suites whose scanning processes may conflict and create performance issues or instabilities that affect performance. At some point, the C-level executives may ask questions regarding the effectiveness of these security solutions and not receive any satisfactory information concerning a measurable improvement in the overall security of the organization. More often than not, the request for yet another new security solution is the response to their inquiries.

Another common scenario occurs when a new CISO comes into the organization and makes the C-level executives aware of duplicate technology solutions and a lack of a coherent plan to utilize these technological investments effectively. The best outcome is for the information security organization to step back from acquiring more disparate security solutions and fully develop a strategic plan on how to best integrate the technologies they have.

Often, this means scrapping some security purchases or modifying the current security infrastructure for others. Until this accomplished, C-level executives may postpone or table further acquisitions of security technology without justification, other than mandatory regulatory compliance requirements.

FUD Fatigue

What is the fastest way to lose both respect and credibility with C-level executives? It is using fear, uncertainty, and doubt (FUD) as a tactic. Some CISOs and cyber security consultants have used FUD as their primary tactic for securing additional budget. The biggest downside to FUD is its overuse. Another reason that FUD is no longer as effective as a tactic for obtaining funding is the growing sophistication of the C-level around cyber security events and their impact on the enterprise. To paraphrase a quote from a famous film, for C-level executives, "This ain't my first time at the rodeo." C-level executives have seen a significant number of security breaches over the last decade and acknowledge that while they may have a significant impact, they are rarely the catastrophic meltdown scenarios described by purveyors of FUD. FUD comes in many variations, such as dubious metrics and return on security investment (ROSI)-based on surveys rather than internal data.

One of FUD's weaknesses is that to fix the scenario it describes requires the creation of an unattainable vision of security, and detracts from real efforts for maturation of the information security program. Using FUD year after year weakens its effectiveness, similar to the famous story "The Boy Who Cried Wolf." The biggest risk of funding via FUD is that when a significant risk appears on the horizon, the CISO will have little credibility by which to acquire supplemental funding.

C-Level Compliancy

Some executives believe that because they have not been breached yet, their luck will continue. The risk is that history does not always accurately reflect future events. The other problem is that it takes an average of 80 days for a company to detect a security breach. It some cases, an intrusion may exist for considerably longer or go undetected indefinitely. Another variation of compliancy is based on the myth that because an enterprise is compliant with some security regulation or standard, it is indeed secure.

True security involves protection of people, processes, and technology against danger, loss, or unauthorized use. The concept is holistic. Compliance is concerned about checking items on a list, passing audits, and successfully managing assessments to get some type of attestation regarding achievement of a regulatory organization's guidelines and standards. Compliance and security are related, but they are not analogous.

Organizations are right to be concerned regarding compliance with industry and governmental regulations because the price for noncompliance can hamper or prohibit revenue-generating operations. For instance, failure to obtain a successful attestation with PCI-DSS standards can prevent an enterprise from taking payment in the form of payment cards. For some enterprises, this might effectively cause the business to shut its doors. Compliance is often the price of doing business. Achieving and maintaining industry compliance with regulatory requirements are great first steps on an organization's security journey.

Compliance-centric organizations view compliance as their last step. These organizations look to meet the bare minimum in terms of compliance and may see additional efforts as wastes of resources. In contrast, *security-centric* organizations continually seek to identify threats and vulnerabilities with the potential to create negative outcomes for the organization, its customers, and partners.

Another cause of C-level compliancy is when a CISO becomes a victim of his or her own success or propaganda. If a CISO boasts too much about the superiority of his or her program in contrast to other organizations, then some C-level executives may see no advantage in providing additional funding. Other C-level executives may believe the old axioms "if it ain't broke, don't fix it" or "don't tamper with success."

There is justification for providing significant budgetary increases to an information security program that is already exceeding its appropriate security level for its identified risk needs based on emerging risk in its threat landscape. However, risks can occur if the actual security posture of the organization is overstated. This may result from the CISO's subordinates providing inaccurate information to please their management or the strategic omission of critical security gaps. The outcome may be that the CISO does not obtain new funding to address these gaps and the gaps create vulnerabilities that are actualized in a security breach.

Waiting for Perfection

Some individuals have difficulty making a decision. They will delay making a decision until they have more information. The more information they obtain, the more they believe they need. This is referred to as *analysis paralysis*. This may occur at the C-level or with the CISO. There can be several reasons why this happens. One reason may be that there is no clear strategic direction for cyber security in the organization. Most decisions appear tactical and are reactive rather than proactive in nature.

The rationale for this behavior often revolves around a decision to delay implementing costly security technology when some innovation might be just down the pike. The result is an endless waiting game. Sometimes the security firms and security researchers contribute to the desire to delay by discussing future technology innovations that are still in the research stages, such as homomorphic encryption. This is another variation of the *silver bullet* syndrome.

The reality in the world of security technology is that there will always be some innovation coming down the road eventually. However, delaying doing anything opens the organization up to current exploits. It is preferable to implement solutions to defend against the existing threat landscape to ensure that the organization survives until the *next big thing* is available and operationally viable. Remember, when this exciting new security technology becomes ubiquitous, attackers will develop new exploits against it too.

They Really Don't Care about Information Security (at Least Now)

This is the hardest one for dedicated information security professionals to hear, but some organizations really could not care less about information security itself. The executives and board of directors might care about fines or other negative expensive consequences, but in terms of accepting security risks, they are more than willing to assume them.

For some organizations, particularly at the beginning of existence, security may be a low priority, especially in light of needing to meet the next payroll. This is a common situation with start-up companies. These organizations need to move rapidly and have a tolerance for risks associated with speed. These organizations have both limited time and budget to achieve their place in the market. There is a significant difference between this type of organization and most others—assets. Start-ups may have limited assets in the case of security incidents that would potentially result in legal actions or fines. These companies have little to lose. Most organizations cannot be so cavalier in their approach to information security risks because of the potential for negative impacts on the organization.

Apathy toward information security is of more concern when it occurs in a mature organization. Most organizations have something to lose after surviving for a number of years, in terms of cash, other assets, or reputation. Part of this attitude is traceable to ignorance of the threat landscape. Some organizations do not believe that they are potential targets for cyber criminals or hackers. Others believe that they are lucky and will not become a victim of a cyber attacker. Some organizations may be comfortable taking their chances with the potential for cyber attacks; to paraphrase the famous line from Dirty Harry,[2] "Do I feel lucky?" Richard Clarke, former special adviser to the president on cyber security, once said, "If you spend more on coffee than on IT security, then you will be hacked. What's more, you deserve to be hacked."[3] Any of these attitudes may radically alter in the aftermath of a security breach and its often-expensive consequence in terms of cleanup and reputational damage.

What Is Normal, Anyway?

Since the beginning of my career in information technology, I have experienced a string of economic downturns and their impact on the companies for which I worked. The reality is that tight budgets have been generally the rule rather than the exception, if you look back on the last two decades in business. I have also experienced supporting products in the last few years of their life cycle.

The basic reality is that management wants to limit resources devoted to the maintenance and support of applications that are heading for decommissioning. This experience in the shallow end of the budget pool gave me an opportunity to hone my frugality strategy, which minimized the effect of limiting resources and still provided adequate (and sometimes excellent) operational effectiveness. The frugality techniques I learned in IT have been easily transferable to the information security function because they address some of the same basic issues and resource drains experienced in operational environments. These tactical approaches use a combination of innovation and a long, hard look at core requirements to accomplish specific functions.

They will not always make you popular with all involved, but neither will they create a working environment resembling a "death march" scenario. Often, these techniques will involve making hard choices, tough decisions, and getting real with staff and clients alike.

Endnotes

1. Richard Nolan, "Managing the Crisis in Data Processing," *Harvard Business Review*, March/April 1979, http://www.comp.dit.ie/rfitzpatrick/ Business%20Perspectives%20slides/Conceptual%20Business%20Models/ Managing%20the%20crises%20in%20data%20processing%20-%20 Nolan.pdf.
2. *Dirty Harry* is a 1971 American crime drama and the first movie of the Dirty Harry series. Clint Eastwood plays the title role as Dirty Harry Callahan.
3. Richard Clark's keynote speech at the RSA Conference 2002.

2
INFORMATION SECURITY MATURITY LIFE CYCLE

Where Is My Team?

During the course of our development, we try new things. Sometimes we love something and "get it" the first time we attempt it. Other times, the experiment is a failure and we swear we are not going to try that again. Often, whether we fail or triumph is not as much a question of aptitude or attitude. It is all about timing. We naturally understand this when we are dealing with kids. The first time a child is put in the water, he or she may beg to get out or acclimate immediately to the new aquatic environment. If the child balks at the water, often the adult pulls he or she out with the knowledge that the child is not ready, for whatever reason, to swim. A child needs to be ready to assume the challenge.

The same is true of organizations. Each organization, including an information security team, has its own unique maturity cycle. Maturation can be rushed. There are many factors that may influence the rate at which the organization progresses, such as the organizational culture, current leadership, business sector, marketplace, and regulatory environment. The information security organization may exhibit a different maturity level than the overall organization in which it exists, based upon a number of things, such as when and how it came to exist as a separate entity. Just like people, some organizations are more mature than others and are earlier in their development. The relative maturity level of the information security team must be a major consideration in all planning regarding the people, process, and technology it will use to create the organization's security posture.

Back in the late 1970s and 1980s, the first models for evaluating the maturity of the information security function first appeared. Dr. Richard L. Nolan developed one of the first models during the early 1970s called the Stages of Growth Model for IT systems.[1] This model is still in use today. I became familiar with the Nolan Stages model while attending Bentley University, where one of the professors introduced me to it. I used it in several papers during my matriculation there to predict the potential maturation of a technology or trend in IT.

In 2006, while researching a way to identify the maturation of information security teams, I remembered the Nolan Stages Model. The Nolan Stages Model offers a qualitative measure of maturity. I adapted the Nolan model specifically for compliance and information security organizations and enhanced it by identifying a set of *symptoms* or dictators for each of the six maturation levels. I introduced my adaption of the Nolan Stages Model for compliance and information security usage at several conferences and summits during 2007. Over the years, I have used this adapted model when performing various IT security assessments, as well as making recommendations for new security practices or technology solutions. One reason I like to use this model is to "ballpark" the approximate maturation level of the information security team to determine if a team is ready to implement a sophisticated security solution or implement a *best practice*. If an information security organization is at a low maturity level, it might be unable to successfully implement or optimize a security solution or practice appropriately. This may reduce the return on security investment (ROSI) of the budgetary expenditure. For example, purchasing costly log monitoring software may not be effective if the team lacks the expertise to understand its output.

Using the Nolan Model Combined with Information Security-Specific Benchmarks

When using any maturity model, it needs to assess the organization's current state of maturity against a set of specific benchmarks that indicate key developmental milestones. In adapting the Nolan Stages Model for use in evaluating information security or other technical-risk management functions, the following list of milestones might be considered as developmental indicators, including:

- Funding and resource allocation
- Information security's role in business

- Planning intervals
- Reactive versus proactive activities
- Use of automation
- Alignment with business strategy
- Focus (internal or external or both)
- Stability of the information security organization, such as history of reorganizations, management changes, or staff turnover
- Overall organizational awareness of information security

While no one benchmark can, in isolation, accurately identify the approximate level of information security function maturation, when considered in their entirety, the benchmarks may offer significant evidence of organizational maturity level (see Figure 2.1 for benchmark chart).

The overall maturity level of the organization does not necessarily reflect the maturation stage of the information security function. Some organizations may not introduce a formal information security function until later in the organization's existence. Often the impetus for its creation comes from influences external to the organization itself, such as regulatory bodies or industry compliance requirements. This may result in a maturity level mismatch in which the information security team struggles to meet the needs of an established organization with limited experience and immature support processes.

The organization's executives may expect that the information security is functioning at a higher level of maturity than it actually is for a number of reasons. One reason is that executives may equate

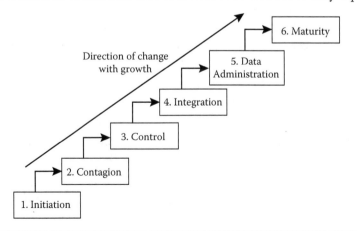

Figure 2.1 Organizational maturity level benchmarks.

technology with maturity. One symptom of an information security organization with lower maturity is a tendency to perceive technology as a silver bullet against risk issues and a failure to understand that technology must be managed to optimize its value. A typical scenario in such an organization is a multiplicity of logging utilities and logs, but staff cannot interpret the data they create. The logs are often in place to cover a compliance regulation only.

Why Assess Information Security Maturity Levels?

Evaluating the maturity level of an information security team has a number of benefits to the organization. It allows an organization to assess itself relative to similar information security teams at other companies. This can provide valuable feedback on whether the team is average, higher performing, or needs improvement.

While average or better-performing teams can always improve, a team that is deficient in specific areas needs a performance plan to get back on track. When auditors or regulators review a security team, they will compare its performance and level of competency against other similar organizations it has reviewed. If the team compares badly with its peers, this might result in lower compliance ratings.

A primary reason for evaluating maturation is to determine a strategy to get the security team to the next level it needs to achieve. This can be especially true if the team has reached a performance plateau and is showing symptoms of stagnation at its current level. The big risk with an information security team is that it gets stuck at a level. When this happens, the next step might be a regression to a previous level rather than a move forward to a higher stage of maturity. This can happen for a number of reasons, such as experienced staff members leaving the team. An exodus of experienced team members can result in the team reverting to a lower maturity stage.

The assessment of team maturation might identify factors that are hindering it from moving to the next level and result in recommendations to overcome these obstacles to get the journey to maturity back on course. These recommendations might provide the justification for projects to achieve increased organizational maturity, such as purchasing training materials or offering opportunities for on-site training in security technologies. This would allow the team to focus on high-benefit opportunities for moving the team along the maturity continuum. By identifying the current maturity baseline level of information security, it provides a continuing basis for measuring future progress toward developmental milestones.

There is a strong correlation between cost-effective security management and maturity levels. Some best practices only become appropriate after an information security team has achieved a specific maturity milestone. This is the case with best practices, which require a formal repeatable process to be successful in reducing risks, such as log analysis or web application vulnerability management. These activities dictate consistent use to develop sufficient history or knowledge to make decisions regarding deploying additional controls, altering current processes, or recommending the acquisition of additional security technologies. It may not be economically prudent to acquire and deploy security solutions requiring highly skilled staff for use before the team is ready for these tools.

A young team at a lower maturity level might make better use of budget funds by purchasing simple multipurpose security tools or hiring consulting resources to assist the team in implementing existing security applications. Most experienced IT professions have experienced a scenario where a group purchased a technology that was beyond its users' ability to effectively implement.

For example, I clearly remember a desktop manager who purchased one hundred copies of a complex publishing application for an organization that was just adopting PC technology. Most users were just learning basic document creation and editing. The end-user committee recommended a simpler application. However, the desktop manager wanted the "best in breed" solution. Three years later, the new desktop manager threw out 97 boxes of the application disks and manuals for a total loss of $90,000. The lesson learned is that the tool must suit the users or its value may be negligible.

The Six Levels of Information Security Maturation

There are six distinct maturity stages, beginning with the Initiation stage and terminating at the Maturity/Continuous Renewal stage, shown in Figure 2.2. Imagine a series of steps that the information security team must ascend to reach increasingly higher levels of

BENCHMARK	LOW MATURITY	MODERATE MATURITY	HIGH MATURITY	OPTIMAL MATURITY
	NOLAN LEVEL 1–2	NOLAN LEVEL 3–4	NOLAN LEVEL 5	NOLAN LEVEL 6
Funding and resource allocation	Funding to cover operational costs/ Lumping of capital and operational costs	Funding to operational costs and planned capital budgeting	Funding to operational costs and planned capital budgeting & strategic budget planning cycle	Strategic budget management/ including multiyear project
InfoSec role in business	Minimal	Compliance-centric/ Tactical	Integrated with business plan	Strategic in lock-step with business plan
Planning intervals	Short-term only/ Under 1 year	Primarily short-term/Under 2 years	Mixture of short & long term/3- to 5-year planning	Mix of short & long term/3- to 5-year planning/ Strategic projects with duration beyond 5 years
Reactive versus proactive activities	Completely reactive	Primarily reactive with some proactive activities	Primarily proactive activities/ Reactive as required for incident	Primarily proactive activities/ Reactive as required for incident
Use of automation	Minimal	Moderate with ad hoc as required	High with scheduling utility	Complete automation
Alignment with business strategy	Minimal	Moderate	Integrated	Embedded within business strategy
Focus (Internal or External)	Internal	Primarily internal with some external focus	Balanced internal and external focus	Strong external focus/assumes leadership role with peer organizations
Stability of the InfoSec organization	Newly formed team/ high turnover possible	Stabilized with core membership/ limited career paths available	Core team/ subteam formed/ defined career paths	Core team/ subteam formed/defined career paths
Organizational Awareness of InfoSec	Minimal/ compliance-centric awareness campaigns	Low to moderate/ regular awareness activities	High/regular & targeted awareness activities	High/regular & targeted awareness activities

Figure 2.2 Six levels of information security maturation.

maturation in its functioning and outlook. Like any set of stairs, it is possible to move in either direction, up or down, depending on circumstances and choices made by the information security team.

While several variations of the Nolan Stages Model exist, I specifically used the six stages model because of its inclusion of the Data Administration stage. The Data Administration stage is analogous to a data-centric security organization that views its data as a critical asset. The following sections provide a brief description of each of the six maturity levels. A checklist of symptoms of each stage is provided in Appendix A.

Stage 1: Initiation

This stage marks the introduction of an information security function/ team into the organization. The creation of the formal function may result from external factors, such as new compliance regulations, or internal causes such as a security breach. The first vestige of security governance may appear in the creation of a high-level information security policy, which provides visible evidence of executive management support for the information security function within the organization. In terms of a budgeting strategy, the information security budget may be only a line item of another operational department's budget, rather than a separate budget to support security-related activities. The result is that security activities may need to compete with other groups' activities for budget dollars. I have heard information security practitioners refer to their team's annual expenditures as "budget lint."

The new information security team is often staffed by former security administrators or other technical staff with limited experience specifically in information security or governance. This stage is often characterized by a rapid proliferation of security tools, ad hoc processes, and limited security governance. The team appears to be purely reactive in its actions.

The main concerns at this stage may revolve around recruiting experienced staff and implementing technology with limited efforts in developing supportive and repeatable processes. Most, if not all planning, is short term in duration. Most security awareness activities are concentrated on compliance-mandated requirements rather than broader behavioral changes designed to prevent user-created cyber incidents.

Stage 2: Contagion

In the Contagion stage, security technology continues to dominate the team's activities with rapid acquisition, development, and deployment of multiple technical solutions. This is a continuation of the search for the silver bullet that will completely ensure the organization's security posture. This continued techno-centric view may inhibit the understanding that even the best technologies need to be combined with skilled practitioners and repeatable processes to function optimally, and that no technology is "bullet-proof."

Planning may remain limited to short-term durations, usually of one year or less. In terms of budgeting strategy, the information security budget may remain as only a line item of another operational department's budget, rather than a separate budget to support security-related activities.

The information security policy set may be expanded to include additional categories of policy documents, such as standards, guidelines, and procedures. This expansion of the policy set may result from feedback from auditors or regulators. A formal exception procedure may appear to manage issues that noncompliant technologies require to support business needs. There is limited use of metrics, often due to frequent changing of the security tools used to accumulate tracking data.

At this stage, recruiting experienced staff remains a concern because many team members, some of which might be internal recruits from other departments, may require training and direction from more senior information practitioners. If budget is tight, the team may look to hire a few subject matter experts to lead projects and implement formal security processes. If the security team has not already done so, it may recruit a senior information security professional to direct the organization. Most, if not all planning, remains short term in duration, much like the prior stage. However, some large security initiatives may require longer planning durations.

Stage 3: Control

The Control stage is the midpoint of maturity development. It represents a changing of priorities from externally focused compliance requirements toward a risk-based model for information security activities.

Rather than continuing to randomly acquire security solutions with no real strategic focus for their use, new technology purchases and projects are justified based on ROSI and targeted risk reductions.

Initially, team members often performed different security tasks as necessary to manage the information security needs of the organization. As the security staff grows and gains expertise, the team members may move away from primarily generalist roles into specialized positions and potentially assume leadership positions, formal or informal, in this area, such as network security or secure application development.

While the focus on compliance remains paramount, the direction of compliance tasks shifts from a primarily external to an internal effort toward the organization's own internal policies. The direction shifts away from the creation of new policies and implementation of security technologies to the effective monitoring and enforcement of what the organization has in place. Organizations at this stage may trim the number of security solutions down with the objective of implementing the appropriate tools portfolio for the organization, while reducing support costs.

Increased maturity will include the establishment of information security as a component of the organization's overall governance process. The information security governance board will be responsible for the final ratification of additions and revisions to the information security policies. The information security team assumes a longer planning horizon, similar to those of the rest of the organization, to ensure an alignment with business strategies.

One clear sign of increasing maturity are repeatable processes. Previously ad hoc processes are formalized into standard project management, risk assessments, and metrics methodologies. These formal processes may adopt an industry standard, such as the National Institute of Standards and Technology (NIST)-800 series, or a custom format.

Stage 4: Integration

It is during the Integration stage that the information security team's activities begin to merge into business processes, rather than remaining within isolated silos. This integration involves a combination of the technology, people, and processes used by the information security team. Information security staff liaises across the various business operations with an objective of embedding security into all processes. An example of integrated activities might be information security's participation in a vendor evaluation team rather than just performing a third-party risk assessment procedure after the vendor selection.

At this stage, the purchasing of tools slows down. New security purchases need to be justified using cost–benefit analysis rather than a knee-jerk reaction to a newly identified risk. Potential solutions look to combine technology, people, and processes rather than just throwing more security tools at a problem. The security team is more willing to think outside the box and work with vendors to customize a security solution to meet the organization's specific threat issues.

The team takes on a proactive attitude by looking for possible ways to add value to business functions, such as by participating in meetings with prospects and discussing security aspects of the products and services offered by the organization.

Information security awareness goes beyond the mandatory compliance requirement and expands to offer targeted training for different employees. This training may be integrated into the corporate training catalog rather than isolated in specific security training events. For example, security training may become a component of every employee's on-boarding or orientation program.

As part of its new proactive attitude, noncompliance is handled in a timely manner rather than allowed to linger until coming up against a compliance due date, such as the annual PCI attestation requirement. By not letting noncompliant areas or expired exceptions age, the security team increases the potential for a successful and less expensive resolution of problems.

As information security matures, it looks outward for opportunities to evolve. This is actually a common trait in the maturation life cycle of both individual organisms and groups. Only by interacting with others are we exposed to new ideas, ways of thinking, and knowledge. At the integration stage, the team looks to extend information security functions to external relationships, such as peer organizations, industry groups, private and public collaborations, such as InfraGard.[2] Members of the team or the entire team might network at the local chapters of profession security organizations, such as the Information Systems Security Association (ISSA) and Information Systems Audit Control Association (ISACA).

External focus provides the team with access to other professionals when encountering new risks, the ability to tap research information offered by security organizations, and other networking opportunities within the greater security community. The relative cost for this expanded universe of security knowledge ranges from free to a couple of hundred dollars a year per team member.

The integration stage is a turning point for many information security teams. The team may flourish through both inner and outward collaborations and connectivity. This may result in a more rapid evolution into the next maturity stage. There is also the possibility that the group may stagnate at this phase. This is more of a possibility if they fail to turn outward in their activities and remain isolated from their other organizational peers and the larger security community.

To maintain the forward momentum toward higher maturity levels requires a competent and progressive CISO and the continuing support of executive management. The role of the frugal CISO may transform from a directive leadership role into a supportive role. The CISO and his or her team at the integration stage may be more of an explorer searching out new potential business areas where the information security team can add value. Once the new opportunity is identified, the CISO can allow the self-directed team to take over; then the CISO moves on with "scouting" missions.

Stage 5: Data Administration

At this advanced stage, the information security team has moved to a new plateau in its evolution. The focus of the team moves away from tactical approaches and toward a strategic concentration on protecting the most valuable asset of most organizations—their data. This is a data-centric strategy with an ultimate objective of protecting information and its value over its life cycle. The information security team needs to ensure that data receives appropriate protection from both external attackers, such as hackers, and internal threats, such as malicious insiders. Big data and the increasing number of data breaches make a data-centric strategy increasingly cost effective and in line with the current regulatory trends requiring the securing of sensitive data.

At this maturity level, the information security team transforms from a service function to a business partner by enabling the organization to take risks by expanding into new areas. A data-centric approach allows the organization to gain a market advantage by using its valuable data, while still protecting these critical assets from exploitation.

During this stage, the information security team will refocus on data protection. Often this can mean the adoption of a formalized data classification model or a retooling of the data classifications based upon the current threat landscape. While revising an existing model may seem the easier of the two activities, even slight tweaks to data classifications can have significant consequences in terms of costs.

For example, if proposed classification requires all personally identifiable information (PII) to be encrypted at rest, this can increase data storage by requiring the use of encryption on many previously unencrypted databases. Enforcing the data life cycle may require collaboration with other internal groups, such as records information management (RIM) and the legal department, to ensure the appropriate disposal of sensitive records beyond their retention period. In at least one high-profile data breach, sensitive data maintained beyond its appropriate retention period played a role in exacerbating the scope of the incident.

The data-centric approach creates the need for a rigorous access control policy and access control audits to monitor and detect risky access profiles. This means strong user provisioning controls are necessary to enforce least privilege and prevent users from gaining risky profile combinations. This might require additional investment in technology and process to provide a single centralized view of all user access across the organization.

In addition to managing the security concerns of data housed internally, a data-centric protection strategy looks to control risks related to sharing sensitive information with external parties, such as business partners and outsourcers. Data-centric security teams need to coordinate closely with internal functions, such as procurement, legal, records information management, and information technology (IT) to ensure that sensitive data stored outside the organizational security perimeter is secured appropriately during its entire life cycle.

At this stage, the security awareness effort needs to focus on the criticality of effectively managing the *people perimeter*. An increasingly porous network means that technical infrastructure alone is no longer sufficient to protect organizational assets. People have become the new security perimeter. One poor decision by a member of the organization can create a significant security breach.

Some mature technical companies have already acknowledged this paradigm shift. One excellent example was the Intel Corporation, which adopted this new paradigm for its technology security strategy several years ago. Intel recognized the criticality of addressing these security risks through behavioral change and a renewed focus on security awareness at every level of the enterprise.

This is a fundamental transformation of security strategy away from the creation of additional restrictions around the use of technology. End-user awareness becomes the primary security strategy that is supplemented by technical security solutions, such as encryption, to defend against the potential for cyber breaches.

Stage 6: Maturity/Continuous Renewal

Only a small number of teams will reach the stage of maturity characterized by continuous renewal. This is similar to the Japanese concept of *Kaizen,* or continuous improvement. Organizations that achieve this maturation stage often have information security teams that have been in place for a number of years, may be in highly regulated business sectors, or have an executive management team or board of directors with a highly evolved social consciousness regarding privacy protection.

Achieving Stage 6 does not mean that the information security team has completed its journey and is "done." In fact, it does not get easier for the information security team once they have arrived at this maturity level. Maintaining this level entails vigilance in sustaining all the people, processes, and technologies, as well as continuing to seek out solutions to emerging risk issues. The security threat environment is dynamic, and the control portfolio needs to be tweaked to adjust to changes in both the general threat landscape and unique risk profile of the organization.

At this highest maturity stage, the team has the appropriate level of controls to manage risks in place based upon a standard cost–benefit analysis process. Security is no longer stand-alone or bolted on, but is embedded in all organizational processes and operations. An example of this entrenchment of security in organization processes would be the inclusion of security requirements in the software development life cycle from the design phase through application decommissioning.

The security team may now include a forecasting function charged with anticipating emerging security needs and technologies, such as looking at regulatory trends, modifications in consumer sentiments toward privacy issues, and technological innovations.

The team will regularly review its existing control portfolio, not only to determine the current level of effectiveness of individual controls, but to determine the possibility of optimizing some controls to mitigate multiple risks rather than using them as single-use controls. This control strategy strives to deploy the appropriate level of controls to manage risks without incurring excessive costs.

In line with the rest of the organization, information security uses key metrics to track its effectiveness with respect to its operating objectives. This provides the frugal Chief Information Security Officer (CISO) with financial justification for the team's expenditures and assists in mapping costs to contributions to business activities, especially revenue creation.

For example, if the business implements customer relationship management (CRM) activities and can utilize a marketing data provider because information security is able to secure the data and maintain the privacy of customers and prospects, then incremental increases in household wallet-share revenues can be correlated to the team's participation in the process. The security team looks to align its performance metrics with business operations, rather than use metrics that are ambiguous or unfamiliar to business groups. Security strives to communicate in simple business language and eschews security jargon. Information security may look to adopt recommended practices (aka *smart practices* or *best practices*) appropriate to a highly mature risk management team.

Security awareness moves away from simple awareness messages toward promoting a culture of compliance. This requires changing the focus from creating fear regarding damaging consequences of noncompliance to touting the positive benefits of real security and doing the right things for their own sake.

A compliance culture shifts the organization in the polar opposite direction away from Stage 1's "do it or there will be hell to pay" message to doing the right things for the right motivation, which influences the entire organization. A compliance culture is the reward at the end of the maturation journey for the information security team. A compliance culture requires regular maintenance and continuing support at the highest level of the organization to thrive and mature.

You Are Here: Determining an Organization's Maturity Stage

The frugal CISO needs to determine where his or her information security team is on the maturation continuum. This is a situation where complete honesty is the best policy because it offers an opportunity to identify issues that inhibit development of the information security team. One shorthand method is to look for key indicators of maturity:

- Budget (percentage of budget compared to overall IT budget or organizational budget)
- Support from the executive level or board of directors
- Staff (appropriate to organization size or inadequate to perform required security tasks)
- Existing policies and standards
- Compliance monitoring tools and enforcement
- Overall organization attitude toward compliance and security
- Business sector
- Regulatory requirements
- Customer and prospect attitudes toward data privacy
- Technology landscape
- Pace of adoption of emerging technologies, such as mobile devices and cloud computing

Approximate Your Final Destination

Not every organization needs to reach the highest level of information security maturity. Organizations in highly regulated business sectors, whose revenues depend upon the safekeeping of valued intellectual property, or that need to maintain the value of their organization's reputation to operate successfully, may need to attain a Stage 6 maturity level. The appropriate level of security is dependent upon the organization and its threat landscape. Factors in determining the appropriate level of security maturity include the following factors:

- Size of the organization
- Inherent risks of business model, such as online sales

- Infrastructure complexity (IT and business structure)
- Value of assets (tangible and intangible)
- Regulatory compliance environment
- Risk tolerance level of management

The desired security maturity level may require revisions based upon internal and external events, such as a security breach, new business area, business acquisition, or emerging regulatory requirements. An organization can move forward or backward between levels depending on internal, as well as external, events, surrounding the information security function.

Skipping Levels

It is possible for an organization to exist on the cusp of two maturity stages, such as overlapping between two steps. This situation is both possible and common. While it is not possible to skip a step entirely, the time spent at a particular level may be brief due to a number of factors, such as effective leadership, generous resource availability, expert staff, and highly motivated executive support. Forward movement requires senior management support because an effective information security program requires top-down support.

Bridging the Gaps

Once the information-security team determines its current maturity level and its desired final stage, it needs to identify any gaps that could prevent it from reaching high maturation stages. Once accomplishing this, the team can prioritize closing the gaps by developing a plan to mitigate issues. The plan should include the following:

- Short- and long-term deliverables and their estimated completion dates.
- An attempt to group gaps as a way to address them in a cost-effective manner.
- One or more key metrics to evaluate progress on the plan.
- Visual "score cards," which are an effective tool to communicate progress.

Stumbles Happen

Setbacks are inevitable in life and development. External and internal events can negatively affect plans and progress. Setbacks can occur for a number of reasons, such as security breaches, financial instability, radical budget reductions, acquisition, mergers, and catastrophic events. Two of the most common sources of maturity setbacks are loss of leadership, such as a CISO leaving, or a major shake-up at the executive level or board of directors. Because "tone at the top" is critical to maintaining the forward momentum of the security maturity progress, both types of leadership losses can slow down or halt the maturation development. It is possible for the information security team to regress one or more levels of maturity.

How the team deals with setbacks is a sign of its overall maturity. It is vital that the information security team always consider *Plan B* options when its primary strategy fails or is put on hold for the time being. Current plans might require acceleration, deceleration, or scrapping altogether.

An example of such a scenario might involve an organization currently at a maturity level of Stage 3 and making strong progress toward Stage 4, which experiences a major data breach caused by lack of encryption of sensitive information stored within the organization's internal network. In this example, a cyber attacker used a phishing exploit to gain a foothold, and once inside the internal network, gained access to unencrypted databases containing PII. The information teams in conjunction with the IT department were in the planning stages of implementing a database encryption solution. Both departments were waiting for budget approval when the breach occurred. The organization received some negative press as the result of the breach. For several months after the breach, the information security team lost its former proactive approach to manage the fallout from the incident. The fallout included the replacement of the CISO and several ongoing investigations from regulatory agencies. However, after the replacement of CISO, the team resumed its forward momentum, despite some lingering impacts from the breach. Rather than focus on the negative aspects of the breach, the new CISO stressed it as a learning experience and worked to justify the closing of identified risk issues.

After a setback, it is important to perform a postmortem and revise the plan to correct the root issues that created the stumble to avoid repeating the experience. To Albert Einstein, "Insanity: doing the same thing over and over again and expecting different results."[3]

Spotting Maturity Landmarks of Progress

It is important to spot positive signs of forward progress for several reasons. If the information security team or CISO does not monitor the maturity development of the team, even qualitatively, the progress can easily go off course or cease to occur. The primary reason to be on the lookout for maturity landmarks is to know the security team is moving in the right direction and that its effort toward maturation is paying off.

If no progress occurs, then it provides an opportunity to correct the team's course or try a different strategy. Peter Drucker, management expert and author, said, "What gets measured, gets managed." Some qualitative landmarks of positive progress toward information security maturation include:

- Demonstrable executive management support, such as statements, participation in cyber security events, or spearheading funding proposals
- Appropriate funding and resources to perform not only basic and required security functions, but offer strategic investment in technology to cost-effectively enhance the organization's security posture
- Use of a cost–benefit approach in determining appropriate security controls
- Consideration of both internal and external risks
- Program approach to security and compliance (versus checklists)
- Use of project management methodologies
- Adoption of recommended, best, and smart practices as appropriate to the organization level of maturation and threat landscape
- Access audits
- Automated monitoring supported by enforcement
- Proactive attitude
- Continuous incremental improvements

Tips for Managing the Information Security Maturation Process

Here are some tips for managing the maturation progress of your information security team:

1. Always keep in mind that information security maturity is situational. The appropriate level of security maturity will depend on the organization, its threat landscape, business sector, and regulatory compliance requirements.
2. The starting point is getting an accurate baseline of where the information security team is on the maturation continuum.
3. Look for key metrics or qualitative attributes to evaluate the team's progress on the maturation continuum.
4. Be willing have the team's plans revised based on internal and external events.
5. Realize that setbacks are normal. Setbacks should be expected. It is how they are handled that makes the difference.
6. Even if the team reaches the highest maturity level (Stage 6), the job is not complete. The team needs to look for ways to continuously improve.

Endnotes

1. Richard Nolan, "Managing the Crisis in Data Processing," *Harvard Business Review*, March/April 1979, http://www.comp.dit.ie/rfitzpatrick/Business%20Perspectives%20slides/Conceptual%20Business%20Models/Managing%20the%20crises%20in%20data%20processing%20-%20Nolan.pdf.
2. InfraGard is a public–private partnership between the FBI and members of the private sector who are focused on intrusions and vulnerabilities affecting eighteen critical infrastructures (taken from www.InfraGard.net).
3. Brainy Quote, http://www.brainyquote.com/quotes/quotes/a/alberteins-133991.html#ZevyTpP5w4J0WpQG.99.

3

REDUCING COMPLEXITY

Complexity and Volume, Oh My

Over a decade ago, I asked a senior IT executive what his greatest challenges were. He responded saying "we have one of everything" and "we can kill anything." What he described was a scenario all too common in large complex IT infrastructure—technological complexity and high transaction volume. Volume is largely a function of business activity.

However, complexity is controllable to a large degree. The reasons for technological complexity varies from personal preferences, technical biases, desire to remain on technology's leading edge, and functional requirements. Only the latter two reasons take into consideration the best interests of the business and its needs. I have seen production applications that are literally a "crazy quilt" of technologies, including unusual hardware and software selections. My personal favorite was the use of an obscure UNIX variant running on an x86 architecture that required end users to have a separate piece of hardware to use one application.

One of the greatest enemies of security and cost management is complexity. Every variation in software, operating systems, and hardware incurs a cost in terms of supporting and maintaining security.

The total lifetime cost of applications is rarely considered during development. After the initial release and acceptance of an application, the ongoing costs associated with the systems often shift to other cost centers. The cost of software maintenance has risen to a whopping 90% of the total lifetime cost of software, and each layer of software complexity puts stress on IT budgets.

When I started in information security in the mid-1990s, the cost of maintaining software security was relatively small and often limited to adding basic security functionality, such as a requirement for passwords. The transition to web applications and the exploitation of software vulnerabilities by attackers increased these costs exponentially due to increased requirements for frequent patching of underlying components and use of protective security software mechanisms.

Complexity creates multiple areas of risk. Complex applications may contain numerous vulnerabilities both in the source code itself, as well as the supporting components and middleware. Software flaws, usually called *bugs*, are almost as old as software itself. It is estimated that there are between five and fifty bugs per thousand lines of source code.

At the same time, the average size of software applications grew to support advanced features. Some web applications require one million lines of source code. Software bugs can trigger conditions in which an application can act in unintended ways. This unplanned behavior can create exploitable security vulnerabilities. Hackers can exploit these vulnerabilities to produce undesirable or unexpected interactions between technologies with the result often being a security breach.

Not all complexity is a target for reduction. Some business functionality may require specialized technology. The organization may need to adopt new or complex technology, such as mobile applications, to remain competitive. The maintenance of some older technologies may require new features to support compliance regulations. However, a great deal of complexity is controllable through requirements based on business justifications, standards, and guidelines.

Some potential areas of concentration for complexity reduction are in-house applications, data stores, and technology platforms. This kind of reduction requires an information security and IT organization at a high level of maturity, equivalent to Nolan's Maturity Model's Integration stage or higher, characterized by the following traits:

1. Integration of risk management functions
2. Security is a component of all applications and architectures
3. Understanding of the criticality of implementation and support of solutions
4. Inclusion of security as a component of all phases of the system development life cycle

A critical step in the reduction of complexity is limiting the overall number of technologies in use and the number of technologies used in software development. Some areas for technology reduction and simplification include:

1. Reduce the overall software inventory.
2. Standardize and reduce the number of components used in the development of applications.
3. Standardize and reduce the number of operating systems (OSs) and OS versions.
4. Standardize and reduce configurations based on business, technical, and security requirements.

Reduction in complexity decreases the overall number of things for which we need to manage security. It provides the collateral benefit of reducing IT costs for managing and supporting seldom-used technology solutions and obsolete legacy applications. This can translate into real cost savings by eliminating costs associated with license renewals, support agreements, upgrades and patching, disk space usage, and processor time. Freed-up resources can be allocated to projects with the potential to truly transform the IT infrastructure to support the business strategy.

Actively Managing the Application Portfolio

Application portfolios bloat when they are not actively managed. A chief information security officer's (CISO's) first step is getting a copy of the application inventory for the organization. The biggest challenge is that an application inventory may not even exist. If it exists, it may not be current or accurate.

Even when an application inventory exists, there may be challenges associated with it:

- Key items may be missing information, such as a basic description or point of contact.
- If separate inventories are maintained by different groups, inventories may be riddled with redundant application names, which might be the same application or different applications with the same name.

Often, the only impetus to retire software is either the termination of a licensing agreement or some other event, such as Y2K, which required costly modifications for software going forward into the new millennium.

Some of the reasons that dubious legacy applications remain on active inventories are:

- There is fear that some unknown group is dependent on the application.
- No individual or group has responsibility for the application.
- It is easier to let obsolete applications remain in active status than deal with issues surrounding their retirement, such as archiving data with records retention requirements.
- There is a lack of understanding of the costs of maintaining inactive applications, such as ongoing licensing and maintenance fees.

While keeping older software is viewed as having no associated costs, this software can create hidden costs and insecurities. Older applications, sometimes called *legacy software*, may suffer from *resiliency degradation* in which the capability of software to resist attacks degrades over time due to changes in technology, threats, and staffing. Older software may not permit upgrades or patching to fix known vulnerabilities.

Older hardware that hosts legacy software may be susceptible to even low-velocity denial-of-service (DoS) attacks. Performing vulnerability assessments on legacy software presents challenges. Older platforms that host legacy applications may not tolerate penetration testing (pen testing) without creating outages. In addition, older platforms lack activity monitoring that alerts staff to outages. The consequence is that pen testing an application and its supporting components may not be possible in production.

Older versions of software can create costs by requiring additional testing of security patches to certify their compatibility with upgrades. At its worst, legacy software can result in exploitable vulnerabilities or failures to meet compliance requirements.

Building a Current Application Inventory

To paraphrase management consultant Peter Drucker, you cannot manage what you don't know about. The number of applications can balloon because nobody knows about them. Applications are created, used, abandoned, and decommissioned without any notification. This may occur because no formal owner exists. Sometimes with a shared application, no one group wants to assume ownership. These applications enter a kind of *twilight zone* in which no one seems to know much about them.

Support and other costs continue to receive payment from old cost centers that no one removed from the general ledger. Unless some specific event occurs or the host platform undergoes decommissioning, they may continue for years.

To obtain an accurate application inventory may require action by the CISO in conjunction with assistance from IT. This means that the information security team takes the lead in the creation or updating of the application inventory. The skills for doing this inventory are tenacity, tact, reasonable understanding of technology, and strong interpersonal communications abilities. It is possible to assign an entry-level practitioner or intern, if they are provided with a script, form, and some guidance. While the process is tedious, the results provide a level of insight not possible to attain in other ways.

This effort can provide a stepping-stone to future joint projects with IT. After creating a draft inventory, joint review meetings can be scheduled. This is a foundational step in the reduction of the applications and supplies the impetus for an initiative to decommission obsolete applications. The justification for such a project is the potential for savings in the support, maintenance, and security of the IT infrastructure.

Appendix B contains two forms to use as a starting point for performing an application inventory. The *Application Inventory Summary Template* is useful in gathering and reporting information about applications at a high level. Once completed for all applications, it provides the basis for the construction of an application inventory. The *Application Detail Template* goes to a deeper level by allowing the reviewer to gather more detail about the types of data managed, processed, and stored by applications. It is useful in identifying repositories of sensitive, high-risk, regulated, or personally identifiable (PI) data for evaluations of controls in place to protect this data from potential breaches.

Reducing Application Complexity

Many applications suffer from overdesign resulting from the inclusion of a rarely used functionality or the desire to *build the resume* (BTR)[1] by using a "cool" technology. As an application support manager in the late 1990s, I managed software applications that resembled college term projects because they used multiple nonstandard or *bleeding-edge* technologies with the objective of producing a "killer app." These applications required excessive support and devolved into kludges. The team kept them running using creativity, common sense, and a sense of humor. However, it was not necessary to manage security risks because these were internal applications and the cyber risk landscape was considerably less threatening. I cannot imagine dealing with these types of complex applications and mitigating security vulnerabilities at the same time.

Unfortunately, the BTR syndrome is alive and well. It has just moved to web and mobile apps. Some "hot" technologies lack basic security and may not be a good fit for the IT strategy or the business functions they support.

Strategies for Reducing Application Complexity

Standardizing components and operating environments shrinks the cost of compatibility testing security patches. It also prevents critical applications from developing a dependency on obsolete components without an upgrade path. One milestone in cutting complexity is an effective collaboration between the CISO and the chief information officer (CIO) or chief technology officer (CTO). This partnership can assist in making a case for standardization during the development process.

Most CIOs and CTOs look to reduce operating costs while increasing efficiency. This objective mirrors the CISO's objective to trim security costs while continuing to provide efficient and effective service. Standardized development components, procedures, and routine vulnerability scanning can contribute to the overall reduction of costly last-minute fixes, noncompliance, and the potential for security breaches.

Fortunately, CIOs and CTOs have significant experience in balancing the adoption of new technologies and the costs of supporting them in production. Many application problems originate from decisions that are made during development but may not be evident until implementation. Each technology evolution increases complexity and requires a balancing of complexity against higher productivity and performance. The use of development standards and guidelines can offer the CIO or CTO assistance in maintain equilibrium between continued innovation and production stability.

Using development standards and guidelines offers five benefits:

1. It reduces unnecessary complexity by providing a standard development tool set.
2. It simplifies maintenance by decreasing the number of products in which developers need to develop proficiency. This can yield major savings because maintenance can account for more than 90% of the total cost of a software application.
3. By simplifying the architecture of the majority of applications, IT can concentrate its resources on applications where cutting-edge functions and innovation have the greatest potential to provide the organization with an advantage, such as mobile applications. This is an application of the *Pareto principle* (the 80/20 rule). This principle tells us to focus on the 20% that makes the most significant difference to the organization.
4. It helps ensure that the handling of security and security-related functions is consistent across all applications. Inconsistency creates the potential for the introduction of errors and other types of vulnerabilities. Cyber attackers can exploit these vulnerabilities to create security breaches or DoS attacks. A common example is Structured Query Language (SQL) injection and other types of injection exploits. SQL injection attacks have been responsible for a number of high-profile data breaches, including Heartland Payment Systems and Hannaford Brothers.
5. Complexity makes security more difficult because there are more "moving parts" to monitor. To use a simple analogy, consider an individual tracking a bunch of bouncing balls on a screen. When the number of balls is low, this is not difficult. As the number of balls increases, it becomes more difficult to monitor all the balls, until it becomes virtually impossible. The greater the number of items that require monitoring, the greater the potential that some will be missed and create an increased probability for exploitation by a hacker.

Why Applications Are the Favorite "Hacker Snack"

Applications often represent some of an organization's most significant assets. Applications also may represent one of the organization's most substantial sources of risk. According to Gartner, 75% of security breaches have applications as a root cause.[2] Many breaches created by applications are the result of insecure development practices. While both the cause and many of the potential solutions have been known for more than a decade, application flaws continue to dominate many of the larger security breaches, such as the 2011 series of breaches at Sony Corporation.

This is the reason that many hackers changed their strategy to focus on applications. It is a simpler and easier route into many organizations' internal networks. It is analogous to leaving a door wide open to a house. Why would a burglar bother climbing through a window when a door is left open?

Web applications offer a possibly more direct route to an organization's most valuable asset, its data. Most organizations have become very proficient at protecting their networks. Unfortunately, the application infrastructure often remains porous and a much more attractive point of entry for would-be attackers.

Applications create security vulnerabilities in two ways. The first way is that applications create "holes" in the organizational security perimeter that hackers can potentially exploit. The second way, and perhaps more serious risk, involves the data that the applications manage, process, and store. Most hackers are not looking to just create disruptions or mischief. The majority of hackers that organizations face have a primarily financial motivation. These hackers are seeking access to data that they can use to make money or sell to others looking to do the same thing.

Application Risk Rating

Identification of Appropriate Information
Protection Classification for Applications

A challenge in dealing with application-based risks may be the sheer number of applications, sometimes numbering in the hundreds or even thousands, used by an organization. Just getting a handle on identifying the entire application inventory can become an expensive and time-consuming initiative (see the section "Building a Current Application Inventory" earlier in this chapter). Even if all the applications and their functions are known, it may not be economically feasible to assure that they are appropriately secure.

When the number of applications exceeds available resources, it becomes critical to apply a risk management triage strategy. In a triage strategy, applications are sorted and allocated resources based upon assessed level of risk. Higher-risk applications receive a priority in threat reduction treatments.

The first step in risk management is the identification of appropriate information protection classifications for all applications, both existing and under development. There are a number of classification approaches available, including:

- Sensitivity of the data managed, processed, or stored by the application
- Location of the application relative to the Internet (Internet-facing, internal)
- Type of application, such as financial, retail commerce, and so on
- Regulatory requirements surrounding data managed, processed, or stored by the application
- Application architecture (mainframe, web application, client/server)

Any of these attributes can become the basis for the creation of an application risk-level classification system. Alternately, a combination of two or more attributes can be used to assess risk based upon multiple risk factors. The decision on which attributes and approach to select will vary with the individual organization's risk philosophy and threat landscape.

Information Classification System

Many organizations may opt to drive the majority of the application risk-level assignment based on the sensitivity of the data that the application processes, manages, or stores. This is because many of the risks associated with applications are at their core data risks. One of

PUBLICLY AVAILABLE	ORGANIZATIONAL PROPRIETARY	ORGANIZATIONAL AVAILABILITY ONLY	ORGANIZATIONAL CONFIDENTIAL OR SENSITIVE
Advertising	Strategic plans	Tactical plans	Social Security Numbers
Job postings	Trade secrets	Legal documents	Health insurance numbers and health records
Press releases	New ideas/ innovations	Human resources records (except "confidential")	Employee personnel files and compensation
Historical corporate information		Policies and procedures	Passport numbers
Marketing literature		Nonpublic financial information	Alien registration numbers
		Information technology data	Payroll records
		Employee work product	

Figure 3.1 Sample generic information classification system.

the easiest ways to drive application risk-level assignment using data sensitivity is by making use of the organization's existing information classification system. If no information classification system exists, it might be a good time to create one. In terms of creating a new information classification system, simpler is generally better. The purpose of an information classification system is to divide the data used by the organization into broad groupings based on its general characteristics and protection requirements. It is a good idea to keep the number of categories relatively small, such as three to five. The primary reason to limit the number of categories to five or fewer is that it is difficult for the average user to remember beyond that number. In the following section and in Figure 3.1 is a sample generic information classification system for the purposes of this discussion.

Publicly Available:
- Information intended for public release
- Information that is publicly available or whose disclosure could not harm the organization

Organizational Proprietary:
- Sensitive information available on a *business need-to-know basis*
- Information whose unauthorized disclosure, use, or destruction would likely adversely affect the organization

Organizational Only Availability:
- High-risk information requiring strict controls
- Nonpublic personal, financial, health, or employment information concerning identifiable past, present, or prospective clients/customers, employees, and consultants, as applicable

Organizational Confidential or Sensitive:
- High-risk information requiring strict controls
- Nonpublic personally identifiable, financial, health, or employment information for prospective clients/customers, employees, and consultants

In addition to the risk levels and examples for each category, each level would receive specific handling instructions to protect the information at rest (storage) and in motion (during data transfers). The determination of the appropriate overall information protection is largely based upon the types of risks associated with a category of data.

The primary objective of an information classification scheme is spending only what is necessary to protect the data against threats. Without an information classification scheme, an organization might need to apply the same level of controls to all its data. This would not be a cost-effective practice. Low-risk data, such as press releases, would receive the same level of protection as highly sensitive data, such as credit card information. Depending on the level of controls selected to protect all the data, some data might be undersecured, while other data might receive excessive and costly overprotection.

Information Classification Scheme and Application Security Rating

An excellent starting point to determine application security levels is to review the data used by the application, including the inputs and outputs the application may include in its processing cycle. Another factor influencing assignment of application risk levels is the function(s) performed by the application. Some organizational functions have greater inherent risks associated with them or need more security to assure their successful outcome. Some examples of more sensitive functions include financial transactions or actions designed to protect human life/safety. Compromise or corruption of these types of transactions could have devastating consequences. Other trans-actions necessitating a higher level of transactional security involve functions regulated by external compliance organizations, such as health information or industry requirements, such as Payment Card Industry Data Security Standard (PCI-DSS).

Another factor in the development of an application risk ranking system is the criticality of the application to the organization's mission or revenue stream. While this application may not process sensitive data, it is nevertheless important to defend it against possible inter-ference by malicious parties.

Application Risk Levels and Definitions

An application sensitivity model exists with four levels:

Level I
- Application processes sensitive, confidential, proprietary, or personally identifiable information (PII)
- Application processes financial transactions, performs monetary record keeping, or manages money/asset transfers (e.g., wire transfers)
- Application manages functions that are designed to pro-tect human life and safety
- Application manages transactions covered under compli-ance regulations, such as Health Insurance Portability and Accountability Act (HIPAA) or PCI-DSS

Level II
- Applications assigned a high availability rating, such as online transactional systems
- Information associated with the creation, processing, or storage of *Organizational Availability Only* data
- Applications used as part of a client service with high availability as a part of the service-level agreement (SLA)

Level III
- All remaining production applications fall within this level

Level IV
- Applications in nonproduction/development and test environments

- Excludes sensitive or unmasked production data in non-production environment

Steps to Implementing Complexity Reduction

The first step is the establishment of standards. This requires effective collaboration between IT and information security. Information security may offer to take the lead in managing this effort. A common concern is that this effort may monopolize too much of the developers' time. This concern may be assuaged by stating upfront how much time each participant will need to commit. Often, the total time commitment can be less than one hour per application.

This project requires the CISO to exercise his/her persuasion skills. Fortunately, this collaboration offers an excellent value proposition for both parties. From an IT perspective, it contributes to the information technology roadmap. The roadmap is a plan that identifies potential technology solutions to achieve the short-term and long-term needs of the business. It considers both current and emerging technologies.

It cultivates a consensus regarding which technologies can best satisfy the business's needs. The roadmap contributes to the creation of a strategic blueprint for technology for up to five years. This blueprint considers current technologies and the adoption of technologies to meet the future direction of the business. The roadmap's collateral benefits include the following:

- Evaluation of new technologies based on their appropriateness for business needs, architectural strategy, and security requirements
- Identification of unusual or one-off technologies within the application infrastructure
- Identification of opportunities for consolidation of technologies
- Identifies inconsistencies between business or technical strategies (out-of-the-ordinary technology choices often stick out like a sore thumb)
- Creates documentary evidence of current and future technology architecture strategy, such as architecture diagrams
- Points out the potential for cost savings through the reduction of technical complexity

- Serves as a chance for the inclusion of information security in the criteria used in setting future technical architecture strategy
- Can be used to create a *technology watch list* to monitor for potential vulnerabilities and exploits
- Identify suitable locations within the IT architecture for the introduction of emerging and innovative technologies, such as virtualization, mobile application, and cloud computing

Using the technology inventory and information technology roadmap, the information security organization can recommend standards and guidelines to ensure applications follow a consistent design and use standard components. These standards and guidelines can include existing and emerging technologies such as cloud computing. Information security can demonstrate that while it supports standardization to decrease costs, simplify support, and improve security, it recognizes the necessity of using specialized technologies to support business requirements.

An exception process supports the need for standardization while supporting innovation for applications that offer the organization a specific advantage in the marketplace. It also provides documentation to justify the use of nonstandard technology.

Legacy Third-Party Applications

Many third-party applications become legacy applications over their production life. They suffer from the same resiliency degradation as in-house applications, which makes them less resistant to attacks. Since the vendor controls the application's source code rather than IT, there is often no way to upgrade, patch, or fix some vulnerabilities without potentially violating the product's warranty or breaking the application.

This can create situations of noncompliance with regulations, depending on the application functions or location within the network infrastructure. Often these issues do not become apparent until after the application fails a compliance audit. At this point, it is often difficult to resolve the issue because the application is no longer covered by a maintenance agreement.

One of the primary reasons that vendor-supplied applications have a tendency to develop critical unremediated vulnerabilities is that they are not consistently monitored. Vendor-supplied applications may be ignored because they perform the functions well without much support. While this situation may appear ideal from a resource management perspective, it can hide unaddressed risks because no one is looking to see if everything is still copasetic.

This situation may go on for the duration of the support agreement. After the support agreement lapses, it is tempting to continue using the product as-is to avoid costly vendor upgrades or delay making a decision. This results in a scenario similar to the one depicted in the movie *The Money Pit*.[3] After a security assessment, problems stemming from unpatched vulnerabilities surface and prevent the organization from passing a compliance assessment. The organization may see any cost savings from delaying an upgrade evaporate in its efforts to remediate vulnerabilities to obtain a complaint rating on the audit. At this point, the organization has five potential options available:

1. Get the vendor to expedite a costly, unbudgeted upgrade.
2. Attempt to patch the vulnerabilities themselves with the knowledge that this will violate any remaining contract provisions and potentially break the application.
3. Rush to carry out a solution search, and then implement the selected replacement application.
4. Evaluate if outsourced or cloud-based solutions are available to assume the function.
5. Make the default decision to do nothing and hope they can get an exemption for the application's noncompliance or offer an appropriate compensating control. This option generally requires implementing a compliant solution within a specific period.

However, by actively managing the security of vendor-supplied applications, this unpleasant scenario is not necessary. It is critical to track all vendor applications from their initial implementation through their decommissioning. Many costs associated with the vendor-supplied applications occur late in the operational life of the application. To minimize costs associated with vendor applications, the involvement of information security beginning with the contractual process is a critical success factor. Avoiding or at least minimizing these costs requires a combination of specific contract language and continuous vulnerability management throughout the application's life cycle.

Strategies for Minimizing Risks and Costs for Vendor Applications

Spell Out the Details of Required Support, Security, and Vulnerability Management in the SLA With an SLA or any other type of vendor contract, the rule of thumb is not to make assumptions. As the adage goes, "the devil is in the details" when it comes to SLAs. Many vendor SLAs do not specifically reference security or regulatory compliance, with the exception of security solutions. Older SLAs may have omitted these clauses altogether.

Even new SLAs may omit specific language regarding security remediation unless explicitly requested by the purchaser. Some SLAs require the customer to notify the vendor of any identified vulnerabilities. This places the onus on the customer to monitor vulnerabilities.

It is common for SLAs to include a clause that terminates or limits the purchaser's support agreement if the purchaser refuses to upgrade release levels. Upgrades often require additional outlay of funds, either for consulting from the vendor or hardware upgrades.

If the SLA is already in place, your best bet is trying to renegotiate the SLA to include security clauses. However, this might not be possible. The CISO is in the best position when negotiating a new SLA with the vendor. In specifying contract clauses for a new vendor application, always attempt to include the following contractual provisions:

- Include explicit contract clauses regarding the resolution of identified vulnerabilities, such as issuing of vendor updates within a specific time frame.
- Require the vendor to notify customers of any vulnerabilities in the product within a specific number of business days of identification.
- If another customer is breached as a direct result of using the vendor's product, your organization should be notified immediately and be notified of fixes and workarounds.
- Require the vendor to identify a specific point of contact for reporting and resolution of security-related issues.

Do Regular Information Security Assessments of Your Vendor Applications Whenever technically feasible, run vulnerability scans of vendor applications on a regular schedule. The determination for the appropriate scan frequency should include looking at compliance requirements, the threat landscape, and other risk attributes associated with the vendor application's function. For vendor applications supporting specific compliance regulations, run the vendor application scans on the same schedule as other compliance checks, such as quarterly scans.

Reducing Data Storage

For most organizations, data represents its most important asset. Data is the most desirable asset for hackers and cyber criminals. Not all data has equal value. Some data is extremely valuable because of its potential to create wealth, such as intellectual property (IP), trade secrets, and proprietary information. These data types have value associated with them because they can be used or sold to obtain more liquid assets, such as cash.

In recent years, cyber espionage, the act of obtaining valuable secret information without authorization, has surged and the current trends predict continuing increases in this category of computer crime. Companies, nations, and individuals can carry out this type of computer crime for both personal and collective gains.

Many organizations underestimate the risks associated with proprietary information, with the result being that they do not implement the appropriate controls to protect these valuable assets. The first step is creating awareness around these issues, such as the value of these assets and the capabilities of the rival organizations. Emerging trends in IT have increased the potential for unauthorized transfers of IP, such as the movement to cloud computing and the explosion of mobile devices. The major challenge for information security will be allowing organizations to reap the many benefits of these technologies, such as lowering computing costs and expediting technology transformations, while providing appropriate protections for IP resources.

PII is another type of data with a high value for hackers who sell it to other cyber criminals using established Internet marketplaces. Information security authorities even branded the year 2011 as the Year of the Breach due to the increasing prevalence of PII breaches during that period. In the United States alone over the past five years, more than half a billion individuals became victims of cyber criminals who stole their PII. Currently, the prevalence of breaches continues to plague most organizations.

Protecting against PII breaches could be one of the most significant potential areas of cost avoidance. For example, in 2011 Sony announced that cyber criminals breached the PII records of 100 million PlayStation Network users. The ultimate total cost of this breach could range from $1 billion to $2 billion, making it one of the most expensive security incidents of all time. These costs do not include the long-term reputation damage created by the breach. As one of my professional peers likes to say, "You do not want to end up as a case study for what your company failed to do."

A comprehensive understanding of your organization's data is the underpinning of strong data security. Data tends to expand to use the amount of storage space available to store it. Data is like the comedian George Carlin's famous routine about *stuff*. No matter how much data an organization has, it seeks more, then buys bigger storage to accommodate it.

There is a tendency to hoard data. Trends like Big Data are fueling the requirements to hold onto large amounts of data. While storage costs have fallen, the costs of managing data have remained high.

Due to the 2006 changes in the Federal Rules of Civil Procedure, excessive data retention can escalate legal costs associated with eDiscovery. According to a 2011 survey by the Association for Information and Image Management (AIIM), legal costs are 25% higher than they could be if organizations followed best practices in records management, including the appropriate disposal of electronic records past their scheduled retention date.

One of the most significant risks associated with excessive data retention is protection of sensitive information, especially PII. The retention of records containing unnecessary sensitive information, especially PII, can magnify the impact of a data breach to catastrophic proportions. In at least one high-profile breach, excess storage of PII magnified the scope of the incident.

By reducing the overall storage of records, especially records containing PII, we decrease the potential impact of data breaches. By collaborating with records information management (RIM), excessive retention of information can be reduced by enforcement of records disposal schedules. In addition to the structured storage of records containing PII, unstructured storage of PII is a significant threat. Data leakage prevention (DLP) tools can identify and inventory unstructured data storage containing PII and facilitate its disposal or encryption based upon business requirements. A collateral benefit is that data reduction projects may pay for themselves in the cost savings generated by freeing up storage space or avoiding purchasing additional disk space.

Steps to Reducing Stored Data

The objective of reducing data storage is not jettisoning useful data, but looking for obsolete and redundant data that tends to accumulate over time. Copies of data, often originating from the same source data, get distributed across the organization. According to a McKinsey Global Institute study, almost 80% of annual storage growth seemed to be redundant copies of other stored data.

Sometimes, when data is no longer required, it continues to be produced because there is no mechanism for stopping it. Older data feeds may contain attributes, such as Social Security Numbers, financial account numbers, and other information we now label as PII. It is logical to believe that some of these older files still exist somewhere on the network. Some of these files have no owner and are essentially orphans. Each of these has the potential to create a security breach.

Strategies for Reducing and Managing Data

I have heard some experts say that one of the greatest and seldom mentioned risks to information security is the amount of data stored across the network infrastructure. Effective data management requires a triad of people, process, and technology. It is not easy. However, the return on investment (ROI) related to getting a handle on identifying the organization's data landscape is substantial. Data reduction offers a benefit in terms of decreased storage, security costs, and a minimization of the potential impact of breaches, if they do occur.

The chief benefit is a diminishment in risk equal to the amount of sensitive data disposal. Few security initiatives yield a one-to-one reduction in risk advantage. For example, if an organization identifies and reduces its total volume of data containing sensitive attributes by 30%, then overall risk diminishes by 30%.

A collateral benefit of data reduction is decreasing potential eDiscovery costs because it cuts the available pools of data during the legal discovery process. In 2006, changes in the Federal Rules of Civil Procedure have placed organizations under greater pressure to produce electronic records as part of the discovery procedures. Legal eDiscovery actions can cost organizations hundreds of thousands of dollars over the duration of a lawsuit.

Steps to Finding the Data

The organization needs to identify its data and its locations. There are two potential mechanisms for accomplishing this objective. The first mechanism is a review of the organization's electronic information inventory. This inventory is an index of all the structured electronic data stores used by the organization. Structured information consists of databases, file stores, supporting files, extracts (for internal use and external transmission), and other digital data used by the organization as part of formal IT processes.

However, significant amounts of sensitive information occur in other types of data, such as electronic documents and other unstructured data types. Unstructured data includes, but is not limited to, tweets, email, blogs, metadata, and health records, audio, video, and analog files. Unstructured information can make up at least 85% of all data in organizations. Gartner predicts that enterprise data will grow by 800% in 5 years, with 80% of it unstructured.

Electronic Information Inventory   The best case is that an inventory of the electronic information already exists that documents the key attributes of all data stores. Organizations with a high level of maturity may already have taken this important first step. The records information management (RIM) team may manage this inventory.

Data Discovery Solutions   Data discovery solutions (DDS) scan the organization's IT infrastructure to identify structured and unstructured data that could contain sensitive information. Data discovery tools use a number of techniques, including pattern matching, hashing, and statistical or other forms of probability analysis.

One common technique is the use of the *Luhn* algorithm to recognize a variety of identification numbers, such as credit card numbers. Some commercial tools allow custom searches for specific metadata and text patterns used within the organization. DLP tools are applied on network egress points, such as Internet portals and external email gateways, to detect and block data containing sensitive information from leaving the organization's network unencrypted.

The Next Steps in Reduction of Obsolete or Redundant Data

The combination of the records inventory and DDS analysis provides a data map of the organization. It can identify redundant or dormant data stores that include sensitive data attributes with a focus on potential high-risk targets, such as PII, proprietary information, intellectual property, and trade secrets.

By providing the CIO/CTO and other key stakeholders with this critical information, it increases the potential for reduction of these potential targets and the momentum for creation of an ongoing data-monitoring program.

Reduce Security Solutions Complexity

Proliferation of security tools and solutions may be a symptom of the early stages of information security that focus primarily on compliance objectives. This is similar to Contagion (Stage 2) in Nolan's Stages Model. The Contagion stage is characterized by a *silver bullet* mind-set characterized by rapid tool acquisition, development, and deployment.

Much of the tool deployment occurs in separate silos targeting specific business or compliance requirements. This can result in the purchases of multiple tools with the same basic functionality, for example, several secure email solutions for external email. The emphasis is on tools acquisition and rapid deployment, not security or cost management.

However, there may be limited acceptance and use of tools because of deficient implementation and lack of adequate user training. Rather than trying to correct these issues, the hunt begins for the *next big thing*, another security tool is purchased, and the cycle repeats again. In addition to the initial purchase price, there are many hidden costs, such as the costs of supporting and training end users on multiple solution sets.

Paring Down Security Solutions

One way to reduce costs while increasing the effectiveness of security tools is to pare down the list of products to one or two per functional category. The first step is the identification of the security solutions that exist and the specifics of each licensing agreement. It is common to have limited licensing agreements for many similar security products with no one licensing agreement sufficient to cover the entire organization.

You need to get an accurate inventory of what the organization has. Luckily, this information might be available in one place, the purchasing organization. The purchasing team usually has this information because acquiring these products involves complex licensing agreements that require input from both the purchasing group and the legal department.

After assembling a current inventory of all security solutions, develop a short list of evaluation criteria for each major product category. These criteria should be broad by design to avoid a tendency to base production evaluations around one existing solution with which team members are familiar. This is a common flaw in some product evaluations that can result in a specific vendor heavily influencing a buying decision. If the team is not familiar with the security product category or has experience with only one vendor's solution, many information security magazines do annual or monthly solution comparisons. The criteria used in these journals are useful in developing a vendor-neutral set of evaluation standards.

It is important to include criteria for determining whether the solution is an appropriate fit for the organization, based upon these nine factors:

1. Organization culture
2. Executive management's tolerance for risk (aka, *risk appetite*)
3. Overall organizational maturity stage
4. IT organization's maturity stage
5. IT infrastructure complexity
6. Business and IT strategies
7. Business sector, such as financial services
8. Current threat landscape
9. Adoption of emerging technologies

Sometimes the evaluation process gets a form of *tunnel vision* in which alternatives are not measured on their appropriateness for the function, but on another nebulous property, such as *best of breed* or *world class*. It is important not to lose sight of the objective of the process, which is identification of the solution's fitness to perform its job.

An analogy would be selecting a vehicle to commute to work. The key criteria would be safety, durability, high gas mileage, delivery of good value for the purchase price, and strong performance in a variety of weather conditions. An expensive foreign automobile might be described as *world class*, but would not be suitable for the purpose described. On the other hand, a compact automobile with all-wheel drive would fit the bill.

The ultimate objective is to identify which security solution or solutions are the best fit for the organization. If it is possible to narrow the selection down to one, that is great. However, because of specific requirements of a specific business area or function, this may not be possible.

By reducing the security solution set, there are cost savings in the ongoing cost and effectiveness of support. Rather than multiple groups supporting siloed solutions, support and training can be centralized. This offers a collateral benefit of higher user satisfaction because support may be more consistent, and available. The net result is a lower lifetime cost for a security solution.

When purchasing a new category of security solutions or researching a replacement for an existing solution, vendor-neutral assessment criteria can clarify what features and key success factors need to be satisfied.

Other Strategies to Reduce the Cost of Security Solutions

These four strategies will also help reduce security solutions costs:

1. Do not purchase components that you do not plan to use, such as application programming interface (API) or scripting tools.
2. Do not buy more of a tool (for instance, more licenses) simply because your organization qualifies for volume pricing or site licenses at a lower unit cost.
3. Avoid purchasing large numbers of licenses for a product to obtain a favorable volume discount when your organization has limited experience with a technology or no concrete strategy for its use. Many times, I have seen a manager negotiate

a great price per unit by committing to volume procurement only to utilize a small number of what they purchased.

4. It is prudent to purchase a small number of units to perform a proof of concept before making a significant monetary commitment to a product.

Reducing Complexity and Risks Created by "Bolt-On" Security

Bolt-On Security

There are two alternatives when adding security to a system. The first is to incorporate security into the system design. The other is bolting on security functionality after the system's design is complete. The *bolt-on* option remains the more popular of the two. Bolt-on security is often the consequence of IT initiatives driven to develop systems as quickly as possible, then adding security as an afterthought.

This failure to include security up front stems from a common myth that inclusion of security within a system design slows down the development project. There is also a current shortage of developers trained in secure development techniques.

Bolt-on security generally includes one to several security solutions that are not designed to work together. The result is a piecemeal security architecture without common communication mechanisms or information sharing capabilities. In other words, the design is a kludge. A *kludge* is a quick-and-dirty solution to a problem. It is the result of a strategy that can be summed up as "if it doesn't fit, I will make it fit." The biggest risks of employing kludges is that they often cannot be extended and are difficult to maintain over time. Neither of these attributes is well-suited to strong security strategy.

Over time, the cost of bolt-on security grows as the application and infrastructure age. This situation can leave the organization exposed to potential security incidents. Some of the hidden costs of the bolt-on approach include the following:

- Bolt-on security adds complexity, which is the enemy of strong security.
- A continuing pattern of software incompatibilities occurs as software ages, either requiring costly rewrites or even uglier code fixes.

- It may not result in optimal security (aka "good enough security").
- It may create issues with patching and upgrades.
- It may be more expensive in the long term.
- It may not offer protection against some exploits.
- It may be disabled by software changes.
- Too much dependence on security mechanisms external to architecture can create the "M&M" scenario.[4]
- Potential for "if it doesn't fit, I'll make it fit," where security mechanisms aren't a perfect match for architecture, but are used anyway.

The use of bolt-on security as a primary security mechanism requires regular diligence to ensure that components still provide an appropriate level of protection. Over the years, some security mechanisms, such as the original Data Encryption Standard (DES) and Wired Equivalent Privacy (WEP) have been broken and no longer offer a sufficient level of protection for most organizations. A more recent security breach involved the use of an older, now crackable, cryptographic function.

Unless bolt-on security controls are tracked and upgraded as necessary, the bolt-on security itself can become an organization's Achilles' heel, ripe for exploitation. Perhaps the greatest risk with bolt-on security is the false sense of protection it offers. This can be similar to the old security fallacy that using a firewall ensures security.

Building in Security: Cheaper and Better

The alternative to an endless cycle of insecure systems protected by a tenuous boundary of bolt-on security mechanisms is to build security into the system from its inception. The advantages of built-in security include the following:

- It is integrated in code, so it does not require separate maintenance efforts.
- It is less likely to create software incompatibilities.
- It is customized to protect against specific risks that the system might encounter.

The primary objective for inclusion of security in the system's core architecture is to increase resistance to a variety of types of attacks.

It seems pretty much like a no-brainer when we look at the data breaches not repelled by the bolt-on security approach. For example, Privacy Rights Clearinghouse (http://www.privacyrights.org) reported that SQL injection attacks were responsible for 83% of successful hacking-related data breaches since 2005.

The standard objection as to why secure development will not work as a viable and better alternative to bolted-on security is that it will cost more and take longer to develop applications. However, a valid financial argument can be made that implementing secure design and development will cost less over the life of a system and reduce the potential for a security breach significantly. With the average cost of a security breach in 2011 hovering at $5.5 million, according to the 2011 Ponemon Study, there is an economic justification for a secure development strategy.

Another area of potential cost savings, and perhaps the most significant, is a reduction in the total cost of the application over its operational life. Applications utilizing a bolt-on security strategy may require more maintenance in the form of remediation of security vulnerabilities and enhancement of existing bolt-on security controls with another level of controls.

Strategies for Embedding Security in Systems

Secure development can be a tough sell. While implementation costs are moderate, it often requires a cultural change for the IT organization. Often, the impetus for incorporating secure development comes from the organization experiencing a data breach as the result of insecure code. The IT development group may resist secure development efforts for a number of reasons, including:

1. Software engineers are already trained in secure development techniques or took classes on this topic while in college.
2. Bolt-on security and firewalls offer sufficient security protection.
3. We are not a target for hackers because we haven't been attacked yet (that we know of).
4. We have secure development materials on the intranet for our developers, so we are all set.

None of these rationalizations is valid in light of the increasing prevalence of security breaches over the last decade. Secure development cannot be sold using fear, uncertainty, and doubt (FUD), but requires a focus on offering appropriate security assurance to allow execution of business strategies and inclusion of emerging as well as innovative technologies that offer a competitive advantage.

The CISO can utilize a number of tactics to promote the adoption of secure development, including:

a. Use of financial justification
b. Use of secure development practices as a pilot proof of concept for select new technology projects
c. Identification of an internal champion for the adoption of secure development
d. Integrate vulnerability testing into the software development process
e. Customize the secure development process to fit the organization

Use of Financial Justification　Secure development offers the potential for cost avoidance in several areas. One significant place where cost savings can be realized from the adoption of secure development techniques is application maintenance and support. While the costs involved in the initial implementation of an application often receive the most focus, 90% of the total cost of an application during its life cycle is maintenance and support.

In recent years, a significant amount of maintenance concentrated on revising applications to remediate security vulnerabilities, such as the potential for SQL injection and cross-site scripting attacks. Many of these efforts would be unnecessary, if secure coding techniques were used.

The cost of insecure coding mechanisms can also create bottlenecks in development after the identification of new vulnerabilities that require the diversion of programming resources to achieve regulatory compliance or close audit findings. This resource deployment can delay new development projects with the potential to provide the organization with a competitive advantage.

The cost of a security breach to the organization can be substantial. For example, the cost of the Sony data breach in 2011 is estimated at

$172 million, which was almost as much as the costs created by the Japanese earthquake and tsunami damage that same year. Security experts predict that the total costs resulting from the 2011 event may top $2 billion, making it the most expensive security breach thus far.

Costs resulting from a security breach include credit monitoring for victims, regulatory fines, forensic investigation, remediation, public relations support, legal costs, customer trust, and revenue losses. An organization can potentially continue to pay ongoing expenses from a security breach for decades. The Federal Trade Commission (FTC) can assess fines and mandate security assessments over a period of up to 20 years for privacy policy violations and significant PII breaches.

Use of Secure Development Practices as a Pilot Proof of Concept for Select New Technology Projects   A proof-of-concept pilot is a common strategy to introduce any significant change to an organization with the potential to transform existing operational processes. Change is often viewed as disruptive, even when it offers substantial benefits. By introducing change in a limited adoption context, resistance is minimal or at least blunted in its severity.

A proof-of-concept pilot provides several benefits. It can serve as a test bed for determining the best approaches to introduce and implement the program. It offers opportunities for early successes that can influence future development projects and organizational acceptance. The key factor in determining pilot projects is to identify high-visibility initiatives involving compliance requirements or introduction of emerging technologies, such as cloud or mobile applications.

Identification of an Internal Champion for the Adoption of Secure Development   The identification of a champion is a great way to bootstrap the adoption of a secure development program. This is often more effective in influencing development staff than bringing in a high-profile consultant. An internal champion will have more credibility and influence over their team members because of existing relationships. The internal champion needs to be a senior and well-respected team member, often at the architect or senior management level.

The internal champion can customize the secure development methodology to uniquely suit the organization and its culture. The internal champion can work with external resources, but remains the point of contact with the development organization. If the organization uses distributed or decentralized IT organizations, make sure that each development team has an internal champion. An internal champion is responsible for the following:

- Serve as an evangelist for secure development
- Make presentations to senior business and IT management
- Identify training and support requirements
- Act as a mentor for other developers
- Promote events that provide visibility for the secure development initiative
- Facilitate the sharing of secure code, such as authentication module code and secure classes, between individual developers and teams

Integrate Vulnerability Testing into Software Development Process   Consider implementing vulnerability scanning into the system development life cycle (SDLC). Scanning should start as early in the SDLC as the vulnerability management (VM) tool allows. The results of the scanning process provide invaluable feedback to developers on the security of their code. It also allows identification of security issues early enough to provide sufficient time for correction.

Customize the Secure Development Process to Fit the Organization   Every organization and IT organization is unique. Forcing a specific flavor of secure development on an organization, instead of adapting to fit the dynamics of the team and existing processes, is often the first step toward failure. Customization will create the least resistance and offer the IT organization an opportunity to give their version of secure development their twist.

Endnotes

1. *Build the resume* (BTR) is a term used by my first manager for doing something for the sole purpose of putting it on a resume.
2. CIO Solutions Group, *CIO Executive Download: A CISO's Guide to Application Security*, http://h30528.www3.hp.com/Security/CISOGuideTo-ApplicationSecurity.pdf.

3. *The Money Pit* is a 1986 comedy film starring Tom Hanks and Shelley Long as a couple renovating their house.
4. In an M&M scenario for security, the security perimeter is hard and crunchy on the outside, but the inside is soft and chewy (once the attacker makes it past the outer perimeter, internal security is limited).

4

FRUGAL HIRING

People, Process, and Technology—In That Order

Strong information security is the intersection of people, process, and technology, in that order. Often the coolness factor of the cyber security technology overshadows the criticality of the human contribution to protecting the organization. While technology can crunch big data by correlating hundreds of variables to identify potential cyber threats and incursions, it is the human capacity to associate what appears to be disparate information in an innovative way to reveal new insights that cannot be accomplished by technology alone.

A notable example of this innately human capacity to recognize threats to information security was documented in the 1989 classic cyber espionage tale, *The Cuckoo's Egg: Tracking a Spy through the Maze of Computer Espionage* by Clifford Stoll. In 1986, Dr. Clifford Stoll was in charge of a number of computers located at Lawrence Berkeley National Laboratory. When asked about a 75-cent variance on a chargeback report, he began an investigation that led to hacker Markus Hess, who was engaged in cyber espionage and selling secrets to the Soviet KGB. At the time of this event, there was very little known about hackers and techniques to investigate cyber incursions.

During this investigation, Dr. Stoll remained committed to identifying the hacker. He demonstrated his tenacity by working long hours and his innovation by commandeering resources. He developed relationships with colleagues and external organizations to assist in his efforts. He did not give up on his conviction or intuition, even when he could not gain assistance from national security agencies, including the Federal Bureau of Investigation (FBI), Central Intelligence Agency (CIA), and the National Security Agency (NSA). By gathering and logging data, Dr. Stoll deduced information regarding the geolocation of the hacker and his possible skill set. He conceived the concept of the honeypot to entice and trap the hacker, which led to his eventual conviction.

The most advanced heuristic security tool still cannot compete with the human brain and its innate capability to combine diverse non-standard data and create startling insights. Of all the decisions that a chief information security officer (CISO) will make, decisions around hiring and managing staff will have the most impact on the success or failure of the information security function.

A bad hire can throw a wrench into what up until then had been a well-run machine, put a drain on company resources, and envelop your team in a black hole of unproductively that hampers talent management. Bad hires can prove to be costly in a number of areas. This is why it is crucial that hiring managers appreciate what they risk when they make a bad hire and take steps to prevent the situation from happening.

Relationship between Costs, Hiring, and Effective Team Management

There is a direct correlation between poor hiring and cost. An organization can incur thousands to hundreds of thousands in costs from recruiting the wrong candidate for a position. The cost of a poor hiring decision starts with expenditures on the recruitment and hiring process itself, such as travel expenses, recruiter's fees, background investigation, relocation allowances, training, and orientation. These costs can be significant, especially for senior-level and management positions. A pattern of bad hiring can result in a need to repeat the recruitment process multiple times with each iteration incurring additional time and expense.

A poor hire can result in an involuntary termination and its associated costs, including termination costs, unemployment insurance, Consolidated Omnibus Budget Reconciliation Act (COBRA) coverage, potential litigation fees in instances of lawsuits for wrongful dismissal, and potentially outplacement/career transition costs.

At least 80% of employee turnover is due to bad hiring, according to the *Harvard Business Review*. The US Labor Department estimates that a failed hiring decision costs, on average, one-third of an employee's annual salary. It is no wonder that staff turnover is often included on managers' performance reviews because these costs can quickly escalate for someone with a continuing pattern of bad hiring decisions. The cost of bad recruitment can add up to five times the annual salary of the bad hire, according to a study by the Society for Human Resources Management, when all the collateral expenses are considered. The longer the bad hire stays on the job and the higher the level of the position, the greater the ultimate cost of their replacement.

The bad news is that these identifiable costs of bad recruitment are only the tip of the iceberg for poor hiring. Indirect costs of bad hiring include damage to staff morale, customer concerns, lost revenue, and lower staff productivity. The long-term impact of multiple bad recruitments can reverberate for years and create additional costs for the organization, for example, recruiters may become reluctant to submit candidates to an organization with a pattern of employee turnovers in the same position.

In addition, some managers develop a poor reputation because of these events, which can affect the entire organization's ability to attract quality candidates for open positions. Individuals doing job searches, even on a causal basis, will often notice when the same position with the same job description is posted every few months, especially more senior-level positions, by the same organization. This can be a red flag for job seekers and recruiters alike.

Finding the Right Stuff and Right Fit

Avoiding bad hires is critical to managing staffing costs, both during hiring and long-term management of employees. Hiring successes usually hinge on two factors—finding the *right stuff* (skills match) and *right fit* for the organizational or team culture. In a recent survey of hiring managers, one-third identified a poor skills match as a leading cause for failed hire. While some candidates may elect to misrepresent their experience and expertise, an effective technical interviewing process may control this during the hiring process. A poor skills match may result from an inaccurate or vague job description.

Another common error that may result in recruitment failures is a conflict between the individual and the organizational or team culture. This can happen when a *right stuff* candidate clashes with the organizational or team culture.

The organizational culture consists of the values and behaviors that define a distinctive social and psychological environment of the organization. It includes the expectations, experiences, philosophy, ethics, and values that act as a "glue" in unifying its participants. Its basis includes shared customs, beliefs, and attitudes. It involves a code of both written rules, such as policies, as well as unwritten rules of behavior, such as "it is not OK to yell at meetings."

It provides a mental model for how the organization and its members interact within the organization and the outside world, including:

1. Ways to conducts business activities
2. How to treat its employees
3. Autonomy in decision-making
4. The power model and organizational hierarchy

Organizational culture does change over time. The organization culture may shift over the years because of events, leaders, and changes in the employee composition, such as increasing numbers of Millennials as Boomers retire, but the process is slow.

The hiring manager needs to be very frank regarding the organizational culture and provide some concrete examples of what that means. Occasionally, there is a miscommunication between the hiring manager and candidate as to the actual culture of the organization. This may result from the words used, which might be vague, such as "employee friendly" or "entrepreneurial."

Sometimes, a hiring manager may get a bit of tunnel vision around the actual organizational culture. That is why examples can be helpful. I once heard a hiring manager in a very rigid organizational culture describe the culture as flexible and employee-centric, despite its "Theory X" management style and discouraging even minimal use of telecommuting (except to support after-hours work). It is a mismatch between perceived organizational culture and reality that creates "fit" issues for some new hires.

To avoid fit problems after hiring, interviews should include questions to determine whether the candidate will fit the culture. The most cost-effective strategy is to try to find a fit for the organization, not just the position.

Job Descriptions or Looking for the Lord Himself (or Herself)

We all want to hire the *star* that exhibits both strong technical expertise and superior *soft skills* (people literacy), as is described in many job postings listed on career websites. One of my former coworkers described these types of posting as "looking for the Lord himself, but willing to take a sinner, when necessary."

Try this exercise: Download some information security job postings from an Internet job board and try to figure out what the position title is without looking at it. Often, the qualifications for entry level, mid-level, and senior-level jobs are strikingly similar in terms of skills, certifications, and experience. This is confusing for potential applicants and may lead the wrong candidates to apply.

Job descriptions need to have a basis in reality of the position when advertised. Many times, if you go to the individual who actually does the job, you get a completely different description of the required job tasks than what appears on the posted job description. To avoid this common error, ensure involvement of individuals currently performing the job in developing the position description, or at least have them review and revise it before posting.

Consider the option of abandoning traditional skills-based descriptions in favor of using a functional approach that reflects the actual job tasks. The functional approach defines the position in terms of both the deliverables and requirements for on-the-job success. This is a better way to communicate an understanding of the real job rather than the typical listing of skills and qualifications.

Another way to construct a meaningful job description is in terms of a *prototype* of the individual who exhibits the qualities, expertise, and other attributes needed to succeed in the position. I learned the concept of identifying a prototype from a senior executive at a technology firm many years ago. A prototype defines a position in terms of the critical attributes required for success in a role, including experience, skills, interpersonal communication, and business acumen. The prototype can be especially effective when creating a new position or redefining a current job in terms of its responsibilities or tasks.

The prototype is not designed to act as an exclusionary tool, but one of inclusion that considers expertise and personal attributes, as well as the aptitude for professional growth in candidates. This executive actively sought out diversity among candidates rather than using a cookie-cutter approach to recruiting new staff, which may result in hiring similar individuals repeatedly. The prototype approach considers who the job candidate currently is and what they can become given the appropriate environment.

A variation of this prototyping is something I refer to as the Weird Science (WS) approach, based on the 1985 comedy film about two male nerds that attempt to create the "perfect woman," who turns out to be so much more. In *Weird Science*, the woman created reflects their requirements (beautiful and sexy), but possesses an understanding of what these young men really need, which is confidence and maturity. The woman provides the two men with opportunities to optimize their potential.

The WS variation is best suited to developing job descriptions for more senior or managerial posting. This approach mirrors the prototype strategy, but looks for candidates to customize the position based upon unique attributes they bring to the table. This is similar to approaches used in some technology positions where candidates define their own position based upon some standard tasks combined with new responsibilities that they themselves specify.

The WS strategy seeks to evolve the organization and reinvent the information security organization by introducing new ideas and services. This strategy is best suited to very mature practitioners with strong skills and a vast range of experience in a variety of positions in different organizations. This assumes the individual can assess the business's needs and develop strategies to enhance current service offerings. The WS approach is appropriate for the recruitment of CISOs, cyber security strategists, security architects, and security evangelists. These types of positions require strong conceptual security skills and an innovative thought process, rather than the ability to perform standard tasks well.

Hiring "On the Cheap"

Some managers use the strategy of trying to get staff "on the cheap," regardless of the current economic environment. While occasionally a manager might luck out by getting a diamond in the rough, more often they hire an individual with a limited skill set or underlying issues. I remember a manager bragging about getting a technician for lower than the posted salary. This individual ended up costing more in lost productivity than the small savings on his lower salary. He could not evolve to do higher-skilled tasks. He was an example of what my brother refers to as "one year of experience repeated twenty times." My manager got the exact value of what he paid for because this individual was an example of the Peter Principle, which states that an individual will be promoted to a position at a higher level until they become incompetent.

This individual limited my manager's flexibility in assigning work. Most of this college's IT manager's prior hires consisted of polymaths drawn from the college's student population with keen intellectual curiosity and the ability to excel at any tasks given. Most of these individuals were drawn to these positions because of access to computing power. They viewed their jobs as a learning environment for future employment opportunities. The economic turndown provided some organizations with the ability to attract staff with more expertise at lower salaries. However, this has the potential to create turnover as employment opportunities improve.

Developing a Hiring Strategy and Tactics for the Long Run

There exist a number of hiring strategies. All might work within a specific organization or work environment. At its core, the hiring strategy needs to be reasonably consistent to develop a strong team over time. While economic cycles do influence the hiring strategy, such as the use of more contactors rather than full-time staff to avoid the creation of hire–fire cycles, the basic hiring philosophy needs to retain its integrity over the long term. However, some hiring tactics can incur a variety of avoidable costs. Some of these costs are tangible in terms of actual cash, while others create intangible costs that can affect productivity in the long term.

From a value proposition, hiring the right people, regardless of economic environment, may result in better long-term succession planning and the development of sustainable staff competencies. Good hires can "hit the ground running" and often possess hidden proficiencies that management can exploit to increase productivity and reduce overall staffing costs in the end.

For example, many experienced IT security practitioners are experienced project managers that can be utilized to avoid hiring staff to perform this function on small projects. It is important to view staffing expenditures from a total cost perspective. High turnover and less-than-optimal hires may result in higher overall staffing costs. In addition, investments in training and developing experience can be lost due to high turnover.

The criticality of hiring strong, credible, and competent management to direct an information security team cannot be overstated. Incompetent or immature management can affect the overall productivity of the information security team and create excessive staff turnover. While tight budgets often restrict or eliminate training dollars, this is one area where investment can yield significant return on investment (ROI) by increasing the value of existing staff and allowing them to optimize their activities.

Hiring decisions are some of the most important decisions that the CISO will make. This is true whether it is a small information security team consisting of a few individuals or a large group employing one hundred or more people. Expediting a hire to build your team may resolve an immediate problem, but can create regrets in the long term. The key to effective hiring is an understanding that hiring the right candidate may take some time, so it pays to be patient, develop a well thought-out hiring plan, and execute it perfectly. Leaving a position open for a while may feel uncomfortable, but no hire is better than a bad hire.

Hiring for the Wrong Reasons

Sometimes hiring managers make a recruitment decision to gain some benefit that they believe at the time will benefit the organization. These are often the most costly decisions they will make in their careers in terms of the organization, team, or themselves. Often the driver behind the hiring decision seems positive. However, its true costs, both tangible and intangible, may not be immediately visible, except in hindsight.

One category of ill-considered hiring decisions involves hiring an individual to ingratiate the manager or the team with another individual, either internal or external to the organization. This can be used to establish a bridge with another group in the organization. On the surface, this looks like a very smart move for the hiring manager's career and team relationships. In the reality, it is often a way for the influencing organization to do someone a favor, while still avoiding hiring the individual in question themselves. This can result in a win–lose with the hiring organization on the losing side of the situation. It can also create bad feelings among current staff, especially those who might have been in line for that opening.

While this situation might always have potentially negative consequences, ask yourself the following question before making a hiring decision based on the influence of other parties:

- Is this individual qualified for the position?
- If they are internal to the organization, is it possible to review their past performance reviews?
- What are the best- and worst-case outcomes for this hiring decision?
- What is the potential gain I can hope to achieve from this hiring decision?

Sometimes, due to the internal political power of the hiring influencer, you might not have an option, but then you need to take some steps to mitigate any negative consequences that might arise.

Some Tactics for Strong Hiring

The following are some tried-and-true tactics to better the likelihood of hiring the right candidate:

Learn to Spot the Candidate with that Je Ne Sais Quoi

Go beyond the job description when hiring and consider the intangible attributes of the position. The French have a term for this attribute—*Je ne sais quoi*—which translates roughly to "that certain something." A candidate is more than the sum of his or her skill set. For most, if not all positions within information security, the employee will need to work with others in a collaborative environment. Consider the candidate's soft skills, such as leadership, innovation, and relationship building, when hiring. I have experienced at least a couple of individuals within information security groups that literally did not talk to their peers and had no actual social skills at all. I always wondered what their interviews were like.

Learn from Past Mistakes and Make a Fresh Start with Each Hiring

Do not use the same old job descriptions or one copied from another company for postings. Even when you are refilling an existing position, take a fresh look at the role. Consider how it could be changed or enhanced to better serve the information security function. Know what you want. Do not recycle past job descriptions because chances are the role has changed. Think about the skills that you would like to add to your team. Avoid listing qualifications, such as having a security certification, that are not necessary for the job, just because they have appeared on other postings by the group. Use a *zero-based* job description strategy and create each posting from scratch based on the job tasks and the team's needs.

Get Your Team Involved

Use your team and internal resources when hiring. This is definitely a case where two or more heads may be better than one. When different people interview candidates, they can bring different insights into how the individual will connect the team. They also may notice different aspects of the candidate's suitability or potential problems. In one hiring situation I worked on, a team member interviewing a candidate noticed that the candidate had some disturbing prejudices that could have been problematic for the team if he were hired.

In addition, we all have personal preferences, which can inadvertently influence our opinions and decision-making process without our conscious awareness. Input from multiple interviews may tend to cancel out any personal biases by team members.

Use available tools and services within your organization. Human resources may have existing relationships with external recruitment firms, and your current staff may be able to offer referrals to potential candidates.

Connection with Candidates on a Personal Level

A good hire in any profession requires the hiring manager to connect on a personal level with candidates to some degree. The interviewer must establish an actual rapport with candidates to get them to feel comfortable and open up. I realize this is not always easy for technical professionals, not even all technical managers. However, it is important to do, especially when evaluating whether the candidate is a fit for your organizational culture.

Avoid Ending on a Poor Note

When you take an acting class, they tell you that the last thing you do in a scene, whether a verbal or a nonverbal action, is the thing that will make the most lasting impression with the audience. Unfortunately, that is what can occur, sometimes inadvertently. Things that can leave a bitter aftertaste include rudeness, lack of civility in the treatment of others (especially subordinates), and uncomfortable (and often unnecessary) questions. I once saw a hiring manager throw a tantrum during an interview.

If you treat others badly in the presence of a candidate, they will generally have one of two reactions, shock or trepidation, or both. If a candidate sees a hiring manager displaying disrespectful or rude behaviors with others, they make the assumption, right or wrong, that this is the normal way of interacting with their staff. Another potential way that a hiring manager can end the interview on a poor note is asking uncomfortable and often unnecessary questions in an attempt to determine how the candidate may act under pressure. This is called a *stress interview tactic.*

During a stress interview, the candidate is placed in a stressful situation to determine how they react. The interviewer may ask difficult or inappropriate interview questions to intimidate the candidate. When this technique is used in the final portion of the interview, it may result in the loss of an otherwise great potential employee who interprets this simply as, "this manager is a jerk."

I have had this done to me on several occasions, such as a hiring manager using profanity (suitable only in adult films) to see my reaction. One manager I worked for became infamous for his final stress interview questions, which resulted in numerous individuals turning down the position when they received an offer.

Whether or not the hiring manager elects to use stress interviewing questions or techniques, it is better to use them in an earlier portion of the interview and explain why this was done after completing that component of the interview process. Then end the interview on a positive and welcoming note.

Avoiding "Halo Hiring"

Just as a good recipe or meal requires more diversity in ingredients, so does an effective information security team. The ultimate success of a team is dependent on its ability to not only combine skill sets, but also the personalities of its members and their unique ways of approaching decision-making and solving problems.

Past studies of technical teams by Stanford University demonstrated that overall team performance improves when composed of individuals with diverse personalities. A diverse team usually does not occur naturally in most organizations. It is even more difficult to achieve team diversity within information security teams because there is a lack of diversity in the profession itself.

According to a 2006 International Data Corporation (IDC) survey, only 13% of information security professionals are women, and other minorities, such as Hispanics, are underrepresented. White males dominate the information security profession, and this trend is expected to continue for some time to come.

This situation can be worsened by a natural tendency all people share, called the *halo effect*, that was first identified by Edward Thorndike in the 1920s. When it comes to hiring, the halo effect can lead to a bad hire. The halo effect is an unconscious bias in which someone's judgments can be influenced by one's overall impression of an individual, often based on physical or personality traits that we prefer or with which we have had positive experiences. Other factors that can create the halo effect include similar backgrounds, interests, or even the college someone attended.

We tend to prefer to hire people like friends, former peers, employees, or ourselves. In a field dominated by white males, this can create some challenges when the best candidate does not possess these traits, but a less-qualified candidate does. It is the reason that some teams seem to be made up of similar people.

I have had an experience with the halo effect's ugly twin, the *horn effect,* in which an individual is negatively biased toward an individual based on their traits. On one occasion, I had a negative reaction to a coworker, Tom, for no specific reason I could identify. One of my friends mentioned that Tom looked like a former employee with whom I had some unpleasant experiences. When I realized that, I stopped shutting down when I interacted with Tom and we actually became friends. The best way to combat the halo effect is to be aware of its existence and its potential to influence our judgments.

Cultivate and Close Your Preferred Candidates

Great candidates may be interviewing for many positions and receive multiple job offers. It is important to always remember that in most cases the candidate has the option to remain in his or her present employment situation and wait for another more attractive opportunity to arise. It is critical that the hiring manager, especially if he or she is the last interviewer in the interview process, "close" the candidate. In sales lingo, the term close means to finalize the deal.

One good way to close the candidate is tell them and show them why they should take your offer over that of another organization. Stress all the benefits of working on your team. Offer an attractive compensation up front, rather than negotiate from a lower starting offer.

We are currently in a *seller's market* when recruiting strong candidates for information security positions. Low-balling your first salary and benefits package can backfire. It is important to remind yourself that the good candidates do not just want the same job at the same compensation that they already have. They want a better job, and in general, a better overall package. Overall salary may not be the only motivation for taking a new position, but it is most definitely a factor in the decision-making process of most candidates.

According to Herzberg's motivation theory, money is a *hygiene* factor, and not a motivator itself. This is likely why giving a current employee a better salary to stay and not go to a competitor rarely works. This is because a hygiene factor does not work in the long term. However, individuals will endeavor to achieve hygiene needs, such as money, because they are unhappy without them. In addition, in our Western society, many people derive a significant amount of their self-worth from external sources, such as compensation.

Herzberg's theory identified the real motivators, such as achievement, advancement, recognition, and development, which are bigger motivators than money. Individuals also have their own personal motivators that drive their behaviors, such as family relationships and maintaining a satisfying lifestyle. By using a combination of these factors, such as sufficient salary plus flexible work schedule, you can persuade the candidate that you are offering the best overall package, thus closing the deal.

Using Recruiters

Recruiters can provide an advantage when hiring for a specialized field like information security. They can be more effective in attracting a pool of candidates that have the right expertise and experience for your open position than posting your job on a social media site. Before you elect to use a recruiter, you need to do some homework about the recruiters themselves.

You want to work with a recruiter who specializes in information security, or at least technology, to identify job candidates with the suitable skills. Unfortunately, that is not always the case. I suggest doing some research on the recruiter before using their services. A social media site, such as LinkedIn™, can provide a quick way to gain some information on the recruiter's background and experience in technology recruitments. I also suggest that job seekers do the same thing before getting involved with a recruiter in their employment search. A bad recruiter can also damage a job seeker's credibility. A quick look-up might reveal an experienced recruiter or an individual that was selling cars up until recently.

Social media and job sites have changed the recruiting field, both for the good and bad. The positive aspects of these technologies is making information about job opportunities available to a broader pool of potential candidates and the ability to expedite the recruiting process by eliminating hardcopy media, like newspaper ads, that were slower and local in their distribution capability.

The negative side of using technology as a recruiting tool is that it lowered the bar of entry for recruiters. The result can be that many recruiters that have limited background in the fields in which they recruit candidates and limited skills in performing the necessary screening activities to identify candidates with the appropriate skills and experience, as well as the personality characteristics required for potential success in a specific job opening. The consequence is wasting the time of both hiring managers and potential job candidates.

Many recruiters primarily utilize a keyword match on specific words found on a job description. This is a one-dimensional approach to identifying strong job candidates. It requires the right type of recruiter and a different type of recruiting process to identify the best person for an available position rather than the best person who posts a resume on a job board.

The recruiter needs to explore the position with the hiring manager from the perspective of their end game for the chosen candidate, such as the outcomes they want to achieve and any long-term career opportunities. This allows the recruiter to gain a better idea of what the hiring organization is really looking for and provide a stronger pool of high-potential, diverse, and undiscovered candidates.

Strong recruiters use a comprehensive strategy to build a strong network of strong (and passive individuals not actively looking for a new position) candidates before a posting occurs. They network at information security events, read trade journals, and join professional associations. This direct approach builds both a database of potential future candidates and referrals.

Since there is no Angie's List™ for technology recruiters, ask your current information security staff and your professional peers who they have used in the past and what they thought of the experience. Some recruiters will request an exclusive opportunity to recruit for higher-level openings, similar to those given to a real estate agent with an exclusive contract on selling a home. The benefit to the hiring manager is that the recruiter will devote more of their resources to pinpointing a pool of the best candidates. This can be a win–win for all parties involved.

If it does not work out, it can waste valuable time in your hiring process. Exclusive recruiting contracts are best reserved for those recruiting firms with whom your organization has had a history of successful hiring or executive search firms for senior information security openings.

Interviewing for Understanding and Motivation

It is important to determine *why* a candidate is interviewing with your organization. In a poor economy, the answer is more obvious, but as the economic outlook improves, the motivation for changing employers is often more complicated.

Candidates may have one or more motivations for interviewing, including:

- Increased compensation or benefits
- Better fit for lifestyle
- Increased responsibility or professional growth potential
- Career change
- Instability of current position
- To acquire new skills and experience
- Organizational culture
- Exploration of what is currently out there in the job market
- Organization's reputation

Often, there is more than one motivation. However, one motivation is usually primary for their decision to interview with your organization. It is important to remember that the most desirable candidates do not just want the same job at the same level of compensation. They want a better job. One of the key objectives during an interview is to probe for the candidate's motivations to join your team. The candidate may not always be forthcoming with this information initially. The appropriate motivation often determines the potential for a successful long-term hire or bad recruitment.

Be wary of candidates whose primary motivation is only monetary. An unfortunate consequence of recent economic downturns is that some candidates interview and accept multiple offers, then attempt to play one organization against another to optimize total compensation. The classic maneuver is to pit a new offer against their existing employer.

I know of several cases where a candidate accepted and started a new position while they were still employed at their existing employer, and then quit the new job after the old employer increased their compensation. These recruitment failures are expensive, unpleasant, and may damage the hiring manager's reputation. I am not going to offer any opinion on this practice, but it is important to understand it does occur.

Interview Process: Identifying the Right Candidate and Closing the Deal

Your goal during the interview process is identifying the potential best employees from the best candidates. Start by providing the candidate with a description of what is expected on the job. Then, ask them to provide their experiences that are comparable with what you just described.

Ask not just what they accomplished, but how they did it. Someone can usually get something done by driving people hard. This cannot be a standard operating procedure. The same goes with the martyr who shoulders the entire burden on themselves to feel like a hero. Both of these strategies cost money because they create the environment for more frequent employee turnovers.

It is important to determine in advance which staff members will be involved in the interviewing process, the types of questions that will be asked, how information will be collected and shared about the interviews, and ultimately who has the authority to make the hire. Develop specific interview questions for the specific position, rather than using a standard list of stock interview questions. Use the list as the foundation for the interview, but allow for some deviations from the initial question to explore some of the candidates' responses.

For entry- to mid-level job candidates, you need to establish that they have the technical skills to succeed in a position. Since technical credibility is important for information security, when dealing with technical peers, it is crucial that these candidates have a basic understanding of the technologies they will be working with on the job. Never assume that because a skill is listed on a resume that the candidate possesses much knowledge or experience in its use. I have had experiences where I asked a candidate a very basic question and from their response realized that they were clueless on the topic.

For higher-level positions, use some realistic scenario questions that ask the candidate to develop a plan or process to manage a cyber security issue. Since at senior levels employees may manage issues independently, you want to insure that candidates possess both the knowledge and thought process to deal with complex situations where they may be on their own.

Watch out for too many stock responses, such as, "my biggest weakness is I am a workaholic." Probe for deeper-level responses by asking about when they used innovation, collaboration, or a nonstandard approach to resolve an issue, increase productivity, or support the businesses needs.

Strategies for Avoiding Excessive Hiring Costs

The hiring process can be long and drawn out or efficient and easy. It depends on your approach. A cost-effective strategy looks to minimize costs by streamlining recruitment to avoid delays in getting vital roles filled rapidly with well-qualified candidates.

Attracting Quality Is Not Cheap

Finding great employees is not necessarily a cheap or easy process. Internet job boards are fairly inexpensive to use, but may not be suitable for more senior positions because they are best at attracting large numbers of candidates, but not necessarily high-quality ones. In recruiting and hiring, you get what you pay for.

Using an experienced recruiter with specific expertise with information security positions is often worth the extra cost in terms of a better candidate pool to select from and time saved in reviewing only candidates prequalified by someone with the appropriate know-how. It is also a quicker way to "get boots on the ground" when replacing a vital role.

Know What the Position Is before You Start Recruiting

Get a complete working job description prior to initiating the recruitment process. Do not expect to get a whole department's worth of skills in one new hire. A comprehensive job description tells potential candidates what the job is and what to expect. Concentrate the job description on the essential expertise and qualifications to be successful in doing the job. Do not focus too much on preferences (the nice to haves), which might not be possible to get and might distract some qualified candidates.

Don't Play Bait and Switch after Hiring

It is not generally an ethical or effective practice to advertise and hire for one position, then change the job entirely after hiring someone. If a candidate takes a job with one set of expectations, but an entirely new set of tasks and responsibilities is substituted, you might have to repeat the recruitment cycle all over again soon. Some positions and companies can become infamous for a regular merry-go-around of post-hire-post again cycles. Some companies may modify the job title, but the description is often recognizable.

Use Recruiters Effectively

Tell the recruiter up front what you are looking for in terms of the specific qualifications and qualities you need in a candidate. Do not use vague phrases, which can be subjective. Explain what you need to your recruiter in clear and precise words. Be clear about compensation levels associated with the position and the degree of flexibility within the range that is possible to offer better-qualified candidates. This information allows the recruiter to target a potential candidate pool more effectively.

If you do not give the recruiter the right information up front, do not be surprised if the recruiter presents candidates what are either underqualified or overqualified and too expensive for the position. This wastes your time and the candidates' time with interviews that go nowhere. All the while, a vital position remains unfilled.

Consider Internal Candidates When Possible

Always look inward first when considering a new job opening. First, survey your existing workforce to promote internal talent. These employees are already contributing to your organization. They are also focused on getting onto a promotion ladder, and if they do not see a pattern of internal hiring, they will go elsewhere. Some organizations may have a negative bias toward internal hiring. They have a tendency to focus on small flaws with their internal candidates, while external candidates look bright and spotless to hiring managers.

It always reminds me of the Carly Simon song called "The Stuff That Dreams Are Made Of," in which the singer considers that perhaps what she currently has, when considered from a different perspective, is better than pursuing a new relationship. Look for potential internal candidates before turning outside. Internal hires provide a variety of advantages, both in terms of monetary saving and intangible benefits, such as increased staff morale.

Mining the existing workforce to identify high performers in advance of actual openings can expedite the hiring process. It also has the collateral benefit of acting as a succession plan for the information security organization during a crisis.

Competition for great information security professionals is rigorous with the consequences of hiring the wrong person being a costly mistake that wastes budget that could have been better spent in other areas to improve the organization. In this increasingly competitive market for technology professionals, organizations need to develop strategic approaches to attract and retain talent.

Hiring internal candidates offers some distinct advantages. The individual involved already knows how the organization functions, so there will be no adjustment period typical with new external hires that need time to learn the lay of the land. The organization saves all the money that you would have spent on recruiting efforts, which can be spent on efforts like training.

Use a Technical Interview

Some candidates brag about their superior technical prowess. This is a time to heed the words of the late President Ronald Reagan, "Trust, but verify." When technical skills or at least credibility count, a technical interview is critical to preventing an incompetent or bad hire. I have worked in information technology and information positions for more than twenty years, and I have seen all types of charlatans con their way into senior technical roles.

My personal favorite was a software engineer from another development team that purported to specialize in the development of DLLs (Dynamic-Link Library). A DLL file is an executable file that permits programs to share code and other programming resources to perform specific tasks. This individual eventually asked me what the acronym DLL stood for.

It was abundantly clear that no one had verified his knowledge or experience beyond reading the resume and making sure that it had the appropriate keywords. I recently encountered an information security manager that had no grasp of the concept of authentication. Always remember one of the favorite phrases of the TV doctor Gregory House (Fox's *House* series), "All people lie" when confronted with an alleged technical expert.

Depending on the technical skills involved, there is a variety of options to determine if candidates can prove their words. One way is an actual skill test to evaluate their abilities, such as for a network security engineer, having the candidate configure a set of firewall rules. For less hands-on roles, a discussion with a technical expert might satisfy your verification requirements.

While most candidates are honest, some are not. Unfortunately, some dishonest job candidates have learned techniques to defeat the technical interview using various means of deception. Based upon the number of unsuccessful attempts at deception that have been related to me by peers, organizations should implement the following controls to avoid any attempts at deception during technical interviews:

- Do not conduct a technical interview of any type over the phone, if that skill is critical to the success of the job. Use video conferencing or the Skype™ service to ensure that the individual participating in the interview is indeed the actual candidate. Some peers noticed a bait and switch scam where another individual took the technical interview for a less technical peer or friend.
- Ask some basic questions at the start of the technical interview to assess the candidate's familiarity with the subject matter. My brother, Bob, a security architect and an experienced application designer, told me that he will ask some almost embarrassingly simple questions, such as "what is application authentication?" or "what does it mean to normalize a relational database?" at the beginning of the interview. Some purported technical candidates cannot answer these easy queries. Bob's point is that one should never make assumptions about the candidate's skill set, despite what is on their resume.

Don't Stretch Out the Hiring Process Too Long

Making a decision is hard, and some folks have a harder time making a decision than others. We have all heard the old adage, "act in haste and repent in leisure." Sometimes, anxiety about the unknown can lead to *analysis paralysis*. This may lead to the need to see "just one more candidate" or request that the position posting be run again, or anything to put off making the actual final hiring decision. However, if you prolong making the final decision too long, you might lose the best candidates to another organization. It is preferable to do all of your deliberations as quickly as possible, then make your selection on a candidate and move on.

I view selecting a candidate for a job opening as analogous to purchasing a home in a seller's market. Some buyers need to see numerous houses of all different types. They do not establish any definite criteria for what they want, so they randomly go to open houses and contact many real estate agents. They agonize over their decision as to the "best" home on which to make an offer because they are looking for one home that includes the top features of all the homes they have visited, which of course, none does.

When they either exhaust the supply of available homes for sale or the real estate agents, they make a low-ball bid on their desired future residence. By then, the prospective buyer has fallen in love with the property. However, they discover that the home is already sold or that the seller has received a better offer. At that point, they have two options, go with the less desirable candidate or start again. Neither option available is optimal.

The same dance occurs when it comes to hiring. Some of this might be the result of behaviors held over from economic downturns. However, this is an effective strategy for the current hiring environment.

Hiring the Transitioning Professional

At a recent conference in Boston, I heard a well-known CISO say that most of the current experienced information security professionals started out doing something else. We were educated for another field. Therefore, we bring some of the attributes and skills of that profession to information security. This can differentiate us from our peers and make us better at our current jobs. For some time to come, the information security ranks will continue to depend on professionals transitioning from another field into information security positions.

When considering hiring an individual who desires to transition their career into information security, there are a couple of key criteria to look for in those candidates:

1. Does the individual possess a security mind-set?
2. Is the individual flexible enough to assimilate new ideas and acquire new proficiencies rapidly?
3. Is the individual willing to put in the time and effort to successfully make the transition?
4. Does the individual appreciate the rapid pace of change associated with information security and that this requires continuous learning to maintain competency?

A security mind-set is not analogous to the hacker thinking. Security mind-set is visualizing the thinking of the users and developing a way to protect their needs, while they do their normal activities. It is identifying the potential threats and then responding with a solution that is both secure and usable. The successful transitioning candidate must seek to understand the end user, whatever their role. They must also understand that security is concerned with enablement, which often involves compromise between usability and providing bullet-proof security.

The transitioning security professional must demonstrate that they are flexible in their thinking and willing to do the work to become proficient with new concepts and evolving technologies. Information security is not the profession for the faint of heart or lazy. It requires a certain amount of *chutzpah* (Yiddish word used to describe someone with "a lot of guts").

5

Frugal Team Management

A Team Is the Sum of Its Ingredients

Building any strong team requires a plan. It seldom occurs organically on its own without some plan or strategy as to what the finished team will be like and what services it will offer to the organization it serves. Team members should complement each other in their expertise and ways of looking at issues. Diversity among team members is what distinguishes some teams from their peers in the ability to attain excellence in today's increasingly challenging risk landscape.

Constructing a team is similar to putting together a great recipe. You need to start with the best ingredients and combine them in the right proportions to achieve the right balance of flavors to get it right. Too much of any one ingredient or the use of an ingredient with overpowering flavor can upset the balance of the dish. Adding a spoiled ingredient to an otherwise perfect culinary concoction assures its destiny in the garbage. Creating teams requires the same level of detail in the selection of the individuals that will compose the team and the foresight to anticipate how the team will function as a whole.

Security Is a Team Sport

Rarely, except in a very small organization, is effective security the result of a one-man-/one-woman effort. Strong security requires acquiring sufficient bench strength to combat the myriad cyber threats in our current environment. Just like a sports team, not all the players can play the same position. The information security team needs diversity among its members to provide coverage for all critical roles. In structuring a team, the chief information security officer (CISO) should seek to balance strong technical staff members ("quarterbacks") with more supportive roles, such as project *managers* ("defensive linemen").

The team should also strive to include individuals at different points in their career from *newbies* to the information security profession to highly experienced cyber security experts. This diversity in experience and ages promotes a wide variety of approaches to problem solving and creates the potential for a strong succession management plan.

While strong players are desirable, the team should endeavor to recruit team players who exhibit the following qualities in their interactions with other members of group:

- Can be counted on to get work done
- Does their fair share of the workload
- Willing to roll up their sleeves and pitch in without being asked
- Communicates constructively
- Honest in their thoughts and communications, but still respectful of others' feelings
- Good listener
- Serves as an active participant on the team
- Shares openly and willingly
- Keeps other team members in the loop
- Doesn't throw other team members under the bus
- Flexible
- Demonstrates commitment to the team
- Problem solver
- Respectful and supportive of others
- Sense of humor
- Credible

There can be a tendency to hire "stars" because they may provide instant credibility to the information security team or have specific expertise in a security technology. This is not a bad strategy, but it is important to ensure that the star will mesh with the overall team. Some security experts may have a tendency to be a bit of a "lone wolf." If you go forward with hiring an individual with this predilection, it may be necessary to buffer this individual by providing a complementary partner whose personality might soften any hard edges of their partner.

Building or Renovating the Information Security Team

They say all journeys start with the first step. For the new CISO, that first step can be a doozy, which is to build an effective, efficient, and innovative information security team. In a perfect world, the CISO could build a new team from the ground up. This new team would be custom designed to meet the needs of the organization, staffed with high-performing professionals, and receive all the resources it requires to get up and running.

While I believe this may occasionally occur, the reality is that most CISOs walk into an existing team created by another manager. The reason that it is a safe assumption is because mandatory compliance requirements persuaded or compelled most organizations into the creation of some type of information security organization. This team, its structure, and membership may not be aligned with the new CISO's own philosophy of the best way to build an information security organization. However, its existence will require the CISO to make some decisions on adjusting the team to better align with his vision of the information security organization.

A Word of Caution: Don't Try to Clone Your Old Information Security Team

There is a tendency to want to re-create a situation or environment in which we have been successful in the past. We might want to relive our "glory years." In CISOs, this tendency may result in trying to re-create the information organization they just left or had the best experiences in managing. It is important to keep in mind that each organization, its threat landscape, IT strategy, and culture creates a unique opportunity for success and failure. The new information security team, whether building a new team from scratch or revamped from the old team, needs to be custom designed for the organization for which it will provide security services.

There are several reasons why attempting to re-create another information security environment at a new employer might not be successful. One issue is that the two organizations might be at different levels of organizational maturation. Some security practices work best for information security organizations at specific stages of maturity. Trying to force best practices, such as advanced data loss prevention (DLP) tools, on an organization in the first levels of information maturity might fail because the team lacks the technical expertise and supporting governance processes to effectively implement the security solution.

Another reason to avoid trying to replicate a former team is that even if the new team has achieved a higher stage of organizational maturity, it may have used a different evolutionary path to reach its current state. For example, the new organization may have developed custom security applications rather than acquiring commercially available tools. Neither a custom nor a commercial tool is necessarily a better decision. It was the decision each organization made based on its requirements. Ripping out an existing security infrastructure to mirror another team may not necessarily achieve better overall security. However, it will be expensive and disruptive with the security value being no better than an existing solution. It may also create the need for costly retraining and the loss of investment in knowledge of existing security solutions.

It may also create an intangible cost in regard to staff that might feel that they are being forced into conforming to the security strategies and philosophy of another organization without consideration of the unique requirements of the current organization. This is an *approach with caution* scenario that requires research and a solid justification before proceeding. New is not always better, and another organization's "best of breed" approach may not be a fit for the new team. A new CISO needs time to review the reasons why decisions regarding security solutions, policies, or other security-related matters where originally made.

Some of the reasons for these decisions might no longer be valid, but the CISO needs to understand their history before dismissing them and proceeding with a new strategy. For example, an organization that was an early innovator in access appropriate to auditing might have elected to go the custom application route rather than commercial software because solutions sufficient to meet their needs did not exist or existing solutions did not provide adequate scalability. These decisions should be revisited, but from the perspective of reviewing a strategy rather than emulating another organization.

It is important to convey to the new team that reevaluating the strategy does not disparage past decisions made by the organization that were made based on the conditions at that time, but to reassess opportunities to renew and revitalize the cyber security function.

Building a New Information Security Team

Building out a new team begins with identifying its basic structure and types of positions it will need. If budget is limited, determine the necessary core functions of the team, then decide what staffing is necessary to provide appropriate coverage for those functions. These decisions depend on the organization and its current threat landscape. It is also important to determine what the information security team cannot undertake at this juncture, based on resource availability, staff expertise, or low priority for providing this service to the organization.

Digital forensics (DF) is an example of a security service that might not be feasible in some information security organizations for a variety of reasons. The organization may have limited requirements for undertaking forensic investigations of computers and networks. DF requires specific expertise and equipment to do correctly, so it may be more cost effective to outsource any requests for DF to an outside cyber security firm.

The bad news is that recruiting the talent you need for your new team is going to be a challenge. Experienced information security professionals are expensive and in short supply. The good news is that it may be possible to fill some openings by transitioning existing technical staff into information security positions with the right approach. Generally, this is a cheaper alternative and these individuals are already committed to the organization.

By slotting existing staff into supportive positions, it is possible to devote more time and resources to recruiting a couple of key security experts to fill vital roles, especially around vulnerabilities management and mitigation techniques. The presence of highly qualified security professionals on the team offers a number of advantages, in addition to their contribution to daily security operations, including:

1. Acting as mentors for junior and technical staff transitioning into security roles
2. Providing in-house training in security topics for the entire information security organization
3. Managing major security efforts, cyber events, and implementations of new security technologies
4. Offering instant credibility when interacting with other technology teams, auditors, and representatives from regulatory compliance agencies
5. In organizations that sell services to other organizations, acting as liaisons for cyber security with client organizations

The hiring of strong information security professions is an example of one of my favorite principles of Frugal Information Security, *spend where it is most impactful (SWIIMI)*. MBA 101 says to make investments where you get the most bang for the buck, also called return on investment (ROI). There is a finite amount of resources available within any organization. The frugal CISO's role is to ensure that the expenditures made using the information security budget have a significant impact on the improvement of the overall security posture of the organization. In making decisions related to budget, this drives their decision-making process for prioritization of spending. Expenditures for good staff and training to maintain their expertise should remain a major priority for the frugal CISO.

I was lucky to work with a very senior expert in my first position within an information security team. He taught me how to think like an information security professional. Each day he handed me a stack of printed information to review to provide me with a background in both the technology and risk management issues of the project I was working on. Many senior professionals have related similar stories of both formal and informal mentoring that influenced their decision to make information security their primary career direction. The value of these types of relationships is vital to creation of the next generation (NextGen) of information security professionals.

It may be a temptation to save some budget by relying on a single security expert on your staff. However, during a crisis, the information security organization needs all its *bench strength* in security expertise to work together and minimize the potential impact of a breach. In addition, one security expert creates the potential for a significant *single point of failure* (SPOF) risk for the organization.

Developing a critical mass of security expertise ensures knowledge sharing, provides coverage for gaps in knowledge, and allows for specialization within team members. One security expert cannot be expected to do it all on their own. Even if they are willing to try, the result is never good. Many security experts are placed in the position of *sole living expert* (SLE), and eventually get frustrated and move on to another organization. I have seen individuals placed into similar positions on many occasions. Because these were highly motivated individuals, they managed to keep up with excessive workloads.

However, many suffer from a condition my mother dubbed *brain overload*. It is the human equivalent of an operating system condition called *thrashing*. According to WhatIs.com, thrashing is computer activity that results in little or no progress toward an actual task. Its root cause is resource exhaustion. A similar condition occurs with carbon-based units (aka humans). When the amount of work overwhelms a security practitioner, he or she may flit from one task to another trying to satisfy everyone, but making no measurable progress.

One issue that sometimes creates a temptation to reduce staff expenditures within the information security area is that it may appear there are long periods of inactivity. This may create the perception to executive management that the team is doing nothing or not busy enough to justify their salary costs. This is because most information security tasks focus on prevention rather than easily visible activities. Often, the information security team is only visible during crisis events.

It is important to prevent this misconception by making proactive efforts to maintain the visibility of the information security team outside of periods of crisis, such as by having them teach classes or become a liaison with other technical or business teams. This is a similar problem to that experienced by another type of first responders, firefighters. Many people seem to think that firefighters do little when they are not actually in the field battling blazes. They are unaware of the time spent doing preparatory procedures to be ready when a fire or other emergency arises.

Revamping an Existing Information Security Team

Today, it is exceedingly rare that an organization has no information security team due to the increasing demands created by regulatory compliance, and the need to adhere to the data privacy and security laws enacted in most states. Often, these teams initially started as a security administrator group and evolved to provide coverage for other information security functions, such as antimalware. However, there is a great deal of diversity in experience, services, and composition of the information security functions across organizations.

Some teams received funding that made it possible to hire expertise in highly technical areas of cyber security, such as penetration testing (pen testing) and digital forensics. Most of these resource-blessed groups are part of large enterprises with significant compliance requirements. These information security teams have been in existence a number of years (or decades) and have achieved a high level of maturity.

Other information security teams are still just taking their first steps toward creating an information security program. These groups are often small, may lack senior security expertise, and are staffed with individuals transitioning from other areas. The maturity of these groups is often on the lower end of the continuum. These teams often result from audit findings, new compliance requirements, or an actual security breach. The amount of C-level or board of directors support for this type of information security is variable.

No matter what the current condition of the existing information security team, it is vital not to take action immediately before the frugal CISO gets to know the organization or the information security team. It is important to heed the old adage, "act in haste, repent in leisure." Your strategy should be primarily listening. The new frugal CISO needs to listen with the objective of:

- Understanding the business (products, services, competitors, industry)
- Understanding the organizational culture
- Learning about the basic threat landscape of organization and industry
- Understanding the IT strategy
- Becoming familiar with the security technology solutions in place and planned implementation of new solutions
- Assessing the team's current capabilities and competency gaps
- Learning about the backgrounds and skills of each individual team member
- Understanding current security policies, standards, and guidelines
- If it is a replacement CISO, finding out the true story of why that individual left.[1]
- Learning about the greatest challenges (from information security team)
- Learning about past security-related incidents, such as breaches
- Obtaining copies of recent compliance reports/audits, such as Payment Card Industry (PCI) Self-Assessment Questionnaire (SAQ)
- Obtaining copies of recent internal and external audit reports

- Learning about the perceptions of the efficacy of the current information security team from peers in other groups, such as finance or marketing

This is the input necessary to began developing a strategy for the team's structure and functions. It is essential to get the basic team structure right the first time. Getting it right the first time means that it will not be necessary to reorganize the team again for some time to come. Reorganization is change and change makes people apprehensive. It also negatively affects the productivity of the team, which increases cost. After determining the new structure, the frugal CISO can begin slotting existing employees in their new roles and identifying key roles that will require recruitment efforts.

Concentrate on the recruitment of key leadership positions and technical security experts because those roles can make or break the new team. Look to recruit internally, whenever possible. Existing employees are already familiar with the lay of the land in terms of people, processes, and technology. It can take new employees several months to a year to become familiar with an organization. Internal hiring may also increase team morale because employees will see it as evidence of the potential to climb the career ladder. However, it is important to recruit individuals for key positions with the appropriate level of expertise to excel in the roles. If identifying an individual with the right expertise is not possible from an internal recruitment, an external recruiting effort should rapidly follow any unsuccessful internal posting.

One of the benefits of being in the information security field for a number of years is that the frugal CISO gets to know the great security experts, either by working with them directly or through reputation. Most senior information security professionals understand the value of networking to get to know the significant players. Efforts to identify information security talent often pay major returns on investment when filling open positions. Some frugal CISOs opt to bring their talent along with them when moving to a new organization. The primary benefits can be summed up as the devil you know often feels more comfortable than hiring a new individual for a role.

You are already comfortable with your former employees and know what to expect from them. This is a reasonable justification for hiring members of your former team(s). However, you should proceed with caution when considering hiring some of your old team.

The first question you need to ask yourself is whether this is the right individual for this position. Just because an individual excelled in their old role does not necessarily mean that history will repeat itself with your new team. This may be a point to rethink familiar patterns and go for the new broom approach based upon the requirements of the new role. Some individuals are successful in a role because they have cultivated relationships and other resources to get tasks accomplished. They are dependent on who they know within the organization. In a new role without these established relationships, they might not be as effective and their limitations may become more apparent.

A significant issue with hiring former employees is how your new employees might perceive your actions. In most cases, their reactions will not be favorable. One common perception is that the CISO is trying to re-create their old team environment at the new company. This certainly does occur, so their suspicions are valid. New team members might also think that the old employee will receive favorable treatment from the new CISO because of their existing relationship. It also may create concerns that the CISO will replace their positions with former employees in the future.

Having Existing Team Reapply for Their Positions

One option in restructuring the current team is to ask current staff to reapply for the job they already have. By using this strategy, the team structure and composition essentially gets a do-over. It can limit risks of discrimination lawsuits if some current employees do not retain their current or similar positions. This process enables the company to retain the best-qualified employees for the new team structure. Options, such as transfers to other open positions, should be considered for existing staff not offered a position on the new team.

While there are benefits to this approach, it can result in anger and frustration for staff. It is important to tell current staff that they need to document their accomplishments and that there is no guarantee that they will be selected for the new team. Prior to announcing the requirement to reapply to the team, it is important to have both the new team structure and role descriptions available. It is important to maintain an upbeat and positive environment during this period.

While the position reapplication strategy is standard operating procedure for some organizations, especially those with a history of multiple mergers and acquisition, it has significant advantages and disadvantages. The obvious benefits are creating a team that best suits the organization's security needs, keeping good employees, and jettisoning staff that is not suited to the new structure. The disadvantage can be anxiety and low morale among remaining staff members. It can result in a later wave of resignations as retained staff leaves after finding new positions. The net impact can be a serious talent and knowledge drain that negatively affects productivity and increases costs. It also creates recruitment costs to fill these positions.

Next Steps after Restructuring of an Existing Team

After the team is in place and positions are filled, the team members need to settle into their new roles. Team members should be responsible for creating an initial plan of action for their new roles. For some existing team members who might be performing many of the same tasks, this may be relatively simple. New hires or team members implementing a new service or function may need to consider any technology requirements, such as vulnerability management tools or security information and event management (SIEM) solutions. Action plans should cover a nintey-day period. The objective of these plans is to focus team members on prioritizing their time on critical activities and hitting the ground running. The duration of the planning cycle should increase over time as the team members acclimate to the new environment and establish regular routines. A collateral benefit of the ninety-day planning process is that it may prevent analysis paralysis or procrastination in implementing security program functions.

Professional Development Planning

Both new and existing teams should have a professional development plan based on their new roles. The plan will differ based upon their specialization. The plan should focus on maintaining current core competencies and acquisition of new skills. Core competencies are the skills and knowledge required to perform tasks in a current role and progress to the next career level. Competencies involve an integration of multiple skills sets, not just technical expertise alone. Information security is not a profession that allows its practitioners to remain static in their skills and expertise for the long haul.

To be successful in the long term, practitioners must evolve with the profession by continuously updating their skills. Steven Covey made the idea of continuously refreshing knowledge and skills when he updated his famous 1989 classic business book *The Seven Habits of Highly Effective People* (Free Press, 2004) and introduced *Habit 8*, "sharpen the saw."

There will always exist some gaps between current proficiencies and those required to move onto the next logical career step or laterally transitioning into another role. After identifying the gaps, the development plan addresses them through an action plan designed to close gaps and to allow the individual to move forward toward their career aspirations.

The development plan is iterative and needs to be reviewed against progress toward its objectives, and adjusted on a regular basis. Appendix C provides some competency/development forms for use as career planning tools for staff.

Stress and Information Security

Information security is an inherently stressful profession. While stress and burnout is common in high-stress fields, finding support and information for handling information security burnout is difficult. In recent years, the profession has begun discussing the issue openly in an effort to make practitioners aware of its warning signs, develop mechanisms to mitigate is causes, and lessen its stigma to make practitioners more willing to reach out for assistance, when necessary.

According to Joshua Corman, director of Security Intelligence for Akamai Technologies and blogger, "We are a nasty group of people. We turn on each other," and "We forget to take care of each other." While security practitioners might not actually be nasty people, we may forget the niceties when dealing with other. This may be related to the common personality types associated with technologists. Sixty percent of IT professionals fall under the Myers-Briggs Introverted Sensing Thinking Judging (ISTJ) type, as opposed less than 3% of all individuals. The Myers-Briggs Type Indicator (MBTI) measures how we look at and interact with other people. My first introduction to the ISTJ and information security occurred when a former manager asked me to see if a coworker who was grieving his mother's death was OK. When I asked why he did not do this himself, he told me that he was an ISTJ, and therefore it was not possible. I am also an ISTJ, but this has never stopped me from relating to others in pain.

Probably one of the best-known examples of this personality type is the fictional Dr. Sheldon Cooper of the popular sitcom *The Big Bang Theory*. The fictional Dr. Cooper exhibits some of the abrasive communication style and lack of *people literacy* traits associated with extreme ISTJ individuals. Whether many information security professionals are ISTJ or not, individuals who pursue this profession tend to have a strong task focus that may be interpreted as a lack of soft skills. When dealing with other practitioners, we feel freer to drop all decorum in our interactions with "our own kind" or take out our frustrations on each other. These frequent caustic interactions may contribute to overall job stress.

In 2012, a Maslach Burnout Inventory (MBI)* was performed on a group of information security professionals. The Voluntary Responses measured the three pillars of potential burnout, including exhaustion, cynicism, and (self-perceived) efficacy in the workplace. The results of the MBI survey confirmed what many practitioners already intuitively knew—all three indicators were exceedingly high. However, it was in the low levels of self-efficacy in which security professionals distinguished themselves from other high-stress jobs. These low rates of self-efficacy might be traced to the very nature of the job.

Information security requires that practitioners remain ready to combat invisible attackers without warning. This means maintaining a continuous state of alertness against an ever-changing threat landscape. Practitioners need only make one small mistake, which a hacker can exploit, to result in a security breach. In addition, the nature of technology jobs can be in itself isolating and may limit the opportunities for human interaction. With an increasing trend for telecommuting among practitioners, many of whom work a non-standard work schedule, the opportunity for regular interaction with peers and coworkers is further diminished.

The frugal CISO needs to be alert to any red flags that might indicate an information security professional is under stress, which might

---

* http://www.mindgarden.com/products/mbi.htm

eventually result in a burnout. Some of the warning signs when the stress level is getting too high include:

- Patterns or changes in behavior
- Absenteeism or disappearing at lunchtime
- A change in appearance (usually for worse or radical new looks)
- Withdrawal
- Not participating in team meetings
- Snapping at colleagues
- Self-medicating with alcohol or drugs
- Physical altercations with coworkers

Tips for Helping Information Security Professionals Combat Burnout

One tactic that could diminish work stress is to get out of the trenches occasionally to provide a fresh perspective, including:

- Mentoring younger coworkers
- Teaching a course
- Having a hobby
- Taking a walk or going to the gym
- Spending time with family or friends
- Writing articles (or a book)
- Speaking at conferences
- Volunteering anywhere

The key is to get away from normal daily tasks. Sometimes security practitioners may feel guilty for taking time away from their jobs, even during vacations or holidays. In addition, mobile devices, such as smartphones and tablets, keep us always connected to work. Information security practitioners are not alone in this mobile device "addiction":

- 90% of 18- to 29-year-olds sleep with their smartphones[*]
- 50% of Americans sleep with their phones next to them[†]

They develop a syndrome similar to that of some technology addicts, where they believe if they complete one more scan, game, or compile, then they will be "done." However, to paraphrase the famous tag line for a popular brand of potato chips, "One is not enough."

---

[*] http://www.pewresearch.org/daily-number/do-you-sleep-with-your-cell-phone/
[†] Ibid

Tips for Employers to Combat Information Security Burnout

One of my former managers often referred to laptops, smartphones, and other mobile devices as "electronic tethers" because they kept individuals always attached to the workplace. This always-on and always-attached technology makes information security practitioners available on a 24/7/365 basis. One option is to force the security practitioners to disconnect for a while on a daily basis.

Some parents do the same thing with their kids to avoid the creation of Internet or online gaming addicts. This does not even work with tech-savvy kids who figure other ways to connect with the web. Several years ago, one conference provider actually held events on ships using a "cruise to nowhere" strategy to limit attendees' access to the Internet and phones. However, I do not see these as realistic tactics to reduce job stress.

Probably a better option is to watch workload and try to offload tasks whenever possible to another less busy team member. Recognize the efforts of security practitioners to their peers and executive management in a public forum. Information security functions may not have predefined completion events, such as project endings or general availability of software releases, for providing visibility of extraordinary efforts by participants, so it important to schedule celebratory events to reward individuals and teams.

Cost of Turnover

Staff-related costs remain one of the most significant expenditures for information security teams. One strategy to minimize unnecessary staffing costs is maintaining a stable workforce. This can result in significant cost savings to employers. It costs organizations an average of 20% of an employee to replace a worker. It is expensive to replace employees because of the productivity loss when a staff member leaves a job, the costs of hiring and training a new employee, and slower productivity until the new employee gets up to speed in their new job.

On average, positions that involve higher educational levels and specialized training have higher turnover costs. These types of positions tend to have excessively high turnover costs as a percentage of salary (up to 200%). The impact of employee turnover on costs is important because annually about one-fifth of all workers voluntarily leave and one-sixth are voluntarily terminated. The actual cause of the employee turnover is not really the critical issue. It is bottom-line impact of the increasing costs to replace employees and the scarcity of qualified information security professionals available for recruitment.

The Great Recession starting in 2008 did temporarily reduce the number of voluntary terminations and employee turnover overall. Many workers stayed in place waiting for the economy to stabilize and improve before risking a move to another employer. At the same time, organizations reduced hiring and did not fill open positions to reduce expenses. While this provided a respite for internal recruiters and managers, it masked a swelling in the number of workers who were unhappy with their present employment and waiting for economic recovery.

As the economy improves, we are seeing this pent-up demand for new employment opportunities actualize itself, at the same time that the overall number of openings for information security professionals has increased. This is a mini version of the perfect storm scenario many organizations faced in the late 1990s in which increasing demand for technology professionals exceeded available supply. If the economy continues to improve, recruiting experienced information security professionals will become more difficult.

Under this set of circumstances, it becomes vital to decrease employee turnover for two reasons. The first reason, already discussed, is reducing expenses attributable to replacing employees that jump ship, which centers on cost avoidance. The second reason is even more important. Numerous open positions may limit an organization's ability to support new projects, innovations, or implement new business strategies.

The core of these issues is the ability of the organization to grow revenues, establish greater market share, and maintain a competitive position in its industry. These revenue-related issues affect the organization's ability to expand and thrive. Organizations cannot stay static, especially in today's global dynamic business environment. To do so is likely a death sentence for the organization.

Turnover of information security employees might result in an inability to staff security roles responsible for assuring the organization's security posture. Insufficient staffing levels might result in a security breach, or in the worst-case scenario, failure to detect an ongoing intrusion and exfiltration of sensitive data by cyber attackers for weeks, months, years, or altogether.

Costs of Excessive Turnover of Information Security Staff

Excessive turnover of your information security staff goes beyond the direct costs associated with loss of productivity and new recruitment efforts. Some of these costs are short term in duration, but others may endure for years. These costs are born by the organization, management, and the employees themselves. By instituting good management practices, significant cost savings can be realized in hard dollars, lost productivity, and human potential. Some of the tangible and intangible costs associated with excessive employee turnover include the following:

- Bad reputation of an organization and team, making it difficult to recruit
- Organization must pay premium compensation (above market rates) for employees
- Frequent illness among staff and stress-related disorders
- Low morale
- Need to use more expensive contract workers to fill openings
- Lawsuits and human resources (HR) actions
- Bad internal reputation
- Loss of investment in staff in terms of training and experience
- Failure to meet compliance objectives
- Team does not step up to the plate in a crisis
- Staff hoards knowledge, creating SLEs
- Failure to mentor younger staff
- Failure to assimilate new technologies
- Frequent disagreement among staff
- Excessive sick time
- Staff disappears or spends work time on frequent job searches
- Increased incidents or delays in identifying events
- Workplace violence incidents
- Damaged career paths
- Bad performance reviews
- Lack of support from the C-level
- Sacrificing long-term for short-term objectives

Tips on Lowering Turnover of Information Security Employees

The majority of information security employees fit into a group referred to as *gold-collar* workers. The term was first coined in 1985 by Professor Robert E. Kelly of Carnegie Mellon University. In his seminal book on the topic, Professor Kelly discussed how this new category of workers differs from earlier workers in what motivates them and how to successfully manage this group of workers.

The term *gold-collar workers* describes highly skilled and college-educated workers who offer employers high performance and demand attractive compensation in return. This category of workers includes late Boomers and Generation Xers. Millennials (Gen Y) are a recent addition to this group. Most gold-collar workers find employment in the high-tech sectors of business and have great flexibility in finding employment opportunities. Gold-collar workers are credited with bringing significant changes to the workplace, such as casual dress codes, flexible work hours, and telecommuting.

Gold-collar workers share common traits, such as enhanced skill set, professionalism, and productivity. They are more highly educated than prior generations of professional workers, such as white-collar workers, and frequently pursue graduate degrees or other advanced educational options. While the gold-collar worker pursues highly compensated positions, traditional benefits may not be the most salient motivators for these workers. In the 1981 book by Tracy Kidder, *The Soul of a New Machine* (Little, Brown, 1981), there is a quote that may best describe the criticality of offering challenging work to the gold-collar worker when one of the engineers states, "They don't work for the money."

Gold-collar workers seek out engaging and fulfilling work with opportunities to develop professionally, as well as personally. They desire opportunities for ongoing education and development. When developing a strategy for increasing retention and lowering turnover of your information security team, it is important to keep in mind the attributes of the gold-collar worker. Some potential tactics to lower turnover in an information security organization include:

1. Determining appropriate compensation for the positions you need to fill and already have. While this might be counterintuitive to good cost management, frequent turnover of information security staff for better-paying positions is more costly

both in the short term and long term than increasing salaries. If you cannot offer competitive salaries, get creative when necessary with benefits, flexible work schedules, and bonus structures.

2. Being flexible where you can be. Consider offering flex hours, telecommuting, or a compressed work schedule

3. Strengthening employee engagement through team interaction and creating a rewarding work environment.

4. Managers demonstrating respect and recognition for staff members.

5. Providing challenging opportunities with room for career growth or at least lateral expansion of job tasks, such as assuming a leadership position on a project or becoming a liaison for the information security team with business groups.

6. Not micromanage employees or nitpicking small issues. A pattern of these behaviors over time can erode employee motivation and morale. This can result in an employee leaving your information security team to avoid *death by a thousand cuts*.

7. Maintaining personal contact with your information security staff, both as individuals and as a group. There can be a tendency to skip staff meetings or one-on-ones when the team is busy. However, the staff meeting, at the very least, allows team members to share information, develop good interteam communication skills, create a sense of cohesion, discourage feelings of isolation, and reduce friction by providing an appropriate forum to air issues and seek resolution. One-on-one sessions assist in providing challenging, clear career paths. Employees want to know where they could be heading and how they can get there. It also is crucial in identifying potential issues that could affect an individual's productivity or create job stress that could result in burnout or turnover.

Retaining and Nurturing Your Information Security Team

The following are suggestions for nurturing your team:

- Be a good example. To quote the late General George S. Patton, "Always do everything you ask of those you command." This means following the same rules as your staff. If you make special exceptions for yourself, it sends a poor message to staff. I have seen management that even asked staff members to cover for their digressions (lie for them). If you behave badly, it may become the norm for your staff. An example was a CISO that developed a reputation as a "bad kid" because he flaunted organizational behavioral norms and went out of his way to irritate executive management. His team admired his chutzpah (Yiddish slang for "guts") and emulated his inappropriate behaviors. Even after he moved on, his former team's reputation remained tainted by their history.

- It is vital to continue to offer opportunities for team members to enhance their value and develop their careers by providing access to both technical training and formal education, such as graduate degrees. If your organization provides tuition reimbursement benefits, make sure that your team is aware of this benefit and how it works.

- Do not throw your people under the bus (to cover your mistakes or the mistakes of others).

- Do not criticize or make fun of team members in front of others, including your peers, other managers, members of other teams, or your own team. It will always get back to the individual and creates bad feelings. It makes others distrust you because they wonder if you will do the same to them when they are not present.

- Do not *trash talk* about your peers or other teams in the presence of the team. The team might emulate this practice, which can create an environment in which disrespectful behaviors and attitudes are acceptable.

- Base promotion opportunities on a defined set of job competencies and provide guidance on acquiring and developing new areas of proficiency.

- Whether you are on the pro or con side of the security certification question, offer these opportunities to your information security team. If there is sufficient interest among staff, consider offering an in-house study group. If your team is sufficiently large, you might have members of the team develop training modules for different security domains in their areas of expertise.

- Celebrate small successes as well as big ones.

- Be a great communicator. Make sure that team members understand why the organization is making certain decisions, especially those most directly affected. People often just want to know why something was done.
- Teach team members how to frame security decisions in a business context rather than a technical one.
- Provide *all* team members with opportunities to gain visibility under positive circumstances rather than while fighting fires in crisis mode only. This allows them to shine.
- Give the credit to the team first for successes. Then point out any team members that made significant contributions to the team.
- Try not to play favorites among team members. Your staff always notices this, and at the very least, it creates disharmony within the team.
- Nurture an open communication environment where honest dissent is encouraged. Being told you are wrong may not be easy, but airing differing opinions creates on opportunity to reexamine a topic, which can result in innovation and improvements. My personal way of getting individuals to share their concerns and reservations about a topic is to query the team saying the following, "Is this OK to do, or am I on drugs to do this?" Strong leaders are open to the opinions of others because they have confidence in their abilities. Weak leaders may tend to squash any opinions that differ from their own.
- Address problems openly rather than allowing issues to fester. I am a great believer in ripping off the bandage to get the air to the wound. It generally heals faster when exposed to air and sunlight.
- Never discipline an employee in front of other staff, managers, or clients. The purpose of discipline is to teach, not embarrass. Several ex-military managers drilled this concept into me. When an individual is embarrassed or put in an uncomfortable position, they may shut down and fail to listen to the message you are trying to communicate.

Why Teams Fail to Meet Expectations

Many teams seem to form with an abundance of advantages, such as great team members, financial resources, and support from the executive level. These teams, on the surface, seem destined for a continuing pattern of achievements that will propel their members onto successful career paths. However, success seems to elude the team, and team members seek avenues of escape onto other teams to prevent the team's poor reputation from affecting their careers.

An excellent example of this paradox appeared in the 1981 book by Tracy Kidder, *The Soul of a New Machine,* which tells the story of the creation of an innovative design in minicomputer architecture realized by a skunk works project team with limited resources. I often refer to these types of teams as *little train that could* teams because they seem positioned against almost impossible odds, but they keeping repeating their manta of "I think I can, I think I can" to anyone who will listen. This skunk works team was only created as a backup plan in case the premier engineering effort failed. However, it was the little train that could that saved the day and possibly the company.

While some teams do fail due to lack of resources, most fall short of expectations for other reasons. None of these challenges has to doom a team to failure. However, they cannot be ignored if an information security team is to remain vital and innovative. Failure to address these types of issues may result in increased costs, loss of productivity, and often the team itself.

Inability to Gel

Often, the success or failure of a team is determined early on, during its formation. At this stage, the members are figuring out whether or not they can connect with each other on an emotional and intellectual level. The essence of a successful team is the establishment of trust among its members. Without trust, the team remains a collection of individuals with a team identity in name only. Interactions with others form trust bonds. Not all interactions are pleasant or enriching experiences. However, they are all necessary.

A normal part of working on a team involves disagreements. Individual personality differences and approaches can create conflict. Conflict is natural. If team members are unwilling to argue, they avoid conflict. Team members are not open with each other in their communications.

When arguments occur without an effective mechanism for conflict resolution, they can become personal. The net result is that the team shuts down, anger builds, tensions mount, and the overall effectiveness of the team is compromised. Team members revert to a strategy of maximizing personal gain instead of team performance.

Cost-avoidance countermeasures: Select team members that balance out each other's talents and weaknesses. Integrate team-building exercises and events into meetings to build trust and communications skills. Create safe environments to reduce conflict by creating opportunities to discuss problems openly.

The Fish Rots from the Head Down

An ancient Chinese proverb says that a fish rots from the head down. Managers may be led to believe everything is OK, because employees tell them what they want to hear and keep complaints down. The Great Recession may have exacerbated this type this behavior. Without direct feedback from people who report to them, the manager may be unaware of significant issues just below the surface. Either productivity suffers or the team may fail to evolve. The true extent of issues may be visible until some event occurs to trigger either an HR review or acceleration of staff turnover. The net result is decreased productivity and increased costs.

Cost-avoidance countermeasure: Utilize the old management practice of walking around to stay in tune with staff sentiments. Create an open-door policy and demonstrate a willingness to listen to opinions that are contrary to your own. If necessary, use a facilitator to create a neutral environment in which team members feel enabled to express their true feelings.

Toxic Element

As the old adage goes, one bad apple spoils the barrel. It is the same with teams. One toxic employee can spoil the dynamics of the team and increase costs due to loss of productivity and high turnover rates. Toxic employees create issues with other employees. They may turn employees against each other or management. While some toxic employees can be high performers or extremely technically skilled, the net economic benefit is often negated by the overstress they create for the team.

One reason that this occurs is that businesses do not have proper performance reviews in place, or their review systems only measure productivity. Information security may not want to address the issue because they feel that it may be difficult to recruit another technical expert or some misplaced loyalty for accomplishments.

Countermeasure: Identify any team members with toxic tendencies, such as efforts to undermine other employees or personal attacks on other members of the team or management. Look to neutralize their behaviors or make it clear that these behaviors will not be tolerated. Make efforts to support other team members affected by the toxic behavior. Often, toxic individuals will pick a particular team member as their favorite target, especially high-performing practitioners who may threaten their position within the team.

If the behavior does not change, find a way to remove the toxic individual from the team. This may be a survival and cost-avoidance strategy because the net impact of the toxic employee may result in the manager's own termination. I have seen a situation where a manager's career was derailed because of their unremitting support for a highly toxic, but extremely gifted team member.

If you want to change the minds and hearts of a team, it is vital to demonstrate that you want to fix the problem and that you genuinely care about them—and show you mean it. If you do not, you are dead in the water in today's competitive climate for information security talent.

Vital Ingredient: Team Learning

Strong teams offer the greatest potential for running cost-efficient organizations and the hope of improving productivity over the long run. There is no magic spell for creating a high-performing team. A strong team needs to develop a culture of individual and team life learning.

Team learning focuses on providing information security solutions to business issues by developing an open approach to questioning. Members of information security learning teams look beyond the standard approaches and experts to a collaborative strategy using the team itself to develop innovative solutions. Team members present both ideas and solutions. This approach promotes open and honest communication exchange, and more importantly minimizes the potential for *groupthink*.

Groupthink is a phenomenon that occurs within teams in which the desire to minimize conflict or promote conformity results in erroneous decision-making. The team reaches a consensus decision without exploration of alternative perspectives. Teams affected by groupthink tend to isolate themselves from external influences, even from other groups within the same organization. A common symptom of groupthink is frequent failures in the assimilation of new team members. Other symptoms that may be indicative of the groupthink phenomenon are idealized remembrances of the team's history and an *us against them* attitude toward other teams or parties external to the team.

While the groupthink phenomenon may look to those affected as team loyalty, it may isolate the team from others in the organization or peers and inhibit innovation or the adoption of best, recommended, or smart practices.

The learning team process is similar to traditional brainstorming, but the process looks to weed out impracticable and unworkable strategies to avoid expending limited resources on dead ends. It considers technical and cultural constraints. By working through the process, it ensures that the team stays together and learns together. At its heart is the shared responsibility of every team member. It views issues from different perspectives to generate the best potential solutions. The learning team highly encourages diversity in opinions and approaches by team members.

Learning is an iterative process that takes place through feedback. We are all used to performance reviews and individual feedback, but rarely do we experience team feedback.

Team learning is fundamental to the performance of a team. Without it, a team can never achieve its full potential. Each iteration of the learning process results in more optimized strategic solutions and improved team performance.

It is important to document each team learning cycle to maximum benefits derived from iterations of the process. This documentation step is critical to supporting a totally objective postmortem review of each effort. A postmortem review of team learning allows the team to identify elements of the process that worked and elements that did not. The net result is a plan for the continuous improvement of the team and a blueprint for future innovations.

A collateral benefit of documenting the learning process is that it may prevent the creation of a false history for the team that is a symptom of the groupthink phenomenon. For example, without objective documentation of a successful project that involved collaboration with external groups, the team may not remember the contributions of other teams, and therefore not seek future opportunities for collaboration with others. This may result in the implementation of technology silos that increase costs across the organization.

Learning is central to the growth of the team. To quote Anthony J. D'Angelo, "Develop a passion for learning. If you do, you will never cease to grow." Both the individual and his or her team need to seek out new development opportunities to incrementally enhance their expertise. *Kaizen* is the Japanese term for continuous improvement. Kaizen is a critical element of cost-effective information security teams. By practicing Kaizen, the information security team will have the knowledge and expertise for future career innovation in the security functions it provides. It is through the Kaizen process that the organization maximizes its ROI in information security and the team itself.

Endnotes

1. I always ask what is the true story of why the person I am replacing left, regardless of the position I am taking, because the answers I get can be very informative.

6

MANAGING EXTERNAL PARTIES EFFECTIVELY

It Takes a Global Village

It Takes a Village was the title of 1996 book written by Hillary Rodham Clinton that discussed the influence of the community on the children growing up within it. In the last two decades, a very similar phenomenon has occurred within the business environment. An apt title for a book discussing the influences of external parties on today's organization might be *It Takes a Global Village*.

Several decades ago, organizations often operated within narrow geographic areas. They purchased their services, hired their employees, and operated within specific geographic areas. Even large enterprises did business like this to some degree with different corporate campuses managed somewhat autonomously and linked by predefined distribution channels. Many organizations were self-sustaining ecosystems that provided most of the services required for daily operations, such as printing and IT services. Staff consisted primarily of full-time employees.

Over the last two decades, organizations experienced an era of profound transformation. We moved away from the traditional big centralized business approach to a global, interconnected, and knowledge-intensive economic model. In order to adopt this new way of doing business, organizations needed to change the way they got things done. This affected every facet of the organization to some degree, including information security. These changes were not without some pain, but offered new economic opportunities with the potential to improve the quality of life for many. However, there have also been unintended consequences, especially around creating new areas of risk.

Two trends that continue to influence the way organizations do business and the risks involved include:

1. Outsourcing of services and functions
2. Expanded use of contract staff
3. Use of specialized security service firms
4. Vendor software

Both of these trends have allowed organizations to expand by reducing costs and optimizing opportunities for innovation and expansion into emerging markets. However, they changed the threat landscape by creation of new risks or transforming existing risks.

According to the Trustwave® *2103 Global Security Report*,[1] in 63% of security incident investigations, outsourced third-party IT support was a significant factor. Outsourcing can help businesses gain effective, cost-friendly IT services. However, businesses need to understand the risk their vendors may introduce and proactively work to decrease that risk.

Outsourcing

A decade or two ago, many organizations existed within somewhat self-contained silos where various internal departments provided services to the organization as a whole, for example, the IT department developed and supported application systems. There was limited need to go outside the organization's perimeter to do operational tasks or undertake initiatives. However, there were issues with this self-contained organizational ecosystem.

There was a tendency for internal service departments to become bloated with administrative overhead and bureaucracy. Internal service departments were not motivated to reduce costs, improve service, or develop innovative product offerings. They were, for all purposes, a monopoly with no competition. This created frustration for internal users. Internal departments exercised their budgetary power by using external service providers to meet the unfilled needs.

The use of external services often resulted in cost savings or better service levels than the internal options. Over time, the utilization of service providers and other types of vendors was not only accepted by senior management, but highly encouraged. Many organizations eliminated internal service departments in favor of outsourcing these functions to reduce costs and improve service. I experienced this in a governmental organization that eliminated its internal micrographic department because of its poor-quality output and refusal to upgrade its service offerings.

Outsourcing of noncore services allowed organizations to down-size and decrease operational overhead. Organizations became more agile. In addition to replacing existing internal services, outsourcing allowed organizations the potential for innovation by engaging new vendor offerings. Many organizations began using domestic outsourc-ing partners in the late 1990s, but in recent years, the pool of potential vendors expanded globally to include relationships with a growing number of offshore partners. Offshore operations can result in vari-ous additional risks because of differences in culture, legislation, legal jurisdictions, government instabilities, and geographic distances.

There is also another significant area of outsourcing risk, which may not be immediately evident. Many outsourcing partners subcontract some functions to other partners. Often, this outsourcing of functions may not be known to the end customer. This may result in the sharing of sensitive data with parties outside of those involved in the original agreement. This creates a requirement to manage the security issues around the protection of sensitive information across multiple locations and organizations. Managing data privacy requirements across a global environment presents new challenges in regulatory compliance and information security. Global outsourcing may make it more difficult to respond to security breaches and other security-related incidents.

A Framework for Cost-Effective Outsourcing Management

Before embarking on or expanding a strategy of outsourcing, it is best practice to create a framework for managing information security of outsourcing relationships that provide external parties with access to sensitive private information, trade secrets, intellectual property, proprietary data, or connectivity to the organization's internal net-work. This framework needs to be sufficiently broad in scope to cover domestic and international outsourcing agreements for operational functions provided both on-site and off-site. Outsourcing partners should be required to adhere to the organization's data classification scheme and the data protection guidelines.

This framework should extend from the initial implementation of the outsourcing relationship through any voluntary or involuntary termination agreements. At the termination of the outsourcing relationship, there is a requirement for the appropriate destruction or transfer of all sensitive residual data involved in outsourced process(es). The outsourcer should remain under the provisions of the framework until a confirmation that all appropriate termination objectives are accomplished.

Outsourcing Framework Objectives

The *outsourcing framework* identifies and manages all information security risks resulting from the outsourcing relationship. It is designed to provide an appropriate level of risk management based upon the specific nature of the outsourcing agreement in an effective and cost-efficient manner. While it remains an option to outsource functions related to appropriate due diligence and security oversight to an external security firm, the final responsibility lies within the organization. In addition, using an external security firm can substantially increase the total costs of managing outsourcing relationships. After establishing the outsourcing framework and its associated procedures, it is often more cost-effective to provide these services through the information security team.

The outsourcing framework needs to be expansive enough to cover a wide range of risks that might occur as the result of a relationship with an external party, including:

1. Protecting confidentiality of sensitive data
2. Minimizing potential for business function outages
3. Legal and regulatory compliance requirements
4. Lessening the potential for misuse of IT resources
5. Fraud avoidance
6. Protecting sensitive data from disclosure
7. Demonstration of adequate due diligence in potential lawsuits
8. Preventing liability resulting from activities of business partners
9. Ensuring adequate controls are in place prior to the start of joint business activities

The outsourcing framework is designed to have wide applicability to business relationships that involve the transfer or storage of sensitive information. Some potential outsourcing relationships might include the following types of external partners:

- Offshore IT development firms
- Direct mailing services
- Data enhancement companies
- Cloud providers: software as a service (SaaS)
- Cloud providers: platform as a service (PaaS)
- Cloud providers: infrastructure as a service (IaaS)
- Joint business opportunity partners
- Email service providers

Before proceeding with any outsourcing risk analysis, a basic attempt to review the outsourcer is a cost-effective way to identify any low-hanging fruit in terms of risks. Fortunately, the Internet has simplified this process. Much of the preliminary research process requires only a good Internet search engine. Other research may require Internet subscriptions to special research sites. The organization's legal or communications/public relations teams may already subscribe to several of these services. The objective is to perform a records and media search that includes the following information resources:

- Public information regarding the principals of the entity under investigation
- Corporate filings
- Licensing and regulatory records
- Court records
- Recent news articles
- Financial reports
- Background on key stakeholders, owners, and corporate officers
- Press releases

This process should be repeated throughout the life cycle of the outsourcing agreement, as necessitated by changes or events affecting the organization or the outsourcing partners.

Outsourcing Assessment Guidelines

Prior to the signing of any outsourcing agreements, a security assessment of the outsourcer may be based upon the identified risks associated with the outsourcing effort. The first step in the process is the signing of standard nondisclosures agreements (NDAs) by all parties involved. The NDAs should be signed prior to any discussions or releases of sensitive or proprietary information with external parties.

After NDAs are completed, the outsourcer is provided with a basic self-assessment questionnaire (BSAQ) designed to identify potential areas of security risk or concerns for further follow-up. Because completion of the questionnaire may require multiple subject matter experts, the outsourcer should be provided with adequate time to complete the document. The self-assessment should consist of multiple sections to cover a variety of common service agreements, such as web hosting services and IT application development, but it cannot cover every type of strategic partnership scenario.

Some basic component parts of the BSAQ might include the following:

1. Generic External Third Party Risk Evaluation Checklist
2. Generic Site Visit Assessment Form

Appendix D contains sample copies of the generic forms.

The BSAQ provides basic information regarding the outsourcing organization, its services, and the nature of the outsourcing agreement. In some situations, it may not be necessary to proceed past the BSAQ because the outsourced function or service is deemed below the threshold of risk for further assessment. By building a decision point into the risk assessment process, cost avoidance is achieved by not requiring unnecessary control procedures for low-risk outsourcing agreements.

The BSAQ may utilize a modular design. The BSAQ should facilitate the collection of basic outsourcer data and the business/technical services covered under the outsourcing agreement. The BSAQ is cost effective because of its standardized approach. It may be used across the vast majority of outsourcing opportunities and may be used across the organization. When a new category of outsourcing occurs, a new module can be created or adapted from an existing module.

Different compliance regulations can also utilize separate modules, for example, the Payment Card Industry Data Security Standard (PCI-DSS). By modularizing compliance questions, it will be cheaper to update these questions when regulations are revised, such as the PCI-DSS Revision 3.0 released in November of 2013. An online version of that BSAQ might further reduce costs associated with outsourcing risk assessment by alerting both the outsource provider or security reviewer to missing information or inconsistencies on the form.

The BSAQ becomes input into site assessment, if the level risk exceeds the risk threshold. The BSAQ provides information security with focus areas where the reviewer should concentrate his or her limited resources when evaluating the outsourcer's site(s). By narrowing the scope of any site assessment, there is the potential to reduce the duration of the visitation and travel-related expenses. The site assessment process consists of a trained risk assessor performing an internal and external site walkthrough accompanied by the outsourcer's representative and key personnel involved in the outsourced function(s).

The site assessment focuses on evaluating the site's physical security perimeter, environmental controls, and business contingency recovery capabilities. The site assessment uses the visit form as a tool to ensure that all infrastructure-related issues receive adequate coverage during the review process.

In advance of any site assessment, the reviewer may request additional information, such as procedure manuals and forms, to supplement and clarify the site's support procedures. This allows the reviewer to specifically identify any critical procedures to observe to determine if they are in compliance with documented policies and guidelines.

Depending on the size of the facility, the process can require one to three days of interviews and observations. The deliverable from the site assessment is a comprehensive evaluation document written from a perspective similar to that provided by an external evaluator. This document allows for the identification of potential infrastructure security issues and actionable countermeasures to reduce residual risk to a level acceptable to senior executive management.

The increasing trend toward use of cloud providers will increase the necessity for outsourcing risk reviews. Investments in automation of this function will lower the costs associated with each review by decreasing the administrative overhead. Combining the BSAQ and outsourcing security review processes with mobile technology could allow information to be entered into a customized in-house developed database to facilitate automation and tracking of assessment status. This database can be mined and data extracted into sophisticated analysis tools to automate much of the assessment process to minimize the cost of providing this security service to the organization.

Information Security and Outsourcing Service Level Agreements

Certain language should be included in all outsourcing contractual agreements involving the potential area of downstream outsourcers. *Downstream outsourcers* are secondary outsourcers that provide services to the primary outsourcer. These risks include the transfer, processing, or storage of sensitive information by another external entity. By including these requirements in any Service Level Agreement (SLA) or outsourcing contract, there is the possibility to reduce legal costs in the event of any security issues cropping up during the term of the agreement or eventual termination of the contract.

1. The external entity must agree to comply with all existing organizational policies and standards regarding the handling of sensitive information, including personally identifiable information (PII), proprietary information, intellectual property (IP), and trade secrets.

2. Contractual agreements must stipulate that external partners are to immediately notify the organization of any cyber or virus incidents at their facility that could potentially affect the organization's information, systems, or network, or that could have any negative effect on the external partner's ability to perform tasks outlined in the contract, even for a limited period.

3. Contractual agreements must stipulate that external partners are prohibited from further subcontracting the service or sharing organizational sensitive information with a downstream processor/service provider without prior explicit approval from the organization.

4. Contractual agreements must stipulate that the organization maintains the right to perform both ad hoc and planned security site assessments of the external partner's facility and those of any subcontractors engaged by the external partner. These site assessments by the organization's information security team or a third-party firm of the organization's choice requires the ability to periodically audit the integrity of networks, systems, and administration practices, as they apply to security access control and intrusion detection.

Contract Staff

The trend toward the increasing use of contract staff began in earnest in the mid-1990s in response to several business needs:

- A shortage of trained technology professionals
- Increasing specialization within technology
- Need for additional staff for large enterprise initiatives, such as Y2K
- Variability in IT budgets created by economic conditions, especially downturns in the business environment

Often, individuals opted to become contractors due to the greater independence and higher compensation levels available for contract engagements. However, since the start of the economic downturn in 2008, an increasing number of organizations are utilizing more contractors rather than hiring full-time employees. Information security teams have mirrored this hiring trend with an increasing number of teams using a larger percentage of contract staff. This situation will likely continue during the economic recovery and beyond.

From a purely economic perspective, contract hiring is a good choice during economic turndowns and financially uncertain times. It prevents the hire–fire cycles, which can create significant hard dollar costs and have a negative impact on remaining team members. A contractor staffing strategy allows the team to increase resources during busy periods or meet project delivery deadlines without incurring the continuing overhead of full-time staff during slower periods.

However, as the employment outlook brightens and returns to a more stable economic environment, the use of contractors to fill critical information security roles becomes more problematic as a long-term staffing strategy. One reason for this is that the rates for contractor staff tend to rise during economic recovery, and there may be an increasing shortage of experienced contractors to fill vacancies.

Contractors may be unwilling to accept short-term assignments or convert to full-time employment. The net result of better economic times may be an overall scarcity of available resources to staff information security initiatives supporting critical business strategies, such as cloud and mobile device integration.

The reality is that prior to the economic downturn, there was already a shortage of experienced information security professionals. The bad economy masked this shortage for a while due to a decrease in IT spending overall and layoffs among information security professionals. However, the brightening economic picture is bringing this scarcity of experienced practitioners to the surface.

While there will always be a number of information security professionals that prefer contract assignments for personal reasons or because their areas of expertise allow them to command high compensation, the number of contract professionals may diminish to some degree with a brightening economic outlook. In addition, many contractors work for information security firms that place them with clients rather than acting as independent consultants. Information security firms often charge organizations a premium for placing their contractors, which may negate potential cost savings from using contract resources.

Risks Associated with Information Security Contractors

Many information security strategies have substantial benefits. However, like most good things, the use of contractors does bring some risks along with the package. The potential for the realization of these risks within a specific information security organization requires consideration when hiring contract professionals, including:

Some Consultants (and Agencies) May Oversell Their Information Security Expertise This issue is not specific to information security, but an issue across most technical areas. It is also not specific to consultants, but also occurs with full-time employee hiring, as well. However, when there is a shortage of consultants, some agencies and individuals may embellish a resume to include areas of expertise in which the applicant has limited experience. The best countermeasure is a comprehensive technical interview.

The problem with this tactic is that your team may have limited proficiency in the area where you need a contractor (why you are hiring the contractor in the first place). If possible, always try to get someone with some expertise in the contractor's area of specialization to conduct the technical interview. This may mean going outside your organization or calling in a favor from a colleague/peer at another organization.

If you suspect that your contractor did oversell their skills and manages to get through the interviewing process, it is important to determine this sooner rather than later. Require an action plan and listing of deliverables within the first thirty days. Procrastination may be a red flag for contractors who oversold their abilities because it drags out the engagement or they are waiting for the miracle to occur.[2] If you are suspicious that your contractor is way out of their league on your assignment, make a couple of calls to your professional network to see if this individual may be repeating a pattern. Also, get a few more candidates in for an interview. You can waste considerable budget if the situation continues and potentially miss project deliverables as well.

Misfit for Corporate Culture   No individual thrives in every organizational culture. Some contractors will be fish out of water in your workplace. This will generally become evident in the first two weeks. I have seen red flags of a total mismatch of contractor to culture in less than one day. While a minor mismatch might be worked around for short contracting engagements or a very specialized proficiency requirement, this situation will create more conflict and frustration than it is worth. It can create costs in terms of lost productivity for existing staff and the contractor.

Serious Limitations in Some Critical Skills   Some brilliant information security experts can manage to be successful despite serious deficiencies in some areas, such as project management, budgeting, and people skills. Sometimes these individuals are aware of these shortcomings, but often they are unconsciously incompetent regarding these issues. In many cases, the individual's expertise makes them worth any inconveniences their limitations create. However, generally it will require teaming or providing another resource to cover areas in which the contractor does not excel. This will cost hard dollars in the case of another contractor or diverting a full-time employee from other tasks. This may be worth the extra cost for specific security expertise.

Difficulty Getting References   Many information security auditors and other cyber security professionals sign NDAs with clients. This may make it difficult to get references from recent engagements. Current or prospective clients should be happy that the contractor honors these agreements because they involve both a legal and ethical duty to former clients.

In general, if you can get a reference from a former peer or manager, this can be sufficient to cover the reference-checking process. In the past, I received a list of glowing references for some individuals, including some internal references from former managers, that were false or at least somewhat deceptive. Some companies have eliminated this process due to its lack of effectiveness. I have received great references for a sociopath and individuals that kept the Human Resources department busy.

Be Realistic about the Length of Your Engagement   I have done contract assignments in the past, so I generally have some idea about how long an engagement should take based on the deliverables. An experienced project manager should be able to estimate, with some level of accuracy, how long a set of deliverables should take. However, I have seen some potential engagements whose projected duration is insufficient to complete the required deliverables. This may be a lack of experience, wishful thinking ("the then miracle occurs" cartoon that many of us are familiar with), or insufficient budget. Regardless of the cause of the insufficiency of the engagement length, the net results tend to be similar, such as failure to complete deliverables, poor-quality deliverables, or cost overruns.

Many skilled information security professionals will not accept contract engagements that they know will not allow them sufficient time to complete the required deliverables or tasks adequately. However, some less-experienced individuals might accept such engagements hoping for an extension or hoping to become a perm-to-temp. Perm-to-temps are long-term contractors. Either of these scenarios can create unexpected costs or create budget overages.

Overhead for Consultant to Learn the Lay of the Land (Your Organization)   One drawback to using consultants is that unless the contractor has worked in your organization previously, the individual is likely unfamiliar with your organization as a whole and its information security team. They must learn the organizational structure of the organization, your team, the basic IT architecture, the policies, and standards, and the specifics of the project or deliverables they will be responsible for producing.

In addition, they must come up to speed on administrative tasks, like time reporting, setting up web meetings, project reporting, submitting travel and expenses for reimbursement, and other requirements of the organization. This can take a regular full-time employee a few weeks. The contractor needs to get these tasks accomplished, while still working to identify the key individuals that will be associated with their work and starting the groundwork for their assigned responsibilities and deliverables.

This means each contractor creates administrative overhead costs before they begin any of the tasks they were hired to perform. The same is also true of employees. However, the administrative overhead created by the learning curve is amortized over a longer period of employment versus a few weeks or months that a consultant might work for the information security team.

There is a great deal of variability in the time it takes different individuals to become adequately acclimated to an organization enough to become productive. Many years ago, I worked with technical helpdesk teams. The average time from hire to becoming fully productive and independent was four months. However, it varied from two weeks to six months for different individuals based on skills, experience, and personality characteristics.

One way to minimize the costs associated with overhead involved in contract staff learning the organization is to utilize a team of contractors that can be assigned to different projects or functions on an as-needed basis. The contractor team could be primarily composed of information security generalists, or its composition could include both generalists and some experts in specific information security areas, such as network security, encryption, or secure application development, depending on the organization's needs. Members of the contract team may be strategically rotated to develop specific skills to increase their flexibility for future assignments.

Attitudes of Employees toward Consultants   To put it very simply, some full-time employees do not like consultants or treat them like second-class workers. I once had an employee at a company where I was working say to me, "If I knew you were a regular employee, I would have treated you better" after discovering that I was an employee.

In governmental organizations, contractors may be viewed as political hacks under someone's patronage. They may receive plum projects and higher wages. This disparity can create tensions with regular employees.

There are several reasons why some employees are not fans or even friendly with contractors. Some consider them hired guns who get higher wages and overtime that they do not receive. Others view them as the modern-day equivalent of scabs (comes from union-busting attempts at some companies that hired nonunion workers as replacements during strikes) that are taking jobs away from employees or a mechanism the company is using to drive down wages.

Poor attitudes toward contract workers are not the case in all organizations, especially organizations that regularly make extensive use of contract labor. It is important to know that these feelings do exist before undertaking the implementation of a strategy of using contract staff to bring special expertise or manage costs. Efforts should be made to integrate contractors into the team to maximize the productivity of all team members, regardless of their employment status.

Generally, You Get What You Pay For (or Less) The improving economic outlook has increased contractor hourly rates. There is also an increasing scarcity of experienced information security consultants, especially those willing to work either short-term engagements or lower pay rates. In addition, many consultants work for security contracting firms that determine hourly compensation rates. This means that wanting to pay less may get you less in terms of skills and experience with the individual you hire.

Before the economic downturn, many of the information security consultants I encountered at the midlevel hourly rate were at the lower end of the security skill spectrum. The differential in rates for an experienced security professional was substantial.

While lower rates for experienced professionals were possible several years ago, this has largely disappeared. This is why it is important that the requirements for contractors identify the actual requirements for the role rather than *nice to haves*, such as security certifications and graduate degrees in information assurance. These add to the cost of recruiting appropriate contractor candidates and the hourly rate required to procure these contractors.

An experienced information security contractor willing to accept an overly low hourly compensation rate may be a red flag. While there are other factors that might influence the individual's decision, such as flexible hours, commute time, or ability to work remotely during part of contract, sometimes this might indicate issues that could affect their performance or other team members. This can easily increase costs through lost overall productivity of the staff or extra efforts to resolve problems.

Early in my career, I interviewed a candidate with what appeared to be impeccable qualifications and a substantial list of references. My intuition was sending out signals that this person was too good to be true. After striking out with all the other candidates and with the time running out, against my better judgment, I hired him. This individual lacked both the skills he purported to have and exhibited inappropriate behaviors with female coworkers. There was a reason this person worked cheap.

Poor Role Selection for Contractor Staff   Not all information security functions can be staffed more cost effectively with contractors. Covering some security tasks may substantially more to both the information security team and any clients being charged for these services. The reason these tasks may not be the most appropriate use of contract staff is that they may involve generally nonproductive hours, such as extensive travel time between locations. Using contractors for these types of security tasks, such as vendor site reviews in remote or distant locations, can incur substantial hourly costs for travel and wait times.

In addition, traveling contract staff will incur expenses, such as airfare, car rental/taxis, lodging, tool, and incidentals. This requires higher administrative costs to review and submit their expense reports. Lastly, because contract staff is paid on the numbers of hours worked, some contractors may have little incentive to multitask, such as drafting reports while traveling, which may also increase costs.

Some tasks may periodically require significant extra work hours, such as cyber security incident management or incident preparedness exercises. It is often possible to give a full-time employee compensatory time off at another time, which will not affect the information security budget.

If your information security staffing strategy involves the extensive use of contract staff, or no full-time staff members currently possess the skills to perform a task, it may be necessary to utilize contractors for certain functions, which might result in incurring higher costs. However, some cost management strategies will be necessary to minimize these expenditures.

BYOD and Contractor Security   Your security team needs to decide whether they will allow contractors to use their own mobile devices during their engagement with your team. A few years back, the need to supply contractors with organization-owned devices would not have been considered an option. However, the trend toward allowing BYOD (bring your own device) has changed standard practice. Depending on the survey you look at, 80% to 95% of all organizations permit employee mobile devices to some extent. Currently, most BYOD officially sanctioned implementations focus on smartphones and tablets rather than laptops or removable media.

While allowing a contractor to use their own personal phone during engagements, permitting a contract or to attach his or her own laptop or removable media produces significantly greater risk in terms of the following threats:

- Introduction of malware onto the internal network
- Theft of sensitive information
- Misappropriation of trade secrets, IP, or proprietary information
- Opening of a channel between the internal network and an outside entity

Depending on the sensitivity or strategic value of the information that a contractor will have access to during an assignment, ramifications of a security breach could range from minor to calamitous for the organization.

A good example of the potential consequences of a motivated perpetrator gaining access to IP during a contract assignment occurred in 2012. A former contract worker at the New York Federal Reserve Bank pleaded guilty to stealing proprietary software code belonging to the US Treasury Department. The individual copied and transferred source code using an external drive. The cost to develop the code was close to $10 million.

When determining whether to allow contract staff to use personal devices, especially laptops and external media, a risk impact analysis is strongly recommended. The cost of managing even a relatively small breach likely far outweighs the cost of providing an organization-owned device to information security contractors. This decision on whether the use of personally owned laptops or external media may depend largely on the information classifications of the data that the contractor will have access to during the course of their engagement. There exists significant risk in allowing contractors with access to PI or PII to utilize personal devices or external storage media. There has been a continuing trend of security breaches involving PII stored on laptops. Breaches involving PII are expensive and embarrassing for organizations.

While many organizations utilize full-disk encryption on their laptops and removable storage media, this may not be true for the personally owned devices of contract staff. Allowing the use of unencrypted devices and removable media may not only incur risks, but potentially violate SLAs and compliance regulations.

Loss of Investments in Training and Experience   Over the course of their assignments, contract staff may gain experience in different technologies or business functions. In some cases, different engagements may require the expenditure of budget to provide training to contract staff, such as sending contractors to external training classes to gain proficiency in a specific technology solution. While there is immediate benefit in terms of accomplishing the task or producing the project deliverables, the expenditure generally yields no further return on investment (ROI) unless the contractor becomes a full-time employee or assumes a long-term contractor role.

Use of Specialized Security Services Firms

Sometimes it is best to stick to that in which you excel, rather than attempt doing things where the end result may not live up to expectations. As the information security profession has evolved over the last decade, there has been an increasing trend toward specialization and more regulatory compliance requirements. A large reason for this specialization is the increasing complexity of security technologies.

While the one-person band may still exist in smaller organizations, it is becoming more difficult for one or two individuals to offer adequate coverage for all critical security functions. Rather than continuing to expand information security teams to staff all specializations, a team may elect to implement a strategy to concentrate their internal resources' core security functions, such as malware control or security administration, and use specialized security firms to cover unique or specialized services, such as digital forensics or penetration testing (pen testing).

The primary advantage is that the specialized security firms concentrate their resources on maintaining experts in their particular area who receive advantage training on state-of-the-art tools and have years of hands-on-experience. The rapid acceleration of technological change makes it difficult for smaller security organizations to maintain proficiency in all security domains without incurring excessive costs.

Larger organizations may need to employ specific security experts in highly specialized areas because of their threat landscapes, compliance requirements, or business sector. For those enterprises, it may be cost-effective to have in-house practitioners with these specializations, such as digital forensics, on call as part of doing business or the volume of incidents requiring this skill set.

The use of specialized security firms offers additional benefits in addition to providing proficient practitioners on an as-needed basis. Security firms often have established relationships with professionals or organizations who may offer other related services, such as breach management firms, which may have contact within regulatory agencies or law firms. A security firm can provide an objective and independent perspective on the issues. They have handled many similar organizations and their associated issues, so they have no learning curve and have a wealth of similar experience upon which to draw. Specialized security firms provide a wide variety of services, including:

- Digital forensics (data recovery and investigations)
- Security breach and cyber incident event management
- Ethical hacking and penetration testing
- Regulatory compliance management
- Electronic discovery

There is some overlap between the range of services provided by different security firms, and some firms may subcontract with a peer to offer a comprehensive service package to their clients.

Digital Forensics (Data Recovery and Investigations)

Digital forensics (DF, or computer forensics) involves the investigation or recovery of all digital data from devices capable of storing it. Originally, the focus was on computers and storage media, but over the last decade, digital forensics expanded to cover the wide variety of devices with data storage capabilities, including media players and phones.

In general, DF is associated with investigation of potential cyber crime. In this digital world, many crimes have either a direct or an indirect digital component that must be included in the investigative process. DF firms attempt to reconstruct the sequence of events by tracing their digital footprints, including:

- Computer forensics
- Mobile device forensics
- Network forensics
- Forensic data analysis
- Database forensics

Because the cost of maintaining the software, hardware, and expertise can be high, it is generally more cost effective to use a specialized firm to perform the required investigative tasks. For large corporations, especially those in highly regulated business sectors, it may be cost-justifiable or a business necessity to maintain a DF team in-house or least one practitioner with DF expertise.

If there exists a potential for an investigation leading to a prosecution or civil legal action, then using a DF expert from the initiation of the investigation is critical. According to Comer's Axiom,[3] the evidence at most cyber crime scenes may be compromised within the first thirty minutes of the investigation, when individuals involved do not always have the appropriate training to handle digital evidence, including which tool suites are most acceptable to the courts. In addition, DF experts generally have extensive experience in testifying in legal cases. They often receive training in serving as an expert witness in court cases.

DF is not solely used for investigative purposes. DF expertise may be required to recover critical files from damaged or corrupted media. Data recovery services are expensive. However, the expense may be cost-justified based upon the business value of the files.

DIY (do-it-yourself) forensics may appear like a potential strategy to reduce costs. However, unless your staff has a strong skill set or experience in DF, it may be as advisable as DIY dentistry. Television programs like *Crime Scene Investigation* (*CSI*), in which they make the process look effortless and fast, likely fueled the interest in this specialty. They are not accurate portrayals of the time and effort required by DF investigations.

The costs of maintaining a highly skilled DF team, in terms of training, equipment, and software, can be extraordinarily high and can generally only be justified by a high volume of requests for investigations. The costs of a skunk works DF can also be high. *DF hobbyists*, with questionable skills and some cobbled together lab could actually *cost* money because the results of their investigation may not meet the standards of evidence required for the courts or could provoke lawsuits. Small internal DF functions are likely best suited for data recovery versus investigations.

One strong prerequisite before embarking on any investigatory activities requiring the utilization of DF is having a specific policy regarding its use:

1. A DF policy provides guidance on what is permissible in terms of evidence gathering, analysis, and under what circumstances a DF investigation can be initiated.
2. A DF policy can help avoid unnecessary legal actions, such as employee lawsuits regarding inappropriate DF investigations.
3. A DF policy can assist in ensuring that legally acceptable evidence gathering and securing procedures are in use.
4. A DF policy defines under what conditions a DF investigation is initiated, what DF procedures are explicitly prohibited, and who can initiate a DF investigation.

The failure to define a DF or cyber investigative policy can be costly in terms of both potential legal actions and morale. A few years ago, a DF vendor related a cautionary tale to me that involved some feuding information security professionals. One of these practitioners decided to use DF as a weapon against his colleague by ordering an internal DF investigation of his peer's laptop based upon his suspicion that the laptop contained pornography. No pornography was found and the individual went to Human Resources to lodge a complaint. The net result was that the external DF firm was engaged to investigate the practitioner who requested the DF investigation. The falsely accused employee left the firm. This resulted in the loss of an experienced practitioner and the investment the firm had made in his training and development.

Security Breach and Cyber Incident Event Management

Security breaches should not be frequent occurrences. However, it is necessary to plan for them. The current wisdom on security breaches is not to consider the *if*, but the *when* of their occurrence. Most organizations have not experienced an actual security breach and may choose to procure a specialized security firm to coordinate the breach management process. Security breach firms have established relationships with the necessary parties that need to be connected in the event of a data breach. For example, they have contacts in regulatory agencies that need to be notified once a breach has been identified. These firms have contacts in the appropriate law enforcement agencies, such as the FBI and state police.

These firms offer *one-stop shopping* in terms of the other services that might be required in the event of a security breach, including:

- Full-service DF
- Public relations/communication/media management
- Specialized legal services
- Cyber incident remediation services
- Full-service investigative services (especially important if the breach points to an inside perpetuator)
- External security assessment/penetration testing/ethical hacking (to prevent future events by identifying any weakness in the organizations security perimeter)

Most of these firms are available on an annual retainer basis or may be contacted for hire in the event of a breach. With a retainer arrangement, the security firm is already familiar with your organization, its functions, and infrastructure. This means no learning curve for the breach management firm. Once contacted, the breach management team is productive from the moment that their boots hit the ground. This decreases costs associated with breaches by potentially reducing downtime associated with breaches. Reducing downtime created by breaches may result in less revenue loss.

The breach management team begins by making an initial analysis of the scope of the breach. It will also determine if the breach is still in progress. Finding out this information is vital for two reasons. The first is that any active security breach needs to be halted and contained as soon as possible. The second reason is that any public reporting of security breaches needs to be as accurate as possible from the beginning.

This is primarily an issue around public perception of the organization, its ability to manage the breach and its aftermath, as well as the candor of the organization around the breach. In past security breaches, some companies frequently changed significant details of a breach, such as the number of records compromised. This created additional concerns around the effectiveness of the organization's handling of the breach and its overall truthfulness to affected individuals. It is cheaper to get important details right (or at least close) from the beginning.

While the retainer is an ongoing expense and may not be used, it may be justified because it provided the organization with a preference in receiving assistance. If several organizations are hit with a breach around the same time frame, client organizations will get services before organizations looking to hire the security firm without an existing retainer. In addition, the retainer might decrease the cost of purchasing cyber liability insurance.

In the event of an actual security breach, a security firm might be able to get your organization up, running, and secure, quicker than trying to accomplish this with internal resources only. This may limit revenue loss and prevent further damage to your organization's reputation. The breach management firm's services may include preparing a postmortem and facilitating a meeting with stakeholders to discuss the report, as well as making recommendations to diminish the potential for future breaches.

Ethical Hacking and Pen Testing

This is another specialty like DF, which seems to attract hobbyists. Like DF, TV programs like *CSI* likely fueled the interest in this specialty.

The rise of DIY ethical hacking dates back to 1995 with the release of *Security Administrator Tool for Analyzing Networks (SATAN)*, an early vulnerability detection tool. Early adopters of cyber security often tried SATAN on their own network infrastructure with the justification that if they did not identify their own organization's vulnerabilities, some hacker would. However, sometimes their efforts backfired and many organizations specifically prohibited using SATAN or similar toolkits on their IT infrastructure.

The SATAN experience created an unwritten rule among would-be ethical hackers (also called *white-hat hackers*) that no penetration testing or ethical hacking of a security perimeter should take place without a "get out of jail free card" letter (also referred to legally as a Letter of Authority to protect the information security team or any external testing firm. There are advantages to performing security testing using the internal team—it can be less expensive, the team has the greatest understanding of the specific security infrastructure, and it provides an opportunity to develop team members. However, there are also significant disadvantages, such as political issues, the potential for unanticipated problems, such as network outages, and the risk of having hacker-type tools available on the network. Many corporate information security policies explicitly prohibit the existence of hacker-type software or tools within the internal network. Some policies impose disciplinary measures, up to termination, for individuals having these hacker toolkits on their corporately owned devices or network drives.

Often, it can be best and sometimes even cheaper to utilize an external security firm that specializes in pen testing and external security assessments. While contracting out these services is expensive, the expense of maintaining information security practitioners with the right level of skills to perform these types of assessments may cost more unless the organization has a requirement to perform frequent security testing. In addition, an independent external security assessment may be required for other purposes and considered more objective.

Purchasing a full suite of commercial pen testing and ethical hacking tools is also expensive and may be difficult to cost-justify for most organizations. While there is always the option to utilize only public domain tools to limit the cost of security testing, using these tools requires a high level of expertise, and network administrators can mistake their use for a cyber attack. These tools also may be more difficult to control, with the worst-case scenario being the creation of server, network, or application outages.

In addition, in order to simulate a cyber attack, it is necessary for the internal security team to establish an external web presence from which to launch the stimulated hacking activity. The external web location could potentially be compromised to launch a real attack during the testing. In addition, housing hacker-type tools within a network infrastructure creates the potential for their misuse by a motivated insider.

The engagement of an external security-testing firm creates many tangible and intangible benefits. The most significant intangible benefit of using an external security firm is that it provides instant credibility to the results of the testing. There is value to brand name, and major security firms have strong brand value that they bring to the table. Established security firms have a wealth of experience that they can apply to the testing process.

They can utilize myriad security testing toolkits, both commercial and public domain. These firms also understand how to avoid inadvertently creating network outages.

An external security-testing firm offers a neutral third-party perspective on the current security posture of the organization. Often, it is difficult for a Chief Information Security Officer (CISO) and his team to judge their own environment because they are so close to it. Security testing firms can offer a different perspective and recommendations for strengthening the overall security posture of the organization.

This independent review may be required by compliance regulations. In some cases, some of the cost of performing the review may be offset by discounts on cyber liability insurance. In the event that a cyber incident occurs, the external security review is visible evidence of a strong due diligence process within the organization.

Be cautious when discussing hiring with external security-testing firms because there is a great deal of variability in the quality of the services they provide. As a cautionary tale, a company hired an external security-testing firm, likely by using the *best price* strategy. The individual who hired the firm did not ask key questions about the potential disruptions that security testing might create. The security firm failed to ask the client important questions about their critical production cycles, such as end-of-month accounting closing processes. The security firm also failed to get some basic information about the composition of the network and its capabilities regarding the detection of server outages. Unfortunately, for this client, this information was critical to avoiding potential operational outages during testing. The security firm implemented testing during a monthly and quarterly close, which jeopardized those critical processes. The organization had an extremely dated network infrastructure with limited monitoring of critical production servers. A low-velocity scan managed to create numerous server outages that took up to an hour to detect and endangered the organization's ability to successfully complete the closing process on time. After the crisis, the organization's technical team reestablished the network. However, there was no appetite to continue with testing any servers considered critical to operational processes. This eliminated 70% of the overall planned internal security testing and removed any testing of critical infrastructure containing sensitive information. This, for all purposes, decimated the business and security value of the pen-testing exercise.

Regulatory Compliance Management Firms

While increased regulatory compliance has benefited the information security team, it has also increased its overall work effort significantly. New compliance regulations are often full of vague language and ambiguities. Often, there is a significant time lag between the passing of the legislation and final rules around information security and compliance.

An example of this time lag is the 1996 Health Insurance Portability and Accountability Act (HIPAA). In August of 1998, the proposed regulations to implement information security requirements were published as the Proposed Security Rule. The Final Security Rule was not published until February 20, 2003. From passage of the initial legislation until the final security requirements, seven years elapsed. Regulatory compliance management firms have their ears to the ground through their contacts inside regulatory agencies to give them a preview of what the final requirements around compliance will include. This can save organizations money because they can direct their spending toward activities that will support likely compliance requirements. It can also reduce costs by avoiding the last-minute rush for compliance that involves incurring excessive overtime, extra staff, and extra resources. Compliance-related activities can be included in the normal budgeting cycle.

It may be possible to include some compliance-preparation activities in projects that provide value not only for meeting regulatory requirements, but also for enhancing the organization's security posture. In some cases, substantial savings are realized by reusing existing functionality to serve compliance-related purposes.

For example, an organization previously created an opt-out field to identify clients that did not want to receive third-party information by phone or email. They were able to successfully repurpose this field to record Gramm–Leach–Bliley Act (aka GLB or the Financial Services Modernization Act of 1999) requests to block information from being shared with unaffiliated parties.

The use of a regulatory compliance management firm can mitigate the tendency some organizations have to overcomply with regulations by adding unnecessary or redundant controls. An example of costly overcompliance efforts was characteristic of some Sarbanes-Oxley (SOX) implementations. A regulatory compliance management firm might aid in narrowing the scope of compliance efforts rather than expanding them unnecessarily. This can save expenditures for implementing unnecessary controls and practices that can cost thousands to millions of budget dollars.

These firms can also get a noncompliant organization back on track to meeting regulatory requirements after failure to pass an audit. This might reduce regulatory files by showing good faith in trying to correct their compliance deficiencies. A regulatory compliance management firm can assist in completing the necessary documentation to file with the required regulatory agencies or have this documentation prepared in cases of an audit. This can actually reduce the overall costs of compliance because the required documentation gets done faster, correctly, and without expensive mistakes that could result in fines or other penalties. DIY efforts can result in errors that can necessitate redoing much of the initial efforts.

Some complex compliance requirements mandate the hiring of a compliance firm at some point in the process. An example is the PCI-DSS, which requires an annual review by a certified external firm.

In addition, the quarterly attestation scans must be submitted by banks. It is often less costly in the long run to engage a compliance firm early in the process to both guide the organization through the initial steps to building out the required procedures and obtaining initial compliance from the regulatory authority. This is especially true for organizations with limited experience with compliance-related activities.

Compliance management firms can assist in developing policies and standards, acquiring security toolsets, and training the organization's staff in performing required activities. These firms may be able to negotiate discounts on purchases of required security tools because of their established relationships with the vendors. This can result in significant savings, especially when acquiring security solutions for deployment across the organization.

The majority of compliance regulations undergo regular revisions to include new technologies or emerging risk issues, such as PCI-DSS, which released version 3.0 in 2013. Compliance management firms may have insights as to what may be included in upcoming updates to regulatory standards, such as guidelines for the use of cloud or mobile device technologies.

DIY compliance efforts may appear to save costs on the surface. However, it may create more costs than anticipated, especially for an organizations with limited experience in information security-related compliance efforts. Any efforts to undertake a compliance project will require a strong and experienced project manager and resources from the organization's legal team.

It is also critical to maintain a documentation trial for all tasks and create a repository for deliverables. Maintaining all documentation related to compliance in one central repository may make the difference between maintaining a compliant status and being assessed costly fines several years down the line when the project is a distant memory. This may be particularly true if a contract resource that managed the compliance efforts or key members of the information security team have left the organization. Unfortunately, key compliance documentation may be misplaced or lost after achieving a compliant status. Since much as of the underlying documentation associated with compliance is maintained only by the organization itself, its loss may result in the need to re-create it or pay fines and penalties. This can be a costly mistake for the organization.

Electronic Discovery (eDiscovery) Firms

Compliance audits and lawsuits can represent major budget drains, and missteps in managing them in the early stages can escalate costs at every successive stage down the line. Both of these situations can create the requirements to gather digital information to defend the organization's best interests and avoid expensive fines and judgments.

Due to the 2006 changes to the Federal Rules of Civil Procedure, digital evidence has become a significant component of most legal proceedings. The 2006 eDiscovery amendments introduced the concept of *electronically stored information* to acknowledge that electronically stored information is discoverable. Electronically stored information includes all types of information that can be stored electronically. The changes are sufficiently broad to encompass all existing computer-based information and elastic enough to include potential technological developments.

The objective of these amendments was to acknowledge that electronically stored information is discoverable. Some of the amendments require the parties to address electronically stored information at the beginning of the discovery process and recognize the importance of managing eDiscovery in order to manage the scope and expense of this process and circumvent discovery disputes later.

Because many organizations have minimal experience in managing eDiscovery requests, it may be cost effective to hire an external firm to manage the eDiscovery process. At an average of $250/hour to review electronically stored information, including emails, structured electronic documents, text messages, and other file formats, the expenses involved in even a small legal action can easily add up to thousands or hundreds of thousands of dollars. eDiscovery firms can assist in reducing the scope of the effort and potentially significantly reduce overall costs.

Vendor Software

Software is the lifeblood of most organizations. While many organizations will always elect to develop a significant portion of their application portfolio to support their core business competencies, at least some software will be purchased from external software vendors. Virtually all organizations use vendor-provided software to some degree, such as desktop and server operating systems, database management systems

(DBMS), office-type applications, and other commercial off-the-shelf (COTS) software.

The large-scale enterprise applications, such as general ledger software or customer relationship management (CRM) solutions have long ruled the IT department in many organizations. Most of the vendors that produce these mature applications have integrated software security and a secure development life cycle process in their release management methodology. They did this as a survival strategy, largely driven by customer complaints and bad press created by insecure releases. They also identify specific dedicated resources to manage recognized security vulnerabilities and release patches to mitigate these vulnerabilities in a timely way.

Back in the 1990s, software vendors rarely considered adding much in the way of security functionality to applications or identifying potential vulnerabilities before the general availability (GA) of software applications. Releasing software on time trumped all other considerations, including stability and security. The result was a deluge of cyber attacks and innovative malware, such as Nimda, Slammer, and Code Red.

The root cause was insecure software that hackers exploited to get their desired results, such as financial gain, mayhem, or enhancing their reputation among the über elite.

To combat this crisis, both vendors and in-house development teams introduced secure development tools, implemented vulnerability management tools, and created tiger teams to review critical code to reduce the potential for code exploitations and leakage of sensitive information. Some organizations, particularly those in highly regulated industry sectors or organizations that had previously been victims of very public security breaches, embraced the secure development paradigm. An excellent example of embracing the secure development paradigm was Microsoft Corporation.

Unfortunately, many organizations have not yet even begun to embed security principles and mechanisms into their application software development process and still rely on bolt-on security to defend against hackers and cyber criminals.

The continuing prevalence of cyber attacks and breaches since 2011 is evidence that after almost thirteen years we still have far to go in developing secure and resilient application software. Currently, the new crop of cyber attackers and exploits continues to take aim squarely at the application layer. It is no surprise that cyber criminals select this avenue of attack. It is relatively easy to exploit and often it is "where the money is" in terms of its potential rewards.

For example, Albert Gonzalez and his Operation Get Rich or Die Tryin' pilfered 4.2 million account numbers from Hannaford Brothers supermarket chain using a relatively simple series of Structured Query Language (SQL) injection attacks. There was a repeat of this pattern of using "low-hanging fruit" in subsequent major exploits, including the Sony breach in 2011.

Existing vendor applications may exhibit *resiliency degradation*, in which the capability of software to resist attacks degrades over time due to changes in technology, threats, and staffing. Older software may not permit upgrades or patching to fix known vulnerabilities. This may create compliance costs in terms of fines and expedited unplanned/unbudgeted upgrades to compliant applications.

New software categories, including social media and mobile applications, as well as deployment options like cloud computing, are emerging as strategic tools to reinventing the way the organization does business. Start-up software companies often produce these new application categories. The software products developed by these companies often have limited history, as do the enterprises that produce them. Because of their relatively short history, the development staff of these new vendors may have limited exposure to concepts of secure development.

In addition, many software vendors do not view security as an important attribute (or selling point) of their applications, especially those that take the position that their product is not responsible for managing sensitive information or will be used only as an internal application.

In order to decrease overall costs of producing their releases, they may not allocate sufficient budgetary funds to security software. For example, they may not assign responsibility for the security of their software to any staff member or make use of secure software development practices. They perceive security as a customer responsibility.

Unfortunately, this situation harkens back to situations in the 1990s that resulted in the software insecurity crisis that continues today. Given the growing dependence on both new and older vendor software applications, it is critical to be proactive in managing the security of software vendors and their applications.

Cost-Effective Vendor Application Risk Management

The cost-effective strategy to manage both the cost and risks associated with vendor applications is at the beginning of the process. The information security team needs to participate in the vendor selection process. Many IT and business managers may perceive information security's participation in the application selection projects as an attempt to control the process and possibly veto a selected vendor product based upon an overly broad definition of potential risks. The primary purpose of the information security team during an application selection project is to facilitate getting the right application for the business's needs with the least amount of risk. This means having a complete understanding of the business needs, application selection criteria, candidate applications, vendors, and threat landscape.

Much of the risk management process for vendor application mirrors the steps for vendor risk management. However, managing application risks entails adding specific steps around assessing both the application's architecture and the vendor's software development process. The most effective strategy is the creation of an Application Risk Assessment Questionnaire (ARAQ) that covers basic questions about the vendor software development processes and overall software life cycle, as well as specific application-focused questions. A sample ARAQ is available in Appendix E.

Use of an ARAQ ensures that adequate information security and controls are available from the vendor application, including the following:

- Identification
- Authentication
- Authorization
- Appropriate Access Role/Provisioning
- Configuration Management
- Database Security
- Secure Development Processes and Life Cycle Management
- Regulatory Compliance
- Industry Security Requirements

The ARAQ provides a cost-effective mechanism to evaluate the overall security of the software vendor and the application itself. If the same software vendor is frequently used by the organization, the cost of the assessment drops because that portion of the ARAQ could be reused. New implementations of the same vendor applications across multiple divisions or business units allows reutilization of the majority of the ARAQ.

The ARAQ modular format allows for the development of new subquestionnaires to cover new application categories or deployment environments, such as cloud and mobile device applications. The ARAQ lowers the cost of assessments and increases the level of maturity of the information security team by creating a repeatable risk management process. The reality is that some software vendors, especially start-up companies, may not have embedded security into their applications. Security may remain an afterthought because these start-up companies:

1. do not see their applications as having any security risks associated with its use;
2. view the application as having internal use only within the organization;
3. look at security as a customer-provided function, such as through a corporate firewall or intrusion detection system (IDS);
4. have a development staff with limited experience with secure development concepts and mechanisms;
5. prioritize functionality or time to market over security in releases;
6. may have a lower level of organization IT maturity, including risk management.

During the evaluation of risks associated with all vendor software, it is essential to consider the product, its functionality, the data it manages, and the deployment environment to develop a true picture of the risks associated with a specific application. It is also important to consider expanded uses of the application, if the implementation is successful, such as a social collaboration application originally intended for internal use that might be expanded to business partners or customers/prospects.

In the early days of ecommerce, applications that were designed for an intranet were often expanded for use on the Internet to allow customers to perform certain actions online, such as placing an order or tracking orders. This situation created the potential for early software exploitation.

Often, the only additional security enhancement to applications ported to the Internet from the intranet involved the implementing of Secure Sockets Layer (SSL) to protect transactions. However, because these applications were designed with the security requirements of the internal network, they were easily defeated by even casual cyber attacks. Exploiting these early online transactional applications was shockingly easy. Often, just copying the source code into an editor and modifying it allowed a cyber criminal to lower unit price, which was all that was required to defraud the seller. It is not difficult to imagine deploying some internal applications utilizing emerging technologies into higher-risk environments, such as cloud or mobile device deployments.

It is important that information security understand current risks associated with deploying these vendor applications and anticipate future deployments of these innovative applications into other less-secure environments in the future. This anticipation needs to go beyond mere conjecture to include both planning and strategies to reduce the risk within the tolerance boundaries of the organization.

The frugal CISO approach would look at creating groupings of security protection mechanisms to create viable strategies to compensate for any risks associated with broad categories of applications. This is a more cost-effective approach than developing protection tactics on an application-by-application basis.

This would also supply a predetermined process for implementing existing internal applications in new risky environments. It also demonstrates an important trait of cost-efficient and effective information security teams—learning. Strong security teams learn from history in an effort not to repeat its mistakes. The best strategy for managing the risks associated with vendor software is best summed up by the words of Albert Einstein: "Learn from yesterday, live for today, hope for tomorrow. The important thing is not to stop questioning."

Endnotes

1. Trustwave Holdings, Inc., *2013 Global Security Report*, http://www2. trustwave.com/rs/trustwave/images/Trustwave_GSR_ExecutiveSummary_ 4page_Final_Digital.pdf.

2. Famous cartoon available at http://avionod.wordpress.com/2009/04/06/and-then-a-miracle-happens/.
3. Information taken from *Information Risk and Security: Preventing and Investigating Workplace Computer Crime* by Edward Wilding (2006); theory articulated by Mike Comer, fraud expert, in 1998.

7

SECURITY AWARENESS

Fluff or Strategic Investment?

What Is the ROI of Security Awareness Spending?

Despite its inclusion in most information security programs, there still exists both controversy and doubt around the relative effectiveness of information security awareness and training. In a series of dueling blogs in the summer of 2012, security experts discussed whether security awareness still had a place with today's information security programs, or if it is time to abandon these efforts in favor of automated security controls.

The underlying question is whether an organization's security posture is improved through the regular application of employee awareness training. I think most security practitioners would agree that to some degree it likely does have at least some positive effect. The bigger question for the frugal chief information security officer (CISO) is whether that positive effect is great enough to warrant spending limited budget on awareness programs beyond what is required by compliance regulations.

One of my favorite frugal CISO principles is *spend where it is most impactful* (SWIIMI). MBA 101 tells organizations to make investments where the most *bang for the buck*, also called return on investment (ROI), will result. Attempting to develop metrics around the ROI of awareness training can be frustrating for information security executives. I have seen many CISOs and information security managers try to do this with limited success. Many of the awareness metrics used often don't pass the *sniff test* with statisticians or even other information security professionals.

One popular attempt at security awareness metrics is to measure the success of awareness efforts by comparing user malware infections before and after awareness campaigns. This is usually not very successful because it is difficult to evaluate the relative effectiveness of the antimalware technology against the contributions of the awareness campaign.

Another popular attempt at developing awareness metrics involves comparing the number of cyber incidents directly related to the end user before and after an awareness campaign. If no cyber security incidents occur that are directly attributable end-user behaviors, then the awareness program rarely is lauded for its contributions to an improved security posture. However, when cyber incidents created by end users occur, then the awareness is considered ineffective and a waste of budget. It seems to be a no-win situation for the frugal CISO.

People Are the New Security Perimeter

In the "good old days" (pre-Internet/proprietary technology)—the *glass house* (data center, usually housing a water-cooled mainframe)—it was possible to construct a strong security perimeter based upon physical and network-level controls. The emergence of open standards and adoption of the Internet created chinks in the previously strong defensive boundaries that protected an organization's "crown jewels"—its data. Over the last decade of continued technical innovation, such as the cloud, outsourcing, social media, and mobile devices, the once seemingly impenetrable security perimeter has become increasingly porous. Currently, the security perimeter more resembles a piece of Swiss cheese than a castle wall. While we attempt to protect and mitigate risk, security incidents continue to occur on a regular basis.

The primary reason is that technical infrastructure is no longer the ultimate security perimeter. Our *people* have become the new security perimeter. One poor decision by a member of the organization can create a significant security breach. Some leading technical companies have already acknowledged this paradigm shift. One excellent example was the Intel Corporation, which adopted this new paradigm for its technology security strategy several years ago. Intel recognized the criticality of addressing these security risks through behavioral change and a renewed focus on security awareness at every level of the enterprise.

This is a fundamental transformation of security strategy away from the creation of additional restrictions around the use of technology. End-user awareness becomes a critical security strategy that is supplemented by technical security solutions, such as encryption, to defend against the potential for cyber breaches.

Are Security Awareness Programs Budget Wasters?

Some security awareness training may be ineffective when weighed against the cost of providing the training. Many security awareness training programs are offered primarily to meet regulatory compliance requirements. These efforts may be limited in their overall effectiveness. This type of training falls under the category of *checklist compliance*, rather than a real attempt to make staff aware of the real security threats they face in the performance of their jobs. Compliance-centric training usually concentrates on the requirements of the regulations or laws that the organization needs to comply with in order to avoid fines or other regulatory penalties.

A good example is that many state data-privacy laws require training on personally identifiable information (PII). One issue with this type of security training approach is that it narrowly defines security protection to the exact definitions of the regulation or law, rather than providing participants with a more holistic view of information protection.

There are a couple of schools of thought on the effectiveness of compliance-centric awareness training. Some security practitioners view this training under the category of "something is better than nothing." The thinking behind this opinion is that these organizations were likely doing little to nothing in the way of awareness training before, so at least making staff conscious of some security risks is an improvement in the overall security posture.

Other information security practitioners perceive this type of training as doing more harm than good for a number of reasons. First, it provides the organization's executive management with a false perception of the security fitness of its staff. Executives may believe that the training programs offer staff a much broader knowledge of security threats and appropriate countermeasures than they actually do. This may result in a rude awaking, if a cyber incident created by an end user occurs, such as the opening of a link on phishing email that triggers a remote-access Trojan that creates a backdoor into the internal network.

At a recent event, a very senior security expert stated that a poor-quality security awareness training program diminishes the value of all such training in the eyes of end users. It creates a perception among staff members that the topic is not valued or taken seriously by executive management. If executive management does not think that security awareness is important, why should staff members?

Have Automated Security Tools Diminished the Necessity for Awareness Training?

Some security practitioners believe that awareness is unnecessary due to the deployment of effective and automated security tools. Some security tools enforce organizational policies and standards that the end user might otherwise choose to bypass for the sake of convenience. Back in the start of the new millennium, some end users viewed security applications as performance hogs or annoyances, so they elected to disable their functionality, such as turning off anti-malware solutions. The consequence was these unprotected devices were easy prey for cyber attackers, especially when combined with sophisticated social engineering techniques. However, it is now possible for the organization's information security team to configure these tools to prevent their functionality from being disabled by end users.

Some security tools detect potentially risky actions and either block the action or at least alert the end user to its possible consequences. However, these tools allow the end user to ignore the warning and proceed with their chosen course of action. The reasoning for allowing end users to bypass risky action warnings in many cases is to handle false positives issued by the security applications, such as download warnings from a trusted website. Most organizations opt to err on the side of convenience to enable end users to get their work done. End users are free to make good or poor decisions based upon their perception of the risk associated with their actions.

Technical security controls have diminished some security threats once associated with end-user actions and inactions, such as failure to patch operating systems promptly or maintaining current antivirus definitions. However, these tools are not a panacea to cease all end user–created security incidents. They are at best a way to minimize incidents resulting from end user errors rather than intentional choices to defeat security control mechanisms. This improvement in the automation and effectiveness of technical security controls does not eliminate the need to consider the importance of the human factor in protecting the organization against cyber attackers.

The frugal CISO can make a strong case for the importance of security awareness training as a component of a mature information security program. The information security team cannot solely rely on technical security controls because cyber attackers will seek out the chinks in these controls to penetrate security boundaries. No technology is foolproof and if one were, it would likely not be cost effective or convenient.

When evaluating security controls, we consider three factors in determining the "best" fit for our needs:

1. Cost of the control
2. Security provided
3. Convenience in usage

Many information security practitioners may focus primarily on the first two factors, cost and security. The basic rule of thumb for efficient and effective controls is that their cost should not exceed the cost of the asset under protection. The degree of security offered by a control is critical to the decision to employ a security technology. If a control is cheap, but provides limited protection against attackers, then its overall value is low. For example, it is cheaper and easier to protect a sensitive document with a password instead of strong encryption. However, this protection tactic offers little protection against even casual attacks, so the security value of the control is negligible. Cost and security must be balanced against each other when determining appropriate technical controls.

The value of the asset must consider both its tangible, as well as intangible, value. With information assets, often the intangible value will dominate the asset valuation. A good example of looking at the cost of a security control relative to an asset's value is the use of hardware-encrypted storage devices to store sensitive information. Thanks to the diminishing cost of technology, the cost of hardware-encrypted storage devices has decreased significantly, making them a viable option for most backup needs. The value of the information stored on those devices continues to increase. If a hardware-encrypted storage device is stolen or misplaced, the value of the actual media (device itself) is relatively inconsequential. However, its ability to continue to protect the information stored remains intact. Therefore, the use of a hardware-encrypted storage device meets the first two criteria for an efficient and effective control.

Security and Convenience: The Human Factor

While information security professionals look at three factors (cost, security, and convenience) when evaluating the "best" fit for a security control, the average end user considers only one, convenience. Humans are very adaptive and innovative when faced with a challenge. This is especially true when individuals view a control as a barrier to convenience.

In the beginning of his 2002 book, *The Art of Deception: Controlling the Human Element of Security*, Kevin Mitnick, infamous hacker and social engineer, uses the famous quote by Albert Einstein, "Two things are infinite: the universe and human stupidity; and I'm not sure about the universe." No matter how much technology you apply to a risk, it only takes one human mistake or action to defeat the technology and open an organization to attacks.

Security vulnerabilities created by individuals looking to reduce barriers to convenience have likely existed as long as the security profession itself. It has definitely been a continuing area of risk in physical security, such as multiple individuals piggybacking through badge-controlled entrances and propping open emergency doors as extra egress channels. Information security has continued to experience the battle between ingenious individuals trying to defeat cyber security controls and strengthening of controls to prevent subversion of their functionality.

One thing that newer information security professionals often struggle to understand is that many common controls were not designed to be *bulletproof*, but only prevent the casual attacker or employee from creating an incident through intentional or inadvertent misuse. Often, to make these controls insurmountable would incur significantly greater expense or make employing the control more difficult for users.

An example of such a control is the laptop anchor. I remember another security practitioner disparaging this effective control in front of a group of end users. His reasoning was that there was a finite set of keys available from one manufacturer for all anchors, and therefore there existed the potential that one user's key might work on another user's lock. I responded that while his point was correct, I have had at least 20 of these cables, and never had any key fit another lock. It was apparent to me that he really did not get this common control's security objective, which is to discourage casual thieves by increasing the work effort associated with stealing a laptop. A good wire cutter can defeat the majority of laptop anchors for a motivated thief. However, this is not really the point. An efficient thief will not bother with a secured laptop, but move on to easier prey.

Technical Security Control Failures via the Human Factor

The current crop of cyber criminals is very proficient in the use of social media. They utilize social media sites, such as LinkedIn™ and Facebook, to identify and perform intelligence gathering on specific employees of target organizations. They use this information to develop targeted exploits, such as *spear phishing* attacks against specific employees of an organization. These targeted exploits utilize social engineering techniques to entice their targets to perform an action, such as opening an email or downloading a file infected with malware.

Like traditional spammers, the cyber attackers use the law of numbers where they send a high number of email messages, but only one of the targeted recipients needs to take an action to accomplish the objective. In many incidents, the objective of the cyber criminal is to plant some type of malware on the target organization's internal network in order to create a foothold for the attack or create vulnerability for future exploitation.

A few years ago, some cyber attackers targeted employees of a well-known security enterprise using a spear-phishing attack. The internal email security tool correctly identified these emails as potential spam and quarantined the suspicious email in a junk email folder. However, one individual removed the email from the junk email folder because the subject piqued their curiosity with a subject line of "2012 Compensation Plan." The phishing email carried an Excel spreadsheet that launched a zero-day exploit that compromised the organization's internal systems by acquiring credentials, scanning and identifying specific servers, and then exfiltrating the source code of its flagship product.

The organization did identify the ongoing attack and immediately initiated a cyber incident response procedure. Despite the quick response, the company ultimately spent millions of dollars directly related to the impact of the cyber attack against its systems. One lesson learned from this incident is the vital importance of employee awareness and IT training policies. While it might be possible to configure protective security technologies in a way that would prevent end users from taking any action not permitted by the organizational security policies, this draconian approach would likely impede the productivity of the staff and create frustration for most stakeholders. However, even if the strictest automated enforcement of security controls were possible and supported by management, it would likely not yield the desired level of security. An innovative end user would likely find a way to divert information or processes away from the official channel into a clandestine channel to avoid security controls altogether.

Human Factor as an Asset to Information Security

Inappropriate judgment about the level of risk may result in security issues when people exercise control of technical controls. However, human judgment can also produce significant benefits in identifying potential security problems. This uniquely human capacity allows us to take in different types of data, sort it out to create new meaning, and then make a judgment call. Human judgment can adapt to myriad complex situations and take in new information as it becomes available. It is this flexibility that may allow an individual to detect issues often before any automated security process.

While Big Data, multicore processors, and software with the ability to learn expected patterns of behavior has vastly improved automated systems' abilities to identify anomalies that might indicate a possible security incident, this functionality has to be preconfigured into the software. Humans have the innate ability to ask the vital questions of why and how when confronted with a new situation and construct a new way to get the answers.

By investing in a solid and well-developed security awareness program, we create a new human network with detection capabilities that complements automated security technologies. The synergies between these human and technological networks could detect or prevent security breaches before they have a major impact on the organization. Staff awareness of security issues is a significant organizational asset and may contribute to earlier detection of cyber intrusions.

In some instances, an organization's employee uncovers a breach after noticing unusual behavior. Dr. Clifford Stoll managed computers for Lawrence Berkeley National Laboratory in California in the 1980s. While attempting to determine the cause of an accounting error, Dr. Stoll uncovered a cyber criminal trying to find and sell sensitive national defense data to the Soviet KGB. At the time of these events in the late 1980s, little was known about investigating cyber events, so Dr. Stoll developed new cyber investigation techniques to use on his hunt for the cyber intruder.

Security-aware staff can also make decisions about initiating specific actions in the event of a potential security incident, such as shutting down systems or network segments. These types of decisions are best left to human judgment because of their potential effects on the entire organization.

Information security awareness training is a layer in an effective *defense in depth* strategy. To quote Ira Winkler, noted security expert and author, "The return on investment for a security awareness program of this form can be huge, even if it prevents a single incident."[1] From the frugal CISO's perspective, it offers a cost-effective way to extend "boots on the ground" in the battle against cyber attacks and enables staff to make better decisions about situations that might create security incidents. It is a solid example of the principle of SWIIMI because a small investment in security awareness training can continue to pay benefits for years and the investment builds over time with repeated reinvestments in end-user education.

Why Some Practitioners Doubt the Effectiveness of Security Awareness

Some information security practitioners, especially the highly technical variety, may doubt the effectiveness of security awareness programs. My guess is that the reason behind their skepticism is their own personal experiences with bad awareness programs. Many information security practitioners view awareness as glorified marketing activities utilizing cute themes and trinkets. While there is no doubt that marketing is a major component of effective awareness efforts, marketing alone is not enough.

All awareness marketing activities need to be tied to the set of security objectives that we need to achieve to enhance the organization's overall security posture. Otherwise, budget spent on these marketing efforts is wasted. Most practitioners have had experience with trite awareness efforts that not only wasted money, but were frustrating to dedicated information security practitioners trying to obtain budget for staff training or technical security controls. They see expensive plastic trinkets immediately relegated to the trash, sometimes in the containers they came in, while they fight for "budget lint" to purchase additional security product licenses.

Why Security Awareness Fails to Meet Expectations

Effective security awareness is *not*:

- Clever slogans
- Costumed characters and mascots
- Plastic trinkets
- Theme-based campaigns
- Skits and videos

While these elements can be components of an effective security awareness campaign, they will not deliver an ROI, unless they support strong actionable messages and plan to deliver those messages. Sometimes the accoutrements may get in the way of the actual awareness being communicated. In many budget-aware organizations, extravagant expenditures, such as *Star Trek*–themed videos, may actually create a backlash against information security because instead of being entertained, end users may resent expenditures on what they view as nonessential "fluff."

Security awareness fails to deliver on its potential when it is offered without a clear plan as to what it wants to convey to end users. Some awareness messages appear to be a succession of topics, such as using strong passwords, conveyed in rapid succession without any underlying goal. While the messages may be valuable, they often become background noise and are largely ignored. A number of popular advertising campaigns were lauded for their brilliance, but ultimately failed to successfully promote their service or product, for example, a series of ads for the popular fast-food chain, won many industry awards, but failed to gain or maintain market share. Clever, innovative, or costly doesn't necessarily drive the message across to its intended audience.

Too many awareness messages divide end-user focus and create confusion as to what is important to strengthening the organization's security posture. Some themed-based awareness campaigns may also obscure the actual message in the background of clever imagery. Sometimes, in an effort to make the message fit the campaign theme, the message itself gets lost in the shuffle. It is generally more effective to err on the side of communication clarity than cleverness.

Implementing an Impactful Security Awareness Program

The overall goal of security awareness is to change end-user behaviors to prevent risky actions and encourage activities that protect organizational assets. It is that simple. The tough part is figuring out what behaviors we want to encourage and what behaviors we want to stop. While on the surface this seems easy, it requires some analysis around the organization's security risk landscape. You need to focus awareness messages where they will make the greatest difference. The frugal CISO principle of SWIIMI is applicable to the implementation of an impactful security awareness program.

To maximize the value of expenditures, the information security team needs to begin by asking a series of questions before embarking on any security awareness plan:

1. What critical organizational assets do we need to protect?
2. How could the "people perimeter" be potentially compromised through risky behaviors?
3. What do we want end users to *do* to make the organization more secure?
4. What do we want end users to *stop doing* to make the organization more secure?

5. What are the most significant threats that the organization will face for the next twelve to twenty-four months?

6. What types of end user–created incidents have occurred in the organization over the last one or two years?

7. What types of cyber security incidents have peers told us about at their organizations that might potentially occur at this organization?

Based on the answers to these questions, the information security team should identify five to seven key awareness messages to support and encourage behavior that is related to or supports these behavioral objectives over a one- to two-year planning window. The next step is to create an action plan to execute these security awareness objectives using some basic principles.

Principles of Effective Information Security Awareness

The following principles are the foundation of an effective information security awareness program. When creating any awareness messages, using some of the following techniques may increase receptivity and retention in your audience:

1. Use KISS (keep it simple and succinct).
2. Stress the *why*.
3. Lump messages around the *why*.
4. Just say "no" to FUD (fear, uncertainty, and doubt).
5. Avoid "security theater."
6. Use stories.
7. Keep it fresh.
8. Require an action.
9. Use *tchotchkes* effectively.
10. Use metrics and statistics sparingly.
11. Avoid trite, silly, or dated concepts.
12. Know your audience and culture.
13. Avoid awareness materials mishaps.
14. Use only licensed content and images.
15. Do not disparage users.
16. Consider generational differences in risk perception.

Use KISS

At some point in our careers, we have been told about the KISS principle (keep it simple and succinct; this is the polite version of the acronym). We need to offer the message in clear and understandable language. Sometimes, we think we are being clear and that the intended recipient of the message understands what we said, but it is not true. I remember having a conversation with an individual in the same basic field of study and using the exact same terms and realizing we were actually talking about different concepts entirely.

Language has numerous nuances that we often do not consider in our daily communications. I have written articles for international journals and questions for international information security exams. In working with the individuals that manage both of these endeavors, I have learned to avoid idioms (unless defined in footnotes) and terms that might not be clear to a global audience.

The basics of KISS are as follows:

1. Avoid idioms.
2. Ban jargon.
3. Avoid cultural references (whenever possible), but especially with a global audience.
4. Keep the language simple. Run materials through one of the many Flesch–Kincaid Grade Level applications and rework anything that scores higher than a tenth grade reading level, which is the standard for most textbooks. Always try for a sixth grade reading level, which is the standard for most newspapers.
5. Don't get too cute or clever, especially when working with an awareness campaign theme.
6. Minimize the word count.
7. Avoid pretentious words; opt for clear and simple words.
8. Know your audience and communicate to them.
9. Don't make up your own words or terms, such as creating your own portmanteau (word created from blending of two or more distinct words or meanings).

Stress the Why

Security awareness training often does a great job at teaching the security *buzzwords* and terminology, such as malware or PII, but forgets to communicate the *why* objective of the behavior we are advocating. Worse, we respond to why questions with some variant of FUD. Humans like to know why something is important. It is instinctual. Anyone who has spent some time around young children understands that we learn by asking *why*.

If we communicate the why of awareness training, we put the behaviors we are advocating into a real-world context. We make it real for our users. This also establishes a foundation for future security learning. Sometimes, reversing the communication process by starting with the *why* can increase the clarity of the message. Rather than lead with the importance of using encryption on external transmission of sensitive information, the message should start with, "We need to protect our sensitive data." The why message acts as a *theme sentence* for the rest of the awareness communications. By keeping the message simple, such as "We need to protect our sensitive data," we create a category for activities that support that objective.

Lump Messages Around Why

When we focus our messages on *why*, we make information easier to remember because it creates shortcuts to memory. Rather than trying to retain many separate pieces of information, such as strong passwords and encrypting sensitive information, we just remember that we need to protect sensitive data. Our brain works by creating separate "containers" (associations) to store information for later recall. I like to refer to this as the *lumping* approach to memory retention.

Many information security professions have had the pleasure of studying for the Certified Information Systems Security Professional (CISSP) exam. One domain that frequently creates some heartaches for exam takers is telecommunications. Some exam takers use a shortcut to lump a great deal of network information by using the International Standards Organization (ISO) seven-layer protocol model and a mnemonic device. The mnemonic is APSTNDP (application, presentation, session, transport, network, data link, and physical), which is learned using the phrase "all people seem to need data processing" (there are several versions of this mnemonic device). Other information is hooked onto this lump to organize it for recall.

One big advantage of the lumping approach around core objectives (the whys) is it creates a basis of future learning that may increase the flexibility, extensibility, and cost effectiveness of security awareness efforts. It allows successive security awareness training events to reference and build upon each other. It creates a context for decision-making in new situations.

Just Say "No" to FUD

Security awareness falls back on "old school" FUD tactics when it cannot come up with a better approach. FUD remains the strategy of last resort, but it is resorted to more frequently than it should be. Sometimes the use of FUD in a security awareness campaign is subtle and difficult to spot. FUD will disguise itself in an ocean of facts and statistics and may be hard to discern. More often, FUD is obvious in its intentions.

Many of us have had the experience of seeing a security practitioner use FUD as his or her primary tactic, such as presenting a Cyber Pearl Harbor type of scenario, which would put a multibillion-dollar enterprise out of business. These unrealistic scenarios only decrease an individual's professional credibility. After more than a decade of experiences with security breaches, many executives have knowledge of the resilience that many enterprises have demonstrated in bouncing back from major data breaches with both their finances and customer bases intact.

The biggest downside to FUD is its overuse. Using FUD year after year as the basis for an awareness campaign weakens its effectiveness similar to the famous story "The Boy Who Cried Wolf." The biggest risk of funding via FUD is that when a significant risk appears on the horizon, the CISO will have little credibility by which to acquire supplemental funding.

Avoid "Security Theater"

Bruce Schneier, computer security expert and author, coined the term *security theater* in his 2003 book *Beyond Fear*. It occurs when proposed security controls offer the perception of greater security, but in actuality add nothing or little to improve security. Some security professionals view some compliance regulations, such as the Payment

Card Industry Data Security Standard (PCI-DSS), as little more than security theater because enterprise executives may view their organizations as "secure" when outside of the PCI-DSS scope, their organization may harbor significant vulnerabilities.

Security awareness gets only a finite amount of time and attention from our intended audiences. We need to SWIIMI, in terms of both time and budget management. To avoid security theater, security awareness needs to place the focus on core behavioral changes rather than trivial procedures.

To minimize the potential for promoting security theater activities, put your awareness campaign on a budget. Develop a list of desired behaviors that support or enhance the security posture of the organization. Derive the list based upon the identified risks to your organization, emerging technology risks, and past user-created cyber incidents. The next step is to rank the desired behaviors based on the number of risks that would be potentially reduced by consistent application of this behavior by staff. Any behaviors that have the potential to reduce significant risks or could reduce multiple risks should receive the highest rankings. Pick the top three to seven behavioral items, depending the size and scope of the security awareness budget (more for bigger budgets, fewer for smaller budgets).

Depending on your annual budget for security awareness, apportion a percentage of your budget to each behavioral objective and review. If the potential available amount does not appear adequate to cover the planned expenditures required, it might be prudent to edit the list of behavioral objectives to cover that year.

Keep It Fresh

Most people enjoy a "blast from the past" and get a chuckle out of dated videos that show cell phones the size of bricks and typewriters. Still, vintage and effective security awareness is not an effective combination. For awareness communications to remain relevant, they must be current and reflect today's threat landscape and emerging technical challenges.

In a world of Facebook, Twitter, and YouTube, "death by PowerPoint" is not going to cut it, especially with younger staff, such as Millennials (Gen-Y) who grew up with the Internet. It is important to consider the relevance of awareness themes to today's workers.

The infamous "Bob and Alice" need to get cooler and more in touch with today. Communicate with people in the way in which they like to communicate by integrating YouTube-style videos, blogs, and social media in your training arsenal. Make it real by including current news stories about security in training sessions. Make sure to include details to make the example more realistic and memorable. Consider letting users contribute their own blogs and videos to a Facebook-style social media site for security awareness. Keep the site fresh by adding new content frequently, such as links to personal security tools and security-related news stories.

Use Stories

People like stories. Before written language, stories were used to relate history, maintain specific behavioral norms, teach ethics, and transfer knowledge. Aesop's fables are an example of using stories as a teaching tool for behaviors. Each story contains a moral and other life lessons. For example, in Aesop's "The Tortoise and the Hare," the basic moral premise is that a slow and steady pace is a better way of winning the race than fast and inconsistent behavior.

Stories can make a point or teach an idea. I taught an internal CISSP exam review class for many years and often used stories to illustrate a point or concept. For instance, to demonstrate the importance of locking unattended devices, I told how my three-year-old nephew commandeered my unlocked email connection and on returning, I found him about to send my boss an email in "French" (page full of random characters).

To be truly effective, stories must promote vivid pictures in the brain of the listener. These images will promote later recall of the information that the stories support because they engage multiple areas of the brain associated with memory.

One master of using stories to relate information security concepts is Ira Winkler, the well-known security expert and speaker. Mr. Winkler's presentations are always memorable and full of vivid details. He frequently uses popular culture and famous stories as unifying themes, such as famous movie spies, *Star Trek*, or the *Wizard of Oz*.

Even a decade later, I can recall large portions of Mr. Winkler's presentations, largely because of the stories he told. I was inspired to try this idea myself and wrote a journal article in 2012 on using fairy tales to teach security awareness concepts. I was amazed at the number of security concepts that I was able to pull out of *Cinderella* and *Hansel and Gretel* without much effort.

Using stories as a mechanism for awareness and learning offers the following benefits:

1. People like to be entertained, and stories are entertaining.
2. Stories are flexible, so they can be customized for different audiences.
3. Stories can be fictitious, so they are useful in depersonalizing controversial, contentious, or uncomfortable issues.
4. Stories help people remember.

One word of caution regarding the use of stories: Do not tell unsavory stories about your own organization. Even if the individuals involved have departed, it is not a good idea.

Make It Actionable

In order to reinforce the concepts presented in awareness training, give the participants some "homework" or a take-away assignment to be performed immediately following the class or event. Every individual has a preferred way of learning—visual, auditory, or kinesthetic. The vast majority of people are visual, which explains why most classroom, as well as online, training is designed with visual learners in mind.

Visual learners like to see that they are learning, which is why they often sit in the front of the room and take copious notes. Auditory learners prefer to hear information. Auditory learners may resort to verbalizing lessons to themselves, when necessary. Some of the past CISSP exam preparation students requested MP3s of lessons, despite the availability of on-demand classes with synchronized slides and audio tracks. I suspect these students were auditory learners. Kinesthetic learners appreciate opportunities for hands-on experience.

While it is true that each of us has a preferred style, combining learning styles can increase retention of information. Stories combine both visual and auditory learning, which might be the secret of why they are an excellent communication technique. Participation in group exercises or games often combines all three learning styles, so it is often a very effective technique for increasing the retention of information.

Follow-up activities or "homework" assignments address multiple learning styles to increase the initial retention of awareness training material. More importantly, they assist in preventing a phenomenon known as *storage decay*. Storage decay occurs when learning that is not quickly utilized is rapidly lost. According to the *forgetting curve*, more than 50% of learned information is quickly forgotten. For example, if you take a class on proper information-classification handling procedures, and then do not use it for two months, you will likely forget most of what you learned in the class.

This is not news to anyone who has ever worked as a trainer or teacher. Lost awareness knowledge diminishes the ROI of providing this training. Therefore, anything that awareness training can include to minimize the storage decay reduces information security costs by avoiding retraining and minimizing the possibility of unnecessary security incidents.

By utilizing new knowledge quickly after the training events, retention is improved both in the near and long term. This is the *learn then do* model for knowledge retention. By giving security awareness class participants an actionable takeaway, such as sending an encrypted email, then sending a follow-up email after completing the requested action, can increase the retention of the information presented in the class. The performance of an action also utilizes an influencing technique called *Commitment and Consistency*, noted by social psychologist Robert Cialdini, in his book *Influence: The Psychology of Persuasion*.[2] When individuals make choices or take actions, it creates internal and external pressure to behave consistently with that commitment. When you verbally commit to an action, it increases the chances that you will follow through with it. This can increase the "stickiness" of security awareness learning activities.

Use Tchotchkes Effectively

Tchotchke is Yiddish slang for a cheap showy trinket, knickknack, or toy. Trinkets are often one of the first things mentioned when creating a new information security program or campaign. The primary motivation for creating and distributing tchotchkes is brand recognition for the program or new campaign.

The biggest drawback of tchotchkes is their cost. Tchotchkes may not appear to cost that much on a per-unit basis. However, they can be expensive to distribute throughout an entire organization. A frequently overlooked expenditure associated with tchotchkes is the cost of distribution of items to either specific areas or the entire organization. Unless your organization has established distribution channels, it can get costly to distribute items that do not fit within a standard envelope, such as mugs or penholders. Alternative methods of distribution, such as leaving boxes of items in common areas like mailrooms, can result in significant wastage.

Tchotchkes can be an effective element of a strong information security awareness campaign. They can also be a significant budget waster, if not used properly to support specific awareness objectives. Several types of tchotchkes are commonly used:

- Water bottles
- Mouse pads
- Magnets
- Pens and pencils
- Coffee mugs and cups
- Hats
- T-shirts

Sometimes, awareness teams use tchotchkes as a lure to get individuals to attend an awareness training session or participate in a postsession activity. Tchotchkes can be used to create relationships between staff and the information security team.

When someone does us a favor or gives us a gift, the natural human response is to reciprocate by offering something in exchange, such as attending an optional awareness event or complying with requested behaviors, such as locking up sensitive items when away from the work areas. It is possible to utilize inexpensive tchotchkes to induce gratitude from the targeted user population.

While the individuals may not be cognizant of this indebtedness, it may contribute to an individual participating fully in the security awareness program. The ROI in this tchotchke is variable and may be worth spending, even on tight awareness budgets, if it plays even a small role in preventing a future security incident. However, cost-effective use of tchotchkes requires discretion in usage rather than making it a default component of all security awareness campaigns.

Tchotchkes may be most effective in terms of both impact and ROI at specific intervals, such as during the on-boarding, the adoption of new technologies, such as cloud or bring your own device (BYOD), or significant changes to the security awareness program, such as implementation of a social media site. The recommendation for use of any promotional items, contest prizes, and other giveaways, should map to specific objectives.

There is a negative side to the use of tchotchkes. It may be associated with awareness programs at a lower level of maturity or less experienced security awareness practitioners who associate tchotchkes with a great awareness effort. It is popular because it looks good and is fun to do. Overuse of tchotchkes and similar promotions can backfire on security awareness practitioners. Workers may perceive these items as a waste of funds, especially if they occur concurrently with reductions in other budget items, like staff training.

A few tips of the effective use of tchotchkes include:

- *Keep it inexpensive:* Look to keep the cost per unit low. Often, expensive custom-created tchotchkes are no more effective than standard items like pens or water bottles.
- *Keep it useful:* Look for something that will not be immediately tossed, but might have some lasting useful life and perhaps everyday use like pens or water bottles.
- *Use it sparingly:* Use tchotchkes as the exception rather than the rule. Include tchotchkes for major campaign rollouts or specific junctions in the employee life cycle, like hiring.

Use Metrics and Statistics Sparingly

Metrics and statistics are like tchotchkes. They should be used sparingly. They can assist in underscoring a point or pointing out the gravity of a risk. However, they are often overdone and hard for individuals to put into a meaningful context.

If a statistic is used, giving its source increases its credibility. In general, very few participants are going to remember statistics after they leave the training session. Another issue is that statistics and metrics from different sources, such as research institutes and surveys, can contradict each other, which can further cloud the true risk issues. They can also distort information, unless you have additional information about the situation.

For example, one popular area of statistical information revolves around the costs associated with data breaches. Recently, it appears that the costs per record involved in a data breach may have decreased slightly. To the average individual, this might indicate that risks associated with data breaches have also decreased. While this might be technically accurate from a metrics perspective, it may not include some additional costs, such as increases in cyber insurance rates and expenditures for implementation of new security controls. Before using a statistic or metric, consider whether attaching a number to risk adds value or creates more confusion for the intended audience of the awareness training.

Avoid Trite, Silly, or Dated Concepts

Along the same line as the keeping it fresh, ban anything trite, overused, or completely dated in building awareness campaigns. It is time to retire the toothbrush-themed password slogan. Remember the "What are the two things you don't share, a toothbrush and a password" slogan? I admit that I used it in 2001. We likely all have. It was great in its time, but everyone has seen it before. It gets boring and bored audiences do not pay attention.

Today's users, who are exposed to every type of social media, are not going to respond the same way that users did a decade ago. If you want to go with a vintage theme, do *real* vintage with current popular themes, such as *Mad Men*, 1960s Mod, or World War II (1940s). You can draw inspiration inexpensively from popular media, TV programs, or movies.

Try to avoid the silly or corny, unless your awareness campaign is willing to make the effort to "make it work" as Tim Gunn of the television program *Project Runway* likes to say. Recycling older awareness materials might also result in a dated-looking campaign. Even if the basic information is still relevant, the message can get lost in the obsolesce surrounding its content. One suggestion to avoid these types of content issues is to have them reviewed by someone outside the awareness group who might have an open perspective on the continued relevance of the materials. Members of the awareness team who might have created the content may be too close to the situation to determine the need to retire content.

Know Your Audience and Culture

Some security awareness campaigns do not succeed, despite great planning, a clever concept, and sufficient expenditures. This can leave the members of the security awareness team scratching their head and wondering what went wrong. The root cause might be failure to connect with the intended audience. We need to know and understand the people we are attempting to communicate with, if we can, to be successful.

First, we need to understand the organizational culture of our intended audience. The organizational culture consists of the values and behaviors that define a distinctive social and psychological environment of the organization. It includes the expectations, experiences, philosophy, ethics, and values that act as a "glue" to unify its participants. Its basis includes shared customs, beliefs, and attitudes. It provides a mental model for how the organization and its members interact within the organization and the outside world.

If awareness communications are not in harmony with the organization's culture, then the messages can fail to click with listeners. For example, at a recent security conference I attended, one of the speakers discussed a short awareness video that was created to communicate the importance of not using unauthorized USB flash drives on enterprise computers. The ad was incredibly effective at communicating its message. There was only one issue. It contained a popular expletive. The organization for which the video was prepared is conservative in its culture. A representative of the organization's HR department said that the ad was effective, but that the offending word needed to be removed to fit into the organization's culture. In a more casual organizational culture, such as a technology enterprise with a younger demographic, the ad would have worked, perhaps even more effectively, with the profanity left in.

Knowing your audience is even more critical when the enterprise is a global one. There are many well-known examples of companies that failed to fully research cultural issues when going global. One particularly well-known example occurred when the Coca-Cola Corporation began promoting their flagship product, Coke®, in China. The enterprise had the product name rendered phonetically, which in the Chinese language sounded similar to the phrase "bite the wax tadpole." Fortunately, prior to the kickoff of its marketing in China, the Coca-Cola Corporation discovered a similar phonetic equivalent that roughly translates to "let your mouth rejoice." Advertising lore is full of these global goofs.

Organizational cultural nuances are important to consider when running training events. A presenter's appearance can influence the amount of attention they can command. In an organization where an authority figure commands the most attention, the presenter needs to mirror the dressing style of authority figures, for instance, wearing a suit and tie. In organizations with laid-back atmospheres, a presenter in formal business attire might have a negative effect because workers might find the authority image off-putting or oppressive. Presenter always needs to consider their appearance based upon their audience and the situation in which they will give their presentation, such as formal corporate function or casual training session in a coffee area.

The same holds true for the choice of language and training aids. Over my career, I have given more than sixty presentations at various conferences. Most of those settings are structured in their nature, so I always wear formal business wear, usually a suit. I am also a very petite woman and wearing a suit and heels offers a more authoritative appearance. It is imperative that awareness trainers consider the impact of their appearance as part of the preparation for presentations.

Avoid Awareness Materials Mishaps

Another budget buster can be ill-conceived or flawed awareness materials. Awareness materials are expensive to design, produce, and distribute. Sometimes a mistake in preparation of printed materials might require the literature to be destroyed. One way I have seen this occur is preparing screen images from production systems, such as screen shots.

This happens because the individual taking the images uses screens that contain the information of an actual employee or customer, and creates a security exposure. I have heard of multiple instances of this occurring. In each instance, the error was discovered before actual distribution of printed collateral. These types of errors can be expensive. They are also preventable by making use of test accounts or test environments in preparation of materials that will contain screen shots. Care should also be taken to avoid leaking other sensitive information, such as URLs or directory paths.

Avoid putting the names and contact information for individuals in printed collateral. Staff members come and go in today's dynamic business environment. By embedding the contact information for specific individuals in printed collateral, it may create the need for premature retirement of the materials because they contain the names of individuals who are no longer filling the function or have left the organization.

It is also a good practice to periodically review both online and printed collateral for obsolete information. I always suggest that individuals perform web searches on themselves on occasion. The first time I ran one, I saw a reference to a PDF created from a document I wrote a decade earlier in regard to tax documentation for vendors. It listed me as the contact for further questions. The document had been copyrighted more than ten years after its preparation and still had my name embedded in it.

The remaining area that can diminish some of the value of printed materials is the poor choice of fonts or font sizes. I used to instruct desktop publishing and graphic classes in the mid-1990s. In these classes, it was important to stress the importance of the readability of materials. One critical issue in the creation of posters is to make sure that they are readable from a normal viewing distance, usually several feet from the poster. Many security awareness posters do not follow this rule of thumb. One particularly memorable one required the viewer to stand about a foot or less from the poster to read the meat of the message.

Here are some rules of thumb for creating awareness posters:

- The poster text should be readable from a distance of 3 to 4 feet (or more, if possible).
- Recommended word count should be limited to a couple of hundred words at maximum.

- *Less is more* in the word count on a poster.
- Recommended font sizes:
  - Titles: 72 or greater
  - Subtitles: 54 or greater
  - Text: 30 or greater

A picture may be worth a thousand words, but too many images or too small an image can make a poster messy, confusing, and just plain unattractive. Novice media designers often fail to edit themselves and may want to use as many images as will fit on the poster.

Creating, printing, and distributing posters is one of the most expensive budget items for many security awareness teams. A poster is often one of the key communication elements of a security awareness campaign. Overly designed or confusing posters may fail to communicate a security message to its intended audience. Some images that look stunning in a smaller size may appear jarring when enlarged. Some bright colors, such as orange or fuchsia, may look garish when they cover large areas of the poster. Placing text over detailed or brightly colored images can make the text difficult to make out.

One particularly ineffective awareness poster I saw used a gigantic detailed image with bright colors with the primary message printed over the image in the same colors as the image itself. Rather than leave white space, small miniposters filled the border area (about 2 inches in diameter each) with 4-point font captions. These were large (and expensive) posters, and they were completely ineffective because of their design flaws. These types of posters are ineffective because they require too much effort by the viewers to decipher the message you are trying to communicate.

One cost-effective way to test readability without making up expensive samples is to print the poster in parts (many publishing packages allow you to print up larger images in a series of pages) and tape them together, then place them on a wall to get a perspective on how the poster will look to the viewing audience.

Then, ask the awareness team and some volunteers to evaluate the posters on the following criteria:

- Can you read the message clearly from the expected viewing distance (3 to 4 feet away)?

- What is the reaction to the color palette used (pleasing, jarring, messy)?
- Is the poster too busy, just right, or too plain?
- Do the images used enhance the message or take away from the message?
- Is there too much or too little white space?
- Is the poster size too big, too small, or just right?

One final note is to determine how the security awareness team plans to distribute posters, and in what types of space the posters will be displayed. Posters designed for display in small spaces, such as coffee/break rooms and mail distribution areas, may often work better on smaller stock or even standard, heavy, letter-sized stock. Larger-sized posters work well in larger display spaces, such as hallways, lobbies, and cafeterias.

A plan for distributing, hanging, changing, or removing posters needs to be in place prior to any poster projects. The awareness team needs to confirm if the use of posters is permissible, and be aware of any organizational standards around their use. Some organizations do not allow the use of posters or limit their use to specific operational groups, such as Human Resources (HR), physical security, legal, or the corporate communications team. If posters are permissible, the awareness team should research any organizational guidelines for their design, such as posters sizes, fonts, and branding/logos.

When creating posters, the KISS principle is the key to successful and cost-effective design. Simpler is better in terms of readability, especially if the awareness team does not have access to a professional graphic designer. Some guidelines for effective do-it-yourself poster creation are as follows:

- Keep your message simple and short.
- Use simple graphics.
- Use large fonts.
- Use only one or two fonts.
- Limit the use of bold and italic font effects.
- Limit the color palette to a few colors.
- Avoid script or handwriting-type fonts because they are difficult to read.

- The amount of text on a poster should be compatible with the poster's planned size. (Larger posters can have more text. Smaller posters should have less text.)
- Use the appropriate amount of space.
- Use standard poster sizes rather the custom-sized poster stock.

When determining font size for other printed collateral, it is good to understand that as people age, most, if not all, become far-sighted. Take care to make sure that an appropriate font size (at least a 12-point font) is used in printed materials so that reading glasses are not required. One way to check this is to distribute draft copies of printed material, such as brochures, end-user policies, postcards, and newsletters, to individuals of different ages on the staff and have them check readability without reading glasses. Be sure to get a few folks in their forties and fifties involved. If they cannot read the printed collateral without their reading glasses, increase the font size, even if it means losing some text or images. It is more cost effective to skinny down the verbiage than to have expensive printed material thrown away because workers do not want to get out their glasses to read your message.

On the same note, avoid the use of colored backgrounds, especially light colors or pastels, with white fonts (reverse effect). These are also more difficult for individuals to read as they get older.

Use Only Licensed Content and Images

One consequence of the vast availability of content on the Internet is that many individuals have forgotten the concept of copyright. They may believe that because they can easily copy images and text, they are OK. Unfortunately, using copyrighted material, such as songs, images, and other forms of content without licensing, may lead to legal actions or the need to pay licensing fees to the creators.

Some individuals are under the false assumption that making some small modifications to the content changes it sufficiently to be covered under the transformative or derivative copyright exceptions. This is rarely true, and any justification for exceptions to copyright laws are best left to legal experts.

Some believe that if the copyrighted content is only used within a small group, it is probably safe to include copyrighted content in materials. The risk is that with the increase in social media and slide-show type sites that promote information sharing, there is a chance that this material could find its way onto the Internet. It might also end up on a search engine, such as Google, and be exposed outside its intended audience.

It is safer to use public domain images and content, as well as pay for the use of any copyrighted images and content. Most licensing fees for content are relatively inexpensive, especially when compared with defending your organization against a legal action for copyright violations. An inexpensive alternative is purchasing media collections. These can often be bought for less than a couple of hundred dollars. It is also important to give credit where credit is due by citing any references in content in security awareness materials, such as survey statistics or news stories, to avoid plagiarism.

Do Not Belittle Users (Even When They Are Not Present)

Similar to the principle of not making disparaging remarks about other employees and managers, the security awareness team should not ridicule users or their errors, even in jest. This type of behavior can quickly ignite a toxic attitude among awareness staff members. This attitude often bleeds into awareness training. It is communicated in verbal and nonverbal messages sent by the awareness team members, such as eye rolls and sarcastic comments. Sometimes, security awareness instructors relay stories that make users look foolish or stupid. If you need to tell a humorous anecdote, tell it about yourself.

This diminishes the value of the budget spent on security awareness training. It also makes individuals less likely to participate in future awareness events or promotions. It is human nature to avoid those we do not like or those who do not respect us.

Members of the team who resist this wave of toxicity may find themselves isolated from the rest of the group or made victims themselves of belittling behaviors. This can result in higher staff turnover, or in the worst case, legal actions against the organization. The distractions created by conflict may decrease productivity and increase costs associated with the team.

There may be red flags that toxicity has seeped into a team by observing team interactions and behaviors. Often, this toxicity bubbles up to the surface and is front-and-center on display. One particular example of toxicity I once saw was a video made by an awareness team that filmed users answering security questions.

The phrasing of the questions made the majority of responders look stupid. By filming within operational environments, it created the potential to expose sensitive information. It seriously damaged the credibility of the security awareness team. In addition to displaying poor judgment, it wasted budget on an expensive joke. The lesson learned is to treat users with appropriate respect and not to use individuals for a cheap laugh. Respect is always earned.

Consider Generational Differences in Risk Perception

Individuals perceive their knowledge of security and attitudes toward risk differently. According to recent surveys, younger workers, called *digital natives* or Gen-Y, believe that they have a stronger grasp of security than their Boomer or Gen-X counterparts. This group also perceives cyber security risks as lower than other age groups. Generational differences in risk need to be addressed as a component of any security awareness plan.

Current studies indicate that younger workers often place productivity before security and view risks as lower than other generations in the worker population. A specific strategy for this group may need to focus on providing guidance around security issues that will not thwart the innovation and creative energy of these younger workers. Some inexpensive strategies for providing cyber security guidance to digital natives might include security mentors, blogs, and live chat services to discuss security issues.

Maximizing Investment in Security Awareness

Information security awareness training is a layer in an effective defense and in-depth strategy. Unfortunately, some organizations have discovered this lesson after experiencing an unfortunate security breach created by a single uninformed end user. Making security awareness more cost effective requires increasing the retention of the information presented. Increasing retention requires getting everyone in attendance involved in security awareness sessions and participating fully in the experience.

This includes the person leading the session. Some security awareness instructors may just go through the motions of presenting the important concepts as part of a compliance checklist exercise. Participants immediately notice this and their level of attention drops. The retention of this information likely does not outlast their walk back to their work areas. The ROI of this type of awareness session is close to none.

I have heard session facilitators talk about how quickly they can get through an awareness training exercise. While we need to be cognizant of the value of people's time, we need to communicate that security awareness education is time well spent. Otherwise, we risk communicating the unspoken message that this is only a mandated compliance exercise, rather than training designed to keep the organization, customer, and employee information secure.

This is exactly the type of awareness session that is more damaging than helpful to information security. It puts it into the category of other unpleasant "chores" like going to the registry of motor vehicles to renew our license or getting a filling at the dentist.

It is because of similar experiences that I advocate that a member of the security awareness team, and not another department, should primarily facilitate awareness sessions whenever possible. Members of the awareness staff understand the value of the information they present, and their verbal and nonverbal language communicate this to session participants.

We need to increase the retention of awareness education in order to build upon the concepts over the length of the worker's employment. One way to do this is by presenting security concepts and practices in small manageable "bites" that are easily consumed. We cannot expect workers to take in the whole menu and retain the whole thing in one marathon session. This is the reason that many mandatory awareness sessions prove not to be cost effective or successful in changing insecure behaviors.

A cost-effective approach is a highly modularized awareness training program where each module builds upon previous modules. This approach allows the individual sessions to be short, which accommodates busy schedules and permits the creation of customized learning plans depending on the individual's job functions, such as advanced social engineering defensive techniques for individuals in positions where social engineering attempts may occur more frequently.

A critical element of maximizing the ROI of awareness training and increasing the strength of the organizational security posture is getting the information to "stick" in the individual's memory. Chip Heath and Dan Heath talked about the "Velcro Theory of Learning" in their book *Made to Stick: Why Some Ideas Survive and Others Die.*[3] Getting anything to adhere to a smooth surface can be frustrating. It gets easier if we roughen up the surface before starting, to increase the chance that something will stick. With each awareness event, we scratch up the surface a bit more, like the little hooks on Velcro®. Anyone that has used Velcro knows its propensity to pick up bits of material that are next to it.

A stickier surface facilitates additional learning by making it easier for new information to attach to existing knowledge, and build a foundation for future training to leverage. The net result is an increase in ROI that organizations can reap from their security awareness training efforts.

Endnotes

1. Ira Winkler, "Security Awareness Can Be the Most Cost-Effective Security Measure: Ira Winkler Makes the Case for the Importance of Security Awareness Training in His Response to a Recent CSO Article Questioning the Value of Such Programs," CSO Security Leadership, July 25, 2012, http://www.csoonline.com/article/712162/security-awareness-can-be-the-most-cost-effective-security-measure.
2. *Influence: The Psychology of Persuasion* (New York, Morrow, 1993) by Robert B. Cialdini, a leading expert in the psychology of compliance.
3. *Made to Stick: Why Some Ideas Survive and Others Die* by Chip Heath and Dan Heath (New York, Random House, 2007).

8

INFORMATION SECURITY POLICIES AND PROCEDURES

Foundational Elements of Cost-Effective and Efficient Information Security

Every information security management textbook starts with the same basic advice on implementing an effective organizational security program—begin with policies. Policies are the foundation of an information security program and provide a basis by which to manage the information security needs of the organization.

The question I always ask is, if policies are vital to an effective and successful information security program, then why do some organizations skip this step in the program's implementation or do a poor job in their creation? Often, the impetus for any organization to create a security policy after years without one is regulatory compliance requirements, such as the Payment Card Industry Data Security Standard (PCI-DSS).

What Are Information Security Policies?

The highest level of the information security policy reflects the organization's vision of security, its objectives for security, and its management strategy for securing information. It is essentially a contract for how the information security function will be managed within an organization. It provides information regarding the structure of the organization, the responsibilities of the information security team, and the responsibilities of other stakeholders (such as data owners, application owners, users) in regards to security. It transfers the authority and responsibilities for security functions from the board of directors and executive management to the information security team. However, while the board of directors and executive management may transfer authority, the overall responsibility for security remains with board and executive level.

Why Some Organizations Go "Naked" (without Policy)

Some organizations chose to go without a formal information security policy because they really do not know better. The lack of a formal information security policy is often symptomatic of an information security organization in the earliest stages of its maturity. This is similar to Initiation (Stage 1) in the Nolan Stages Model. These organizations may focus on technical security issues, rather than considering the creation of policy. Toward the middle or end of this stage, it is common for the information security organization to develop its first high-level information security policy.

However, this is not always the case. This is common with teams with a primary focus on the technical aspects of cyber security, such as firewall management and antimalware implementations. Strong technical leaders of these types of teams may view formal policy as unnecessary or busy work without much return on investment (ROI) in terms of the organization's security posture.

Sometimes a team goes "naked" simply because no member of their current team has the skills or the experience required to develop an information security policy. This may be more common with teams that started out as security administration teams rather than a planned information security function. Rather than hire an outside resource, these groups might skip this step entirely until a new influence, such as an upcoming compliance regulation or when a C-level executive requires the creation of some type of information security policy.

Some information security teams elect not to have a formal policy because they believe it provides them greater flexibility in the way they manage information security. These teams view formal policy as too restrictive. This is often the case with start-up companies. These organizations need to move rapidly and have a high risk tolerance associated with speed. These organizations have both limited time and budget to achieve their place in the market. There is a significant difference between this type of organization and most others—assets. Start-up companies may have limited assets when faced with security incidents that would potentially result in legal actions or fines. These companies have little to lose. Most organizations cannot be so cavalier in their approach to information security risks because of the potential for negative monetary impacts on the organization.

An example of a cyber security incident that can severely affect an organization monetarily is illustrated by the 1996 case of malicious insider Timothy Lloyd. Mr. Lloyd worked for Omega Engineering, a company in New Jersey. He allegedly could not get along with his coworkers and Omega fired him. However, Mr. Lloyd saw this event coming and took steps to plan his revenge. He managed to gain control of all backups. He also planted a software time bomb on Omega's servers that, in six lines of code, purged the servers of the all files. The results of the attack devastated Omega Engineering by creating more than $12 million in losses and causing more than eighty employees to lose their jobs.[1] Effective information security policies and their enforcement might have prevented or at least mitigated this unfortunate outcome. The need to limit risks creates the requirement for information security policies in most mature organizations.

Why Does an Organization Need an Information Security Policy?

Information security is, at its essence, a business issue rather than one of technology. Policies are just a set of rules—the dos and the don'ts of information security within an organization. Security allows businesses to take risk to further their mission, and in many cases, create more wealth for stakeholders. Data often represents an organization's most significant assets, especially in our global economy, and organizations must assure the confidentiality, integrity, and availability of these assets. Information security policy is the tool to accomplish this goal.

Beyond creating a framework for the protection of assets, a policy provides the information security function with the authority to monitor and enforce the protection of assets. Most high-level information security policies identify the structure and functions of the information security team. In the absence of a charter or vision statements, the information security management policy provides an overview of what the team is designed to do, what it wants to accomplish, and how it will do so. It is, in essence, the *why* statement for information security within the organization.

Benefits of Information Security Policy

An information security policy provides myriad benefits. The purpose of having an information security policy is to tell the entire organization what is expected of it in terms of protecting the organization's assets, especially its data. It is the basis of all security activities. It offers legal protection against claims by management, staff, and other stakeholders that they were not aware that assets of the organization needed to be secured, especially its data. While this might appear to be commonsense to most business people, it needs to be stated explicitly in the form of an information security policy.

It also demonstrates the board of directors and executive management commitment to protecting critical information assets. It exhibits a commitment to stakeholders, such as employees and customers, that the organization is vested in protecting their best interests, as well. It signifies to compliance bodies that the organization takes its responsibilities in regard to security seriously. Information security policies also create awareness of risk-related issues for the organization's personnel.

Policies Ensure Standard Ways of Doing and Measuring Security Activities

Security policies ensure that the various parts of an organization perform security activities in a standard way rather than each group developing their own procedures within isolated silos. Policies can assist in supporting consistency by offering direction, assigning specific responsibility, and laying out the consequences for noncompliance. Standard ways of performing and measuring security activities allow for the creation of metrics and a mechanism for the evaluation of progress on security initiatives. Failure to standardize security activities can make it difficult to create meaningful measurements in regard to the overall strength of the organization's security posture or evaluating its progress against outstanding issues.

One good example of where lack of standardized processes created difficulties involved an organization attempting to evaluate progress on remediating host configuration vulnerabilities. For example, the information security staff assigned to different organizations each claimed to be using different policies for achieving compliance than the enterprise security policies dictated. According to some groups, they used a higher bar for host compliance than their peers in other parts of the organization. This created difficulties in estimating the percentage of compliant servers on the internal network.

It was not until after the automation of host compliance checking across all hosts using a common baseline that enterprise security discovered that some groups had not been as complaint as they claimed to be, even the less-stringent requirements.

Creates a Foundation for the Rest of the Policy Hierarchy

The top-level information security policy acts as an anchor for the rest of the policy hierarchy. While the high-level policy provides the basic direction, structure, and objectives of the information security management program, it does not offer specifics of how to achieve the program's objectives. To use a popular terminology in compliance, the high-level policy is *vendor neutral*. The lower-level policies, standards, guidelines, procedures, and technical directives put forward the specific details on how to effectively manage that organization's information security program.

This layered structure provides the advantage of allowing the underlying policies to remain relatively stable, while allowing updates to portions of the policy hierarchy to accommodate changes in technology strategies and the technologies themselves, such as the addition of mobile devices and cloud technology, to the overall IT strategy. The addition of standards and guidelines may occur, as necessary. The fleshing out of the hierarchy is common as the information security team matures. This is similar to Control (Stage 3) in the Nolan Stages Model.

On occasion, some organizations will opt to skip the creation of a high-level information security policy because they do not view it as a necessary part of the set of information security policies. Alternately, these teams may opt to construct their information security policy as a single document with a primarily technical focus. This approach may result from an organization quickly trying to achieve compliance with technical requirements of a specific regulation or law, such as PCI-DSS or state data privacy/breach reporting law. The various approaches to the creation of policies are discussed in the next section.

Communicates to Stakeholders Proof of Commitment to Security

When an organization goes through the effort of publishing a policy, it symbolizes an executive-level intent to embed information security into business processes. The very existence of this policy may convince stakeholders, including potential customers, partners, and investors, how serious the organization is about security. Over the last decade, the number of organizations requesting solid evidence of adequate security controls from external parties with which they do business has increased dramatically.

When I began performing external security reviews of vendors and business partners almost fourteen years ago, many organizations were not familiar with the concept. Now, the procedure is a routine component of many vendor and third-party business relationships.

When doing any type of external security review, one place to start is with the organization's information security policy. The absence of any type of information security policy or specific contact for security-related issues is a red flag that the organization has not invested in security protection for its information assets. Therefore, it probably will not do so for another organization's data either.

Demonstrates a Commitment to Security to Regulatory Bodies

Regulatory bodies like organizations that play well with others, especially the regulatory agency itself. Regulatory bodies look for demonstrable evidence that an organization wants to fulfill its compliance obligations, rather than finding creative strategies to avoid them.

Some business sectors have specific regulatory and legal obligations around guarding the integrity and confidentiality of sensitive information. A good example exists in organizations that offer medical services, such as hospitals and clinics. These organizations are required to comply with the Health Insurance Portability and Accountability Act (HIPAA). HIPAA obligates organizations creating, handling, and processing personal heath information (PHI) to protect this data against unauthorized access using a well-defined set of rules.

To provide evidence of appropriate due diligence in this regard, it is imperative that these organizations have published policies. Information security policies reveal the philosophy and security strategy of an organization's executive management. The policy is tangible proof of the organization's commitment to information security.

Shows a Pattern of Due Diligence to Auditors in Business Operations

A significant part of an auditor's job is to observe the environment. Much of this observation involves looking for positive as well as negative indications of the security culture of an organization. One of the most visible signs that an organization takes security seriously is the existence of a formal information security policy. It also provides auditors something to audit against during their engagements. The executives of some organizations mistakenly believe that the absence of an information security policy will result in an easier audit because there are no objectives to audit against during the engagement. However, just the opposite may occur.

When an IT or compliance auditor does not have a specific policy or standard against which to audit, the auditor will use best practices and general IT control standards as the guidelines for his or her assessment. The auditor may also choose to apply implicit policies, such as what the organizational representatives say they do, or determine that specific practices are allowable because management is aware of these behaviors and has taken no action to curb their occurrence. The absence of an explicit information security policy based upon the specific risk landscape of an organization can result in more audit findings than an audit using an information security policy developed specifically for that organization. Auditors can deem the absence of an information security policy a risk finding.

Provides Guidance for Acceptable Use of Assets

Organizations vary greatly in what is permissible and prohibited in terms of activities with the potential to create security risks. Something that is OK in one organization, such as using personal USB drives on organization-provided devices, may be grounds for termination in another organization. This is part of the organizational culture. Some organizations, especially smaller privately held companies, may place greater trust in their employees. It may also result from inherent and regulatory risks associated with a specific business sector.

An organization's staff can be either its strongest or weakest link in terms of information security. While security awareness is essential in communicating the appropriate actions to ensure that the organization's security posture remains strong, it is only one part of the total security program. Unfortunately, the information security team, with the support of executive management, needs to convey the penalty for noncompliance with security policies, otherwise known as the *sharp stick*. An information security policy puts people on notice by delineating what can and cannot be done by users, and assuring that end users are aware of standards. It avoids the potential for users pleading ignorance for infractions of the policy.

Provides Demonstrable Evidence of Executive Management

Let us be truthful; end users are not always information security's biggest fans. The objectives of information security may conflict with the desires of end users. This can create resentment and frustration from senior-level positions against the information security team. They can perceive information security as an obstacle to productivity and convenience. Often, these conveniences are trivial, such as a five-minute configuration check to ensure that a remote device is secure, in comparison to the risks involved in exposing internal network and sensitive assets to potentially insecure devices or malware.

An information security policy serves as a directive from the board of directors or executive management that authorizes the information security team to enforce decisions that may not be liked by other staff. This prevents information security from having to continuously defend their actions.

Limits Liability for Organization and Staff

Using an information security policy can protect both the organization and even the staff itself from legal actions. Increasingly, new legal cases have held the organization, and even its employees, liable for failure to address security risks or provide appropriate controls to mitigate security breaches when they do occur. These cases have found an organization and its staff liable for security incidents based upon a failure to practice due care, negligence, and breaches of fiduciary duty.

In some cases, the potential for criminal charges being brought against management and technologists may exist. The existence of a comprehensive information security policy has proven useful with the courts in showing that the organization and its management was concerned and is addressing security risks.

Information Security Policies are Expensive to Create and Maintain

It requires substantial resources and effort to develop the first set of written information security policies for an organization. This initial policy set would outline the philosophy, functions, organization, and authority of the information security team. The vast majority of this initial set of policies would remain static throughout the organization's existence or at least for several decades.

Often, the organization's information classification scheme may be included with the initial set of policies. Information assets have varying degrees of sensitivity and criticality. Establishing an information classification scheme allows the organization to establish guidance for the handling of different types of information. An appropriate information classification scheme is critical to the frugal chief information security officer (CISO) in reducing risk and avoiding excessive control costs for the overprotection of low-risk information assets.

While data classifications may remain relatively stable like other high-level information security policies, there may be a need to reexamine the classifications of data by its need for protective controls and handling procedures, based upon regulatory requirements and consumer sentiments.

For smaller organizations, the costs of developing an initial set of policies may be relatively low, depending on the development strategy pursued by the organizations. Usually, smaller organizations can use a relatively simple high-level policy structure.

Larger organizations, especially organizations consisting of multiple business entities, require complex policies. These policies may need to define the roles associated with a distributed security organization or a wider variety of security roles. Global organizations may need to develop their policies on a country-by-country basis to accommodate differences in local laws, regulations, and culture. Even with global concerns, it may be possible to develop one overarching high-level information security policy that acknowledges the organization's commitment to protecting its information, its responsibility to stakeholders to adhere to the privacy and security laws of countries where it does business, and executive management's support for the information security organization.

The cost of developing a set of high-level information security policies for larger or complex organizations can be very expensive. A basic rule of thumb for most projects in the security realm is that with greater complexity comes greater cost. Additionally, size does matter when it comes to security projects. Bigger projects cost more to do. Creating an information security policy for a larger organization will generally cost more as well. One of the reasons for the greater cost may be the need to gain consensus from multiple people and multiple groups in order to ratify the documents with all stakeholders. This can incur significant administrative costs.

The development of information security policies is not a project in which doing a fast and cheap job is an appropriate strategy. Security policy development is a good place to practice the frugal CISO information security approach, spend where it is most impactful (SWIIMI). An investment in a solid security policy can create ROI for decades. A weak or inappropriate security policy can create costs that recur on a regular basis, such as regulatory fines, increased legal fees, or defending the organization against audit findings.

Over the life of the information security policy and related documents, there exists an ongoing need to regularly ensure that the organization remains compliant with data security laws and other regulatory requirements. The annual information security budgets need to include a line item for policy maintenance and revisions. Even if the policies or supporting standards do not require annual updates, they need reviews on a regular basis to ensure they remain current and applicable to current operational functions. New policies and standards are necessary to ensure emerging technologies are properly secure, such as mobile devices or cloud computing, or to manage compliance requirements. Policy development is an iterative activity that needs to remain adequately funded in information security budgets.

Initial Policy Development Costs

A number of factors may influence the cost of developing and maintaining information security policies. Each of these factors contributes to the total cost of security policies. One significant cost is the size of the team required to develop the policies. In smaller organizations, it may be possible to have one individual develop the policies. In larger organizations, this effort may require a team of individuals. The complexity of the organization for which the security policies are being developed also influences the final cost of their development.

The following attributes contribute to the complexity of the organization, and therefore the overall cost of writing a set of information security policies to meet its needs:

- Business sector(s) in which the organization operates
- Regulatory environment in which the organization exists
- Organizational culture
- Country or countries in which the organization operates
- Organization's financial structure, such a private, public, or partnership
- Past history of cyber incidents or negative audit findings
- Existing information security sanctions, such as Federal Trade Commission (FTC) requirements for ongoing audits
- Organization's overall level of maturity
- Information security team's level of maturity
- Organization's overall governance structure
- Information security's experience in governance processes
- Types of products or services offered by the organization

All of these factors can potentially influence the amount of work effort required to review, ratify, and issue information security policies. Another major factor is the total quantity of policy documents that needs to be developed. If the organization only wants to develop a bare-bones policy that covers only high-level information security program essentials, the effort may be considerably cheaper than the development of a more extensive policy set that covers the majority of activities undertaken by the information security team.

Another thing having some bearing on policy development cost is whether the team needs to hire an external resource to write the policy set. The cost of an external resource or resources will increase the expense associated with policy creation considerably. A quick way to estimate the cost associated with policy creation might look like the following:

Time (person – hours) required to develop the policy documents

× cost of resources responsible for development

= Cost of preparation of organization's information security policy

However, this estimate covers only the basic costs associated with writing the policy document itself. Much of the costs associated with the creation of the information security policy may occur after the completion of the first policy draft. With the exception of very small organizations, there exists the potential for significant debate before the ratification of the information security policy by the organization and initial implementation.

The information security team will often need to spend its time and resources holding a series of meetings to review the policy documents and making revisions based upon this feedback. There may need to be several iterations of revisions before finalization of the policies.

After finalizing the policy document, the information security team will need to work to gain consensus among stakeholders to get the document ratified. The formula to evaluate the total costs associated with policy creation might likely look like this:

Time (person-hours) required to develop the policy documents

× Cost of resources responsible for development

= Cost of preparation of organization's information security policy

+ Cost of policy document revisions

+ Cost of gaining consensus with stakeholders

= Total cost of the organization's information security policy

Since the total cost of the creation of an information security policy can be significant, it needs to be included as a major line item in the budget for the security organization. Future year budgets need to include specific line items for review and revisions to policies and related components of the supporting policy hierarchy.

Approaches to Creating an Information Security Policy

Organizations can utilize a number of approaches to the development of an initial set of information security policies. The decision regarding the appropriate approach is dependent upon the organization itself. The information security team needs to consider a number of factors before making the decision on how to proceed. A big influencing factor will be the organization's information security level of maturity. Security organizations with a lower level of maturity may elect to use some purchased or pre-packaged policy materials as the foundation for policy development. Younger security teams may not have practitioners with experience in policy development in the group. Budget availability will also have an effect on how the security policy is developed. As previously stated, policies are expensive to develop. If a team has limited budget availability, its only option may be utilization of preprepared templates as part of its policy development strategy.

Complex, large, and highly regulated organizations will usually have no choice but to develop their policies from scratch to meet their organization's specific requirements. However, these organizations are likely to have sufficient budgetary resources or experienced practitioners on staff to guide the policy project. There are four primary approaches to security policy creation:

1. Use prewritten policy templates
2. Develop a custom policy
3. Use another organization's policy and make adjustments
4. Outsource policy development and maintenance

Use Prewritten Policy Templates

A small organization with limited resources may elect to use a prewritten information security policy template as the basis for its policy development process. These templates are readily available from a number of sources. Some good templates are available online from information security organizations. Some templates are available for relatively small fees through publishers. There are a number of excellent books on the topic of information policy development. Many of these books have become classic textbooks. Most authors who write policy books include the policy templates, often on CD-ROM or web downloads, with their books or on their websites for purchasers. Whether an organization decides to use a prewritten template or not, policy textbooks and templates may prove a valuable resource to the policy development process because they offer insights and approaches to the activity.

The advantage to using a prewritten template as the basis for information security policy is that it offers a starting point for the rest of the process. This is important when the information security team is relatively new and no team member has been through the experience before. Templates can be especially helpful to teams in earlier stages of maturity, similar to the Initiation (Stage 1) phase in Nolan's stages model.

Templates are useful in getting the basics down, but rarely can be used *as is*. Templates are best used when adjusted to meet the unique requirements of the organization. Omissions and additions to the template will optimize the prewritten text.

Carefully review all the boilerplate text provided in the template. Some policy items may be aspirational for smaller or less-mature organizations. Aspirational policy items may not be currently attainable by the organization. Aspirational policies may result in expensive audit findings for noncompliance or other undesirable consequences.

Be cautious to avoid the creation of policies that are aspirational or unenforceable in nature, even for mature or larger organizations, because auditors will use them in the evaluation of security control objectives. The organization may lack the technology or resources to effectively monitor and enforce policy statements. After completion of adjustments, it is always recommended that all information security policies undergo a complete review by a legal resource before proceeding to the review stage.

Develop a Custom Policy

Some organizations are just too big or specialized for the use of prewritten policies. Templates are best suited to small to medium-sized organizations with limited regulatory requirements. Most available boilerplate focuses on domestic organization rather than business with a global presence. Organizations need to consider developing a custom information security policy if they possess any of the following attributes:

- Large organization
- Specific industry or regulatory compliance requirements

- Global entity
- Multiple business lines (products and services)
- Distributed administrative functions
- Multiple subsidiaries or legal entities
- Complex technical infrastructure

Writing a custom information security policy is a nontrivial project that requires both appropriate budget and resources to manage the project. Custom policy development takes time. Often, adding more sources to the policy development team may not expedite the process. The team responsible for authoring the high-level policy documents needs to remain small for collaboration. Later in the policy development, the project leader can delegate various components of the policy set to different team members to speed up completion of documents.

The majority of the effort in developing customized policies often occurs prior to the start of the policy's first page. The policy development team needs to do extensive research on the organization itself, its products or services, any regulations or industry-specific compliance requirements with which it must comply, the organization's structure, and organizational culture. It also needs to be aware of other types of policies that already exist for the organization, such as human resource (HR) and employee policies, privacy policies (Internet and internal), HIPAA, internal audit and finance policies, record information management (RIM) policies, and ethical behavior policies. Knowledge of existing policies is central to avoiding conflicts between the new information security policies and the rest of the organization's policies.

One area to check for potential conflicts or overlap is acceptable use policies (AUPs). An acceptable use policy, also known as a fair use policy, is a set of rules the organization establishes around the use of organizational assets, such as networks, computing devices, and phones for nonorganizational activities. Initial implementation of acceptable use policies began around the use of phones and photocopiers in the workplace.

The objective of the early AUPs was to avoid excessive use of organizational resources for personal use. Today, AUPs govern the use of computer resources, such as the Internet, by workers, and in some circumstances, customers. AUPs describe what is both permissible and prohibited in terms of behaviors, such as engagement in illegal activities. The AUP may outline enforcement and penalties for violations of the AUP. AUPs reduce the potential for legal action against the organization for actions of workers and customers.

After completion, it is always recommended that all information security policies undergo a complete review by a legal resource before proceeding to the review stage.

Use the Information Security Policy of Another Organization and Making Adjustments

Some organizations may choose to use the information security policy of another organization by copying it and then tweaking it for their own use. Often, information security practitioners may carry with them a policy used by their former employer or files given to them by another information security professional.

For example, an information security practitioner told me of being given a hard copy of information security policies of a famous enterprise and being told to create that organization's new information security policies based upon the documents. The policies were elaborate and reflected the threat and compliance issues of another business sector. The new organization was a small private enterprise in a different business sector.

While reviewing the information security policies of different types of organizations may be enlightening for practitioners, rarely can one organization's information security policies be essentially cloned and used by another organization without extensive modification. This is especially true of sophisticated policies created for organizations of vastly different sizes, ownership structures, or industry sectors.

Copying another organization's security policy is different from using prewritten templates. Templates are generic by design to allow their utilization by different types of organizations. Often, template policy designers will offer several versions of boilerplate for different size organizations and industry sectors. Templates may include instructions for making modifications to accommodate the security practitioner's own organization.

To adapt another organization's security policies requires a highly experienced practitioner. However, this type of practitioner is often not available. This is often the approach of an organization looking to save on the cost of developing their information security policies or an inexperienced practitioner with limited resources available.

In the long run, trying use another's policies may actually end up costing the organization significant sums of money. The information policies of a mature or larger organization may be aspirational or unenforceable policies for smaller or less-mature organizations. Unfortunately, it is these policies that they will face during future audits. The organization may lack the technology or resources to effectively monitor and enforce policy statements.

Aspirational policies are policies that may not be currently attainable by the organization. Some mature organizations may purposely opt to put in place aspirational policies as a kind of "reach" goal for improving its security posture. Aspirational policies may result in expensive audit findings for noncompliance or other undesirable consequences unless their objectives can be achieved with a reasonable timeframe.

Outsource Policy Development and Maintenance

A recent option available to organizations is to outsource information policy development to a third party, such as a subscription service or an outside security firm. These firms offer prewritten security policies with regular updates. A new information security team might want to explore this option rather than using static prewritten templates. The cost of using a subscription policy service may offer a sweet spot in terms of cost between using prewritten templates and maintaining an internal policy development group. However, prewritten policies may still require modifications specific to an organization's unique needs and environment.

Security organizations at higher maturation can use policy subscription as a resource to their own internal policy development group, especially for security policies involving emerging technologies, such as bring your own device (BYOD), cloud, or virtualization.

Steps in Creation of the Information Security Policy

An information security policy is not just a document someone can sit down and write in isolation from the rest of the organization, although I have seen this approach used by some organizations. To create a strong and long-lasting information security policy requires going through a series of steps to ensure that the policy reflects the organization's risk landscape, business sector, regulatory requirements, risk appetite or tolerance, organizational culture, available monitoring and enforcement mechanisms, and other unique organizational attributes.

The following are the frugal CISO's basic steps in developing an information security policy. Depending on the approach and objectives, some steps may be eliminated, combined, or abbreviated. If the organization's objective is the development of customized policy using in-house resources, most, if not all, of the steps are required to be successful.

1. Identify the security policy team.
2. Collect background research material.
3. Prepare a coverage area list.
4. Design a policy standard structure.
5. Develop policy content.
6. Perform review and revisions involving key stakeholders.
7. Obtain ratification and release the policy.
8. Have a formal exception process in place.
9. Develop a policy rollout plan and awareness campaign.

This is a simplified process flow and additional steps (and costs) may be necessary for a specific organization. However, it offers a plan and budget guide to manage the costs and requirements associated with the initial costs of creating an organization's first information security policy.

Identify the Information Security Policy Team

Identifying the members of the policy team is critical. The number and experience of team members will affect how expensive the policy development effort will become over its total course. If possible, the team leader, in addition to being an effective leader, should have past experience in policy development. Past experience with policy development or the governance process means that they understand the challenges of the project and will be better prepared to deal with the eventual bumps in the road when and where they occur.

If there is no member of the team with specific policy development experience, it might be a good investment to consider using a contract resource with this experience, at least at the beginning of the project. While this will increase the expense of the policy development effort, it can save unnecessary costs, such as restarts or total rewrites later in the project.

The team leader needs experience in reaching out across the organization throughout the life of the project to build rapport and check in with the stakeholders necessary to ratify the security policy once complete. The lead should do regular check-ins outside the team. This is especially true when policy items have the potential to create disruptions in existing processes or add substantial costs. One way to do this is the creation of a policy council composed of stakeholders from across the organization. A policy development effort may literally have to start again from scratch if it fails to gain consensus from key stakeholders and the result can be lost effort and budget.

Depending on the team's size, it is optimal to have a strong business writing resource. Policy development involves a great deal of writing. The policy development effort needs an individual that is comfortable writing quickly and can turn around first drafts and subsequent revisions in a timely manner. The policy development team also needs a strong project manager. A policy project can become a budget buster, if not well-managed. Most expenses are person hours and these costs can mount up quickly if not watched.

Collect Background Research Material

An information security policy touches all three key aspects of an organization: people, process, and technology. The team needs to understand this before it can begin to ensure the policy will work for a specific organization. If aspects of the new policy are not a good fit for existing business processes and technologies, the fallout can create extra costs or noncompliance.

It is a failure to understand the business and its needs that is one of the most common criticisms of information security. The information security team needs to acknowledge its responsibility to ensure that the organization can fulfill its missions and minimize risks associated with its activities because information security is mitigating the potential for the exploitation of those risks. A single policy statement could have the potential to create tens of millions in costs with limited reduction in risk exposures. Only with thorough research and understanding can this possible scenario be avoided. It is critical that the policy team not exist in isolation from the business of the organization in order to perform optimally.

Prepare a Topic Coverage List

The policy team needs to decide what areas the security policy will cover in its first iteration. The availability of budget and time will influence the number of topic areas covered in the initial policy release. Regulatory requirements will also influence what areas must receive coverage in order to achieve compliance with the appropriate authorities and laws.

An information security policy hierarchy is often developed over several years to achieve full maturity, and needs to be continually revised to handle changes in technology, threat landscapes, business strategies, societal influences, organizational culture, regulations, and the law. It is never *done*, much like the information itself.

If budget allows more than the development of a high-level foundation policy, such as the establishment of the information security program, team structure, information classification scheme, and functional responsibilities of the team, then other policies may receive coverage depending upon their criticality in assuring the organization's security posture. Emerging technologies, such as mobile devices and cloud, may take priority over older technologies in creating policies because of their potential values and risks to the organization.

Design a Policy Standard Structure

Currently, there is no one standard format for what defines the content and structure of information security policies. The International Standards Organization (ISO) 27001 provides guidance in this area, but it is up to the individual organization to determine what works best.

Before the actual writing starts, it is important to determine the basic policy format. All policies should use more or less the same structural elements to make it easier for users to interpret and find the necessary information. The best format is as simple as possible, while providing the necessary information for the policy's use.

The use of a standard format assists in the effective management and updating of policies. It enforces consistency among documents. Some common elements include the organization name, policy name, author, original creation date, and last revision date. Other information included in the standard policy format, in addition to the actual policy content, might include the following:

- Introduction
- Purpose
- Scope
- Limitations of use
- Glossary
- Approvals and acknowledgments of ratification
- Date policy went into effect

Many sample formats are available on the Internet or may be purchased from policy subscription services, policy textbooks, and as prewritten templates. It is not necessary to create a unique format, just one that works for the organization and its users.

It is important to use standard and consistent terminology. The inconsistent use of language may create ambiguity and inconsistency in the application of policy statements. Some words may create debate about the flexibility assigned to performance of a policy item or may be interpreted differently by different users. Some words that may appear to be clear, such as the word *required*, may create questions regarding the applicability of a policy item and under what circumstances is it permissible to violate compliance with the item. One key area for application of consistent language and meaning is in the compliance rating, which provides the reader with desired behavior or action expected for a policy item.

The following terms are examples of unambiguous policy language:

- **Required/must:** It is necessary and compulsory to comply with the policy item without a formal exception.
- **Recommended/should:** It is suggested that users observe compliance with the policy item. This policy item represents a best or recommended security practice.

- **Strongly recommended:** It is suggested that this policy item always be observed. There are two permitted exceptions. The information security team receives an executive sign-off for non-compliance under a specific instance or an exception is in place.
- **Prohibited/must not:** Behavior or action associated with a policy item *must not* occur unless a formal exception is in place.

All policy documents should include a version number. The version number clearly identifies which is the current version of the policy and assists in maintaining a version history of each policy document. Maintenance of a complete policy version history is not only a best practice from a document management perspective, but it may prove useful as a means of preserving digital evidence for future legal actions. It exhibits the organization's commitment to information security by updating its policies on an ongoing basis.

Develop Policy Content

Based upon prior steps in the policy development process, the writing of the policy content begins. If possible, the policy author should have prior experience in writing policies. If not, the best strategy may be using prewritten templates as a starting point for developing new policies or hiring an external resource to jump-start the writing phase.

When developing highly technical policy, such as a secure development policy or cloud computing policy, the individuals creating the majority of the content need to be fluent in the technologies involved. This is important for credibility with the target audiences for this category of policy documents. The text and terminology utilized must reflect that of a technical expert to be acceptable to technologists that will use it. If not, the best strategy may be to borrow a technical resource from another organizational team or hire an external resource.

The most important attribute of any information security policy is that it needs to be clear and understandable to its target user populations. Not all policies are meant for everyone in the organization to read and understand; for example, the average end user is not expected to read and understand the firewall management policy. It is permissible to use technical terminology in policies governing the use of technology, but not in policies designed for end users.

Write policies in plain and simple language. Avoid the use of legalese, which may be difficult for the average user to read and understand. If the information security team does not employ a specific content development resource, such as a writer or communication specialist, it might be a good investment to hire a technical writer or experienced editor to simplify the policy's verbiage. While this may increase the costs of the policy's development, the decreased support necessary to respond to questions regarding the policy will offset this cost and may pay dividends in the long run.

All documents targeting end users should use *policy in plain English* (PIPE). PIPE translates security terminology into easier-to-understand language. Always run content through a Flesch–Kincaid grade level application and rework anything that scores higher than a tenth-grade reading level. Tenth-grade reading level is the standard for most college textbooks. Always try for a sixth-grade reading level, which is the standard for most newspapers. If the organization has a graphics department, it might be effective to develop some colorful graphics to include with any printed collateral or place on the web pages containing end-user policies.

Information security policies that target end users should be short, no more than two pages in length. End-user security policies are the one possible exception to the standard format rule for a policy document. End-user policy documents need to be structured and formatted to attract and maintain the attention of end users, as well as highlight critical elements.

Policies and policy-related documents should be placed into separate categories by type and purpose, rather than mixed into a massive policy document. Keep policies, standards, procedures, guidelines, and technical directives in separate documents.

Policies are the most general and highest-level statements created under the specific direction of executive management or the board of directors. Standards are subordinate and much more detailed than policies. Standards ensure consistency in technology and operational practices. Guidelines are the *gray areas* within the policies because they provide flexibility in their application. They offer recommendations and operational guidance on use of specific technologies. Procedures are step-by-step directions on performing a task or achieving an objective. They are usually the lowest level within the

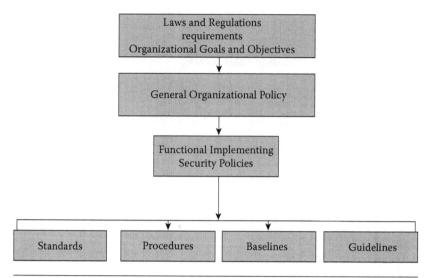

Figure 8.1   Illustration of policy hierarchy.

policy hierarchy chain. Some organizations may include technical directive documents within the policy hierarchy. Technical directives are specific configurations and directions for using approved security technologies.

There is a direct relationship between how understandable a policy document is and the costs associated with its use. Poorly written policies increase costs in two ways. If a document is difficult to understand, it will increase the number of questions received regarding the policy and the support costs associated with the policy rise significantly. Errors and omissions resulting from mistakes in the interpretation of policies can cost considerably more than answering questions regarding policies.

The failure of one individual to correctly follow a policy or mistakes in application of an approved standard configuration can open the organization to potential exploits. The fallout from mistakes can be extremely expensive to manage, up to millions of dollars in total costs, in addition to damages to the organization's reputation and other assets.

It could also create audit findings and regulatory fines for non-compliance with requirements. While these consequences are not as serious or expensive as a security breach, the consequences can be costly and erode confidence in the information security team's competence.

Perform Reviews and Revisions Involving Key Stakeholders

The worst-case situation for an information security team developing a policy is to get to the end of the process and have it summarily rejected by the organization's stakeholders. This does occur and its consequences include wasted budget and embarrassment for the information security team as a whole. Some of the causes of this nightmare scenario include developing the information security policy in isolation from the rest of the organization or not having the right individuals from other parts of the organization on the policy team.

It is important to ensure that the policy review team contains the right membership. Make sure that the team has representation from major business areas and that they can express their thoughts and bring up issues during meetings. Remember, just because someone is extremely vocal doesn't mean that the individual speaks for the whole group.

Policy committee members that frequently request minor revisions may not identify significant issues with the policy that may delay or prevent its successful ratification.

The best mitigation strategies for preventing last-minute surprises during the policy review and ratification process is early and frequent reviews by stakeholders from influential or major business areas. These stakeholders often have the most to lose, might face considerable expenditures if a policy specifies unrealistic requirements for their business functions, or might be required to undertake expensive retrofitting of technologies. What might appear to be a trivial requirement might actually create a need to modify numerous application programs or negatively impact infrastructure performance.

Policy reviews should start with the first draft and be held at regular intervals throughout the development process. This strategy should be repeated for all revisions to high-level policy or new policies with the potential for significant change in the way the organization conducts its activities, such as BYOD or cloud computing.

Obtain Ratification and Release the Policy

In order for an information security policy to succeed, a consensus on its adoption needs to be obtained from the majority of organizational stakeholders. This is especially true for the influential and powerful stakeholders.

If these individuals are not in agreement with the new policy, they will find avenues to disparage or nullify the policy using their influence, political strategies, or other tactical maneuvers.

The frugal CISO needs to be front and center in promoting the ratification of any new information security policy. This means face-to-face meetings with security and technology stakeholders, the stakeholders' teams, and even the stakeholders' own managers. While these meetings might cost time and money, the ROI is gaining approval for the new policy, and potentially support for future security projects as well.

The CISO needs to be strongly associated with the policy. This is because executive management has delegated their authority for managing security-related issues to the CISO. It is vital that the frugal CISO assume a leadership role around all policy development. Policies are essentially the laws of the land for security issues and the frugal CISO must be intrinsically familiar with these policies. Some CISOs may allow the policy project manager to assume the leadership role during this phase of the policy initiatives. This may be cost effective for lower-level policies. However, it is often inappropriate for higher-level, high profile, or controversial policies.

The reception that the initial policies receive may set the tone for future interactions between the information security team and the rest of the organization. Rough waters around the adoption of a new information security policy can serve as an omen for a pattern of continuing conflicts between the team and the organization. This is an excellent time to correct any existing conflicts and create a fresh start.

Have a Formal Exception Process in Place

It is not possible to follow all policy items to the letter at all times. This can be true for a number of reasons. For example, older applications may not be flexible enough to be completely compliant because of their age or the use of legacy components. Another noncompliance situation may occur when an organization is waiting for a vendor to supply a patch or fix to resolve a policy issue. These are expected and normal reasons why 100% compliance with policies may not be obtainable. It can also result from policies created in isolation without appropriate input from business areas. These policies may create compliance problems from the start of their use.

It is safe to assume that with policy comes the necessity for exceptions to policy. It is preferable to have a formal process for requesting and approving policy exceptions. A process for the submission of written exception requests should be created in advance of the information security policy "going live." This acknowledges that the first need for an exception will likely occur shortly after the policy goes into effect.

In addition to having a formal exceptions policy, an exceptions committee needs to be identified as well. Exceptions meetings need to occur on a regularly scheduled basis and exceptions should require the approval of one or more managers within the organization. All exceptions must have a defined time frame, such as six months to a year, before they must come up for renewal again. The exception should require clear and detailed documentation. There should be an identified of each specific exception.

Open exceptions require tracking until resolved. Adding automation to the exception tracking process, such as the use of a tracking database, can reduce the cost and increase the accuracy of exception monitoring activities. Access to information regarding exceptions, especially open exceptions, should be restricted to specific information security staff and individuals directly involved in the exception. The information contained in open exceptions may provide details with the potential for exploitation.

Develop a Policy Rollout Plan and Awareness Campaign

After the ratification of the information security policy, the next step is an organizational rollout. Particularly, if the security team is relatively new or recently reorganized/refreshed, this can become an opportunity for the team to introduce itself to the organization. A specific security awareness campaign or series of campaigns needs to be planned around the new information security policy. Because not all security policies are pertinent to every individual, the rollout effort may choose to target the specific audiences for each category of policies, in addition to one overall effort to promote the general end-user policy.

Information Security Policy *Faux Pas*

A number of factors may restrict the overall effectiveness of an information security policy. Some policy *faux pas* occur in the initial design of the policy itself, such as an overly lengthy policy. Some policy issues occur as the policy evolves in an effort to improve policies by introducing new requirements to strengthen the organization's security posture. However, the new policy items may be difficult to impossible for the organization to comply with at that time based upon its current technical and resource capabilities. Policy *faux pas* detract from the overall perception of the effectiveness of the information security policy. Some common *faux pas* in the development and maintenance of information security policies include the following issues:

1. Policy *Faux Pas* 1: The Overly Long Policy
2. Policy *Faux Pas* 2: Policy Cannot Be Monitored or Enforced
3. Policy *Faux Pas* 3: Aspirational Policy

Policy Faux Pas *1: The Overly Long Policy*

Some information security policies are incredibly lengthy with forty to one hundred pages of content. An information security policy that lengthy is not a policy at all, but a *security tome*. These types of policies violate the basic premise that a policy is a short, one to three pages at most, high-level document. The tomes are the whole security policy hierarchy in one unwieldy document.

These policy documents mix policies, standards, procedures, and guidelines into one document. To add to the confusion created by mixing different components of the policy hierarchy, the document targets multiple audiences from technical specialists, such as firewall administrators, to regular end users. By creating these mammoth documents and requesting everyone read and understand them, the organization is assuring that the opposite will occur.

The driving force behind these information security policies "from hell" is most likely *checklist compliance*. This is an attempt to substitute compliance for actual security. The creation of these documents often coincides with a new compliance regulation or security law. These documents are the electronic equivalent of *shelfware* and rarely deliver much ROI in their creation.

Policy Faux Pas *2: Policy Cannot Be Monitored or Enforced*

Some policy items create problems because there is no mechanism to verify their compliance status. The organization may lack the technology or resources to effectively monitor and enforce policy statements. To avoid creation of a policy item lacking the potential for monitoring or enforcement, ask the following questions about any proposed policy item:

a. What method(s) could be used to verify compliance with the policy item, such as manual inspection, automated scanning tools, or audit logs?
b. If no automated monitoring mechanism is available, is it economically feasible to monitor compliance manually?
c. Is this a theoretical risk or have exploits been verified outside of a research laboratory?
d. What is the estimated annual cost of monitoring compliance with the policy item?
e. What is the value, in terms of risk reduction, of implementing the policy item?
f. Will this policy item assist the organization in achieving compliance with a specific regulatory requirement or law?
g. Are there currently any open audit findings related to the risks this policy item is designed to reduce?
h. Is this considered a common best practice in information security?
i. What is the real possibility of the risk associated with this policy item being realized within the organization's environment?

The answers to these questions offer a method to evaluate the costs and benefits of a proposed security policy objectively. This is one area where information security professionals are their own worst enemies. Policies associated with low-probability risks may create unnecessary conflicts and costs, especially for the IT folks.

An overly rigid security practitioner may insist upon a questionable (and expensive) policy item with little realization. If the only justification for a proposed policy item is a theoretical journal article, it may be a good idea to reexamine the issue. This can be a case of failure to pick the right battles. This battle ends up losing the war because it solidifies information security as creating unnecessary costs, being unreasonable, and inferring with the business.

Policy Faux Pas *3: Aspirational Policy*

Sometimes in an effort to increase the strength of the organization's security posture, smart information security practitioners make dumb mistakes. These practitioners usually possess a strong focus and actively work to maintain their skills by reading technology journals and visiting security research sites. The problem is that some excellent practitioners have limited real-world experience with production operations.

These individuals may successfully lobby for the inclusion of policies that may be aspirational in nature. Often, some of the risks these policies are designed to reduce have a low potential of occurrence and require extensive resources to implement. The bottom line is that aspirational policies have a very low ROI. The worst case of aspirational policy exists when implementing the necessary policy controls negatively affects business activities, such as increasing development costs or decreasing transactional performance. This contributes to business's frequent perception that information security practitioners "don't get it."

There are two possible strategies for avoiding the cost and potential conflicts that might emanate from insistence on aspirational security policies. The first strategy is providing security staff with a better understanding of production environments. Security staff should have the opportunity, on a rotating basis, to act as a liaison to production support groups. Another rotation might include a stint in a development team. These experiences might allow information security practitioners to assess the potential impact of proposed controls on operational environments.

The other strategy is to have the security practitioner estimate the total cost of implementing the proposed controls. While most security practitioners are proficient at estimating the total cost of security-related activities, practitioners without direct experience in application development or support may not be familiar with these categories of costs. This was evident when an extremely senior security professional suggested that retrofitting the requirements of a policy change would have no cost impact if performed concurrent with other code maintenance activities. He failed to recognize that the additional code changes, testing, and other activities would create additional, likely unbudgeted costs, and push other business-related maintenance requests off the release schedule.

Best and Cost-Efficient Practices in Information Security Policy

Certain practices make policy creation and revisions easier and cheaper to do. These practices decrease the costs of a policy over its life and increase their effectiveness in promoting appropriate behaviors that support a strong security posture. I collected this list of *best, smart, recommended* practices over the last decade from working on multiple information policy development initiatives, creating policies, working on policy review committees, and implementing policies within business areas. Using these practices can assist an information security team in maturing its existing policy management program.

Strong Version Control

Policies should follow recommended practices in document control and have a policy version number. The policy version number is more than just an administrative convenience and a way to maintain a version history of each policy. The version number identifies the version of the policy that was in force at a specific time. Workers terminated for policy violation can potentially sue and claim that they were unaware of a policy (otherwise known as the "nobody told me" defense) if older and out-of-date policies were available on different organizational websites. During legal proceedings, it can be important to determine which policies were in effect during an incident. It is also visible evidence that the organization regularly reviews and revises its information security policies based upon the current threat and regulatory landscape.

Policy Review Committee

It is more efficient, in terms of costs and time, to establish a standing policy review committee to evaluate, revise, and ratify the initial policies and all subsequent policies and revisions to the policy documents for a specified time interval. Committee membership should be refreshed from time to time as members' roles change or individuals move on to other organizations. Some organizations choose to rotate committee membership among a group of individuals. The policy review committee should contain representation from across the organization, especially key stakeholders or business areas. The committee should include representation from business areas as well as technology.

It is important that the role of the information security team members on the committee be as facilitators or consultants. The role of the committee should be to discuss policies by evaluating the costs, benefits, and potential impacts on the organization that are associated with a specific policy. Out of these discussions, the committee should request revisions to policy verbiage, make requests for additional information on risk issues, agree to ratify a policy, or reject a policy as currently written. The policy review committee should never be a "rubber stamp" for the information security team. This review committee is appointed by administrative authority to provide control and direction regarding information systems security polices for the entire organization. The review committee's responsibilities include the following:

- Oversee the development, revision, and maintenance of the information security policies, including security policies and related recommended guidelines, standards, procedures, and technical directives
- Ensure related regulatory compliance requirements are addressed and met, such as privacy, security, and administrative regulations associated with federal and state laws
- May oversee the process of requests for formal policy exceptions
- May recommend the creation of new policies or other policy-related documents based upon emerging or existing risks

The most important qualification for membership on the policy review committee is a deep commitment to security and seeing its role as beneficial to enhancing the organization's activities, rather than restricting them.

Regular Reviews

Information security policies need regular review to remain effective and reduce costs associated with remediating security incidents.

Rarely do high-level policies change; however, the more technically oriented portions of the policy hierarchy require updates to remain current with technology and the threat landscape.

Determine Policy Ownership

Each information security policy should have specific identified owner, author, and executive sponsor. Defined policy ownership acknowledges information security's responsibility for updating and maintaining information security policies. In most cases, the identified owner of the information security policies will be the CISO or the individual currently responsible for the organization's overall information security functions. Providing an author offers a point of contact for individuals with questions regarding a policy.

Some organizations do not regularly review or revise polices. The result may be information security policies that are so outdated that the author often is no longer with the organization. A review of all policies for dated references should be included as part of a annual policy refresh planning process. Information security policies need to have an executive sponsor, such as a board member or C-level executive, who "blesses" the policy set. This executive sponsor serves as demonstrable proof to all stakeholders that the organization takes information security seriously.

Determining When a New Policy Is Needed

The annual policy refresh and planning process should have the objective of identifying the need for new policies, as well as revisions to existing policies. However, sometimes the need for a new policy may be driven by risks from emerging technology trends, such as BYOD or cloud computing, or new regulatory compliance requirements. Often, these risks need to be addressed immediately instead of waiting for the next annual policy planning cycle.

There is one more motivation for the creation of a new information security policy—the occurrence of a security breach or a *near miss* cyber security incident. These events will often create the impetus for the fast-track development of a policy to outline appropriate use of a technology.

Policy Management Applications

Some organizations still distribute information security policies in hard-copy form. On my first day on an information security team, I remember receiving a set of five thick books that looked like they had been typed on an IBM Selectric[2] typewriter. However, few organizations print policy books because information security policy has become too dynamic to make it economically viable to print and distribute policy in that manner. Some organizations briefly experimented with CD-ROM distribution, but that also quickly faded away. The most common way of distributing an information security policy and its supporting documents is via an organizational intranet site.

Over the last few years, automated solutions for managing information security have emerged as a popular trend, especially for larger organizations. There are different solutions to automating policy management, which range from general document management applications to highly specialized policy management solutions, including:

1. Simple file hierarchy and spreadsheet/general database
2. General document management/version control software
3. Automated policy management solutions

Simple File Hierarchy and Spreadsheets/General Database

This solution just places the policy in a simple file structure that mirrors the logical hierarchy of the policies, starting with the root (highest level) information security policy. To add document tracking, a spreadsheet or simple database is created to provide information about versions, file name, author, file path, and other metadata. The spreadsheet entries may include a link to the current policy document.

This solution may work for smaller organizations with a relatively uncomplicated policy hierarchy. The main advantage of this solution is that it is cheap, easy to understand, and requires no special training to implement. It also has significant drawbacks. It has no built-in version control features. It depends on the policy administrator to maintain accurate and current information about the status and location of each file. It is easily corrupted by human errors.

General Document Management/Version Control Software

Document management/version control software is a general software application designed to manage and track changes to documents, software programs, website components, and other collections of digital information. Each change is identified by code or level, which is automatically updated for each subsequent revision. Each revision contains metadata, such as a time stamp and the individual who made the change.

Operations can be performed on revision levels, such as comparisons, restoration, and merges. The use of document management software offers a way to organize and control revisions, especially in a collaborative environment where a team of people may work on the same files.

Many organizations where document management is employed for policy management already utilize the same application across the enterprise. The incremental cost of managing policy documents is therefore minimal for extending the licensing to cover additional files or a new application instance.

In addition to the potential lower cost of implementation, this category of application supports collaboration by offering check-in/check-out functions to prevent updates from conflicting with each other. However, these applications do not offer specific functionality to support the unique needs of policy management, such as providing users with a mechanism for acknowledging reading and understanding of policies. If this functionality is required, it is necessary to provide the acknowledgment feature through another application or create it in-house through an application.

Specialized Policy Management Solutions

Policy management is a time-consuming task. A specialized policy management solution adds automation to the workflow by supporting the policy life cycle, such as editing, updating, version control, approval, and publishing of documents. Features provided by popular policy management solutions include a customizable intranet portal with multiple views based on user roles, quizzing features to test policy knowledge, and policy acknowledgment functionality to manage user acceptance of policy documents for compliance requirements.

Some policy management solutions provide complete audit trails of all policy management activities.

Policy management solutions are often best suited to larger, highly regulated, or complex organizations because of their high cost. Often, these solutions may require specialized skills to implement and maintain that add considerable overhead to the policy management function, often on a continuing basis.

In larger organizations, decreased costs associated with policy management, such as tracking user policy acknowledgments, may offset the cost of the software and its associated expenses.

Policy management solutions may be part of larger governance application suites that include functions, such as third-party risk management, enforcement, and exception tracking, as well as offering automation for other security tasks. These application suites represent significant capital and operational expenditures for organizations and their acquisition may involve a lengthy process.

Going Naked (No Information Security Policies)

Some organizations choose to proceed with no or limited information security policies. While this occurs less frequently today, it does still occasionally occur. However, with the majority of the states having some type of data privacy or breach reporting laws, it is more difficult for an organization to assume this strategy without risk. In most situations, an organization might chose to create a bare-bones policy that just states that the organization does have an information security policy and not much more. Some of the reasons that organizations decide to adopt this strategy include:

1. They view it as way to save the expense of developing an information security policy, and perhaps funding a specific information security function within their organization.
2. They believe (wrongly) that if their organization has no explicit policies, they cannot be audited against them.
3. They simply do not know better or do not see themselves as having any specific security risks.
4. Their executives believe that they are lucky and will not become the victim of a cyber attacker or identified as part of a

regulatory audit. Some organizations may be comfortable taking their chances with the potential for cyber attacks; to paraphrase the famous line from *Dirty Harry*,[3] "Do I feel lucky?"
5. They feel they have nothing to lose, which is often the case with start-up companies.

Unfortunately, the "naked" strategy, while it might create some cost savings in the short term, can be extremely costly, for both the organization and potential executives, when things go wrong, such as:

- A security breach occurs.
- An audit is required.
- A regulatory agency gets involved.

The lack of an information security policy does not impede audits. If there is no existing policy, auditors will use best practices and generally recommended IT control mechanisms to evaluate the organization.

This can be a considerably higher bar than might have been required if an information security policy had been in place that was customized to the organization's specific risk profile. The cost of remediating or contesting audit findings can be substantial. One case with which I am familiar resulted in almost half a million dollars in legal fees, and the organization ended up conceding and accepting the audit findings and a fine in the end.

Audit and regulatory agencies see the absence of a formal information security policy or a very scant policy as a potential red flag that the organization's executive management is not concerned or does not care much about security in general. This might have the result of making the audit team more vigilant in performance of the engagement. This might involve increasing the amount of substantive testing rather than using compliance (observational) testing procedures. This could increase the costs associated with the audit substantially.

If a data breach should occur, the economic consequences could potentially be grave for the organization, executives, board, and potentially the technical staff. Increasingly, new case law has held the organization, and even its employees, liable for failure to address security risks or provide appropriate controls to mitigate security breaches when they do occur. These cases have found an organization and its staff liable for security incidents based upon a failure to practice due care, negligence, and breaches of fiduciary duty.

Regulatory bodies, such as the Federal Trade Commission (FTC), can assess significant fines and require costly privacy/security audits for up to twenty years after a single cyber security breach. The severity of these fines and associated costs may be mitigated by tangible evidence that the organization made best efforts to promote security within the organization. One of the most visible proofs of this commitment to security by executive management is a well-developed information security policy hierarchy. The absence of information security policies may act as a red flag to the courts and regulatory bodies that executive management has not performed the appropriate level of due diligence in regard to the security of the organization. The outcome may be a magnification of the costs assigned by the courts and regulators.

This is in addition to remediation and other expenses associated directly will the cyber event. The organization's assets could be wiped out. The organization might cease to exist in its current state. Its loss in reputation might also doom the organization. While some organizations have thrived after a cyber breach, others have not, such as CardSystems Solutions.[4]

Some organizations take another avenue to avoiding information security policy development by "faking it" in a way. The organization's representative downloads an information security policy from the Internet and uses it to get around any regulatory or state data security laws. This is an example of *checklist compliance*. The primary symptom of this is a mammoth information security policy that has very little to do with the actual security practices of the organization.

Unfortunately, this strategy may result in cost savings in the short term, but can be extremely costly, for the organization and potential executives, when things go wrong, similar to having no explicit written policy. In the case of an occurrence of a security breach, audit, or regulatory review, the organization will need to substantiate implementation of the information security policy. Often the organization cannot do this because it lacks the people, processes, and technology to do so. This might be an instance where no information security policy may be better than having a fictitious one. The failure to create and use an information security policy is negligence. Courts and regulatory agencies could construe a fictitious policy as fraud.

One way for the frugal CISO or other security practitioner to point this out diplomatically is to ask specific questions about some policy items and how a security objective is accomplished. For example, "Where do you perform the disk degaussing process?" if the policy item specifies using a degaussing device to permanently remove all traces of magnetic data from a disk storage device. Since fewer and fewer organizations have such devices, this might prompt a review of all policy items and the removal of inaccurate information. The question as to whether an organization requires a specific, complete, and valid information security policy can be answered this way: "Only if the organization, its executive management, or staff have any assets that they prefer not to lose."

Major Policy Renovations

No matter how well-constructed, many information security polices will require revision at some point in their life cycle. This occurs for a number of reasons. One is that the policy was overly aspirational from the beginning. What sounded like a reasonable idea might have been infeasible or become that way as complexity and volume of information increases within the organization.

Many current policies predate the "renaissance" of information security that started in earnest with the rise of the Internet, electronic commerce, and increasingly skilled cyber attackers. Back in the day, information security policies were documents printed in books that received only minimal attention outside of IT audits and a few stakeholders. It was also an environment with considerably fewer regulatory requirements.

Policies written a decade or two ago, may not have considered the impact that technical innovations would have on information security as a whole. Often, the organization has expanded either in size or into different business areas since the information security policy was implemented. Whatever the reason, when the high-level information security policy needs revision, it is a big project. Big projects in security can get expensive, and those expenses can increase if missteps occur that necessitate going back to the drawing board and restarting the process at some point during the project's duration.

A common driver for information security is the changing regulatory environment faced by many organizations. It is difficult for most organizations to avoid dealing with at least some type of compliance requirements, such as industry sector, governmental, or other regulatory body.

In addition to facing a dramatically enhanced regulatory landscape, older security policies may conflict with emerging societal changes. Consumers, employees, and other stakeholders have increased their expectations surrounding the security and privacy of their personal information.

Many in these groups of stakeholders also expect to have more options in how, when, and where they receive their information. This is part of the growing trend in the consumerization of IT. In IT consumerization, the consumer market adopts technology products first, such as in the case of the iPhone, and then extends the use of these products into business and government sectors. The appearance of consumer markets as the principal driver of technology innovation is a noteworthy shift away from the decades-old model in which technical innovation emerged initially in the business sector.

Renovating an existing information security policy can be a fresh start for the frugal CISO and the information security team. It should be looked on as a type of "do over" with the objective of creating a policy document that endures as long or longer than its predecessor.

However, with this new iteration, it is even more critical to avoid falling into common policy traps that often plague the initial information security policy, such as:

- Not doing sufficient background research on the organization's structure, current business strategies and areas, culture, past audit findings, regulatory compliance requirements, IT systems, and long-term strategies
- Not getting sufficient involvement and support from key organizational stakeholders
- Not getting first drafts out for review early in the policy development process
- Not considering the economic and performance costs of some required security controls dictated in the policies
- Not evaluating the impact of proposed policy controls on legacy systems

- Failure to include all regulatory requirements, including federal, industry sector, and state, in revised policies
- Porting policy items that were aspirational when the policy was initially created and still are

Of course, the actual test of the mettle of a policy will be its endurance over time. However, a policy developed to evade common pitfalls of policy revision will be more likely to last until significant shifts in the business, technical, or regulatory space require another round of revisions.

Emerging Policy Areas

It is better to address emerging technology areas with policy sooner rather than later. Sometimes, even the frugal CISO silently hopes that some new technical trend or product category will just fade away. Unfortunately, that is rarely the case.

Sometimes there is a belief that by not directing a specific security policy at an issue, the organization can avoid being mired in complicated details. However, just the opposite may be true. By not having a policy that encourages the secure inclusion of these technologies in the workplace, workers may go underground while using them with sensitive files and create bigger risks.

A good example of an emerging risk area is BYOD. In BYOD, workers utilize their own mobile electronic devices in the workplace to perform business and personal tasks. The BYOD trend began under the IT radar in many organizations. Many organizations have now embraced BYOD as a way to cut costs, while increasing worker productivity and satisfaction.

This is an example of consumerization of IT trends, which includes not only BYOD, but other emerging technologies, such as cloud services and applications such as cloud storage and social media. These trends are driven by reasonably cheap, accessible, and ubiquitous technologies that increase flexibility by allowing individuals to work anytime, anywhere.

By endorsing BYOD and other technologies associated with IT consumerization, organizations can benefit from these innovations, while developing a strategy to reduce security risks, financial liability exposure, and operational chaos. The first step to successfully managing the myriad risks associated with these emerging technologies is creating specific security policies to codify their use. A policy-driven strategy allows the balancing of security risks with the benefits of BYOD and other types of IT consumerization when combined with a solutions infrastructure. This reduces potential costs associated with risks, such as legal actions and breaches, by managing sensitive organizational data and limiting liabilities on personally owned devices. In the past, there have been different strategies for handling new technologies, including:

1. The river called "Denial"
2. Toothless policies
3. Technology without written policies
4. Combining policy and technology

River Called "Denial"

Under this scenario, the technology is used in a covert manner initially. Its use is ignored, despite being common knowledge among workers and management. Management fails to acknowledge use of the technology or its risks. "The river called Denial" strategy leads to a wink-wink tacit acceptance of an insecure practice with potential exposure of sensitive information.

Denial is a delaying tactic for the most part. The problem with denial is that by the time the problem receives attention, a significant amount of risk may have occurred. Often, the impetus for addressing the issue is a security crisis or scary *near miss* situation. It is usually more expensive to fix at this point because the fix requires expediting to manage a crisis situation.

Toothless Policies

A policy with no provision for monitoring and enforcement has no teeth. Most people might ignore a toothless dog and they do the same thing with toothless policy. A good example of a toothless policy at a government agency occurred in the mid-2000s when the employee of a government agency took home an external drive containing millions of individuals' personally identifiable information (PII) against organizational policy. The device subsequently created a breach. The episode was a public relations nightmare for the agency. The agency ultimately paid $20 million to the victims, in addition to the direct costs associated with handling the breach.

The toothless policy often just delays a need to create monitoring and enforcement mechanisms. Like the denial approach, by the time the problem receives attention, a significant amount of risk may have occurred. Often, the impetus for addressing the issue is a security crisis or scary *near miss* situation. It is usually more expensive to fix at this point because the fix must be expedited to manage a crisis.

The toothless policy may actually create greater risks and could potentially be more expensive to fix than even the denial tactic. In the case of the toothless strategy, the organization acknowledges the potential for risk and detrimental consequences by having a policy, but does not do anything to support it. The consequences of a security incident, especially a significant breach, could be fines, regulatory sanctions, and punitive court judgments. On top of these costs, the organization will bear any direct expenditure associated with a security incident should it occur. It is usually more expensive to implement a security monitoring and enforcement solution after a crisis or near miss because executive management may want to expedite the process to avoid future security incidents.

Technology without Written Policy

An organization may implement security controls to reduce the risks associated with an emerging technology, but fail to issue a formal written policy. This may occur for several reasons. One is that the organization's executive management does not believe that a separate policy is required because they think that existing written security policy is sufficiently broad to cover the new technology.

However, some technologies and their associated trends are, by their nature, transformative enough that existing policies may be insufficient. Some technologies, such as BYOD, social networking, and cloud computing, will create significant, fundamental changes in the enterprise, according to Gartner 2013 IT trend predictions.[5]

These technological revolutions can potentially transform the way organizations do business, in ways similar to how the emergence of the Internet in the late 1990s/early 2000s changed the way we work and live. They also bring with them myriad risks that organizations will need to manage through both policy and technology.

Combining Policy and Technology

The "old standard" for managing the risks associated with emerging and ubiquitous technologies is recognition of the risk and recommendations for its secure usage through issuance of a formal written policy combined with control mechanisms to mitigate its risks. This combination approach holds the most potential for making users aware of both the benefits and security risks associated with a technology. It provides tangible evidence of appropriate due diligence by executive management. It may offer the most effective strategy because it may prevent security incidents and breaches from occurring, thereby avoiding unnecessary expenditure. It may diminish costs by allowing the information security team to consider various security solutions and implement their selection without any additional costs to expedite the process.

Policy Grandfathering

The organization may not be able to implement all items included in an information security policy quickly, easily, or in a cost-efficient manner. This is especially true of a category of application known as legacy applications. Legacy applications are older systems that often utilize older languages, operating systems, platforms, and techniques than current technology. Many legacy applications still meet critical business needs. Some legacy applications may eventually undergo conversion to newer technologies, but this is not always the case. Older COBOL[6]-based mainframe applications may have software life cycles that span several decades. Older technologies may interface with new technologies, such as web applications using middleware components.

Many security tools do not provide coverage for legacy applications. For example, most software vulnerability scanning tools do not work on a mainframe environment or source codes, such as COBOL. Even if scanning tools ran in these legacy environments, different vulnerabilities and risk landscapes occur within the legacy environment. Therefore, many of the security policy controls might be inappropriate for legacy applications.

Even if it were possible to apply the same policy controls to legacy environments, applying these protection mechanisms might have detrimental effects on performance of the applications, especially mission-critical or core application systems. Retrofitting new policy requirements, especially on older legacy applications with large code bases, might prove extremely costly and time consuming. In the vast majority of cases, verifying or enforcing some policies may be virtually impossible and possibly create audit issues similar to those caused by aspirational policies.

If the organization has a number of older or legacy applications as part of its software portfolio, it is recommended that at least one member of the information security team have some familiarity with these systems, the platforms that support them, and the specific risks associated with their use. If this is not possible, the information security team needs to identify a contact within the organization to consult with on legacy systems security issues.

There are several approaches to handle possible incompatibilities between the new security policy item and legacy applications. One is to grandfather all legacy applications under the older policy or to require compliance to policy only for applications created after a specific date, or create a category of applications, such as mainframe applications, that are not covered by the policy.

Another potential option to manage the legacy system issue is through the formal exception process. While this is an option, it is a misuse of the exception process. Exceptions are not meant to be indefinite in duration. An exception could be an option for a legacy application nearing the end of its production life, such as an application system with a planned decommissioning date within two years. However, many legacy systems remain vital workhorses for revenue generation, so it might be a poor precedent to use an exception for this purpose.

Besides grandfathering or exempting legacy applications from the policy, you can require appropriate compensating controls. Compensating controls reduce the risk of exploitation of existing or potential control vulnerabilities.

There exists a potential hidden landmine for the frugal CISO, if information security insists on applying inappropriate policy controls to legacy applications. Often, legacy systems provide a significant revenue channel with a low risk of exposure for many organizations. To insist on implementing costly controls where there is no need for the sake of consistent policy application can be an example of winning a battle and losing the war of support at the executive level.

Often, some highly technical security practitioners who are committed to best practices lose sight of the basic wisdom that the cost of policy controls should not exceed their potential return on increasing the organization's security posture. It is more unfortunate when they persuade a CISO to back them in their insistence on low return on security investment (ROSI) policy controls. The frugal CISO should ask a couple of questions before insisting on implementation:

- Can the risks this control will reduce be quantified or can a specific example of occurrence be documented?
- What are the potential costs associated with implementing this policy control (labor, software, performance, lost opportunities for revenue enhancement, such as implementing other features to increase market share)?

If the costs significantly outweigh any potential benefits, grandfathering the legacy might prove a better course of action for both information security and the rest of the organization.

Information Security Policy: Final Words with a Cost-Saving Checklist

An organization's information security policy is the foundation of its program and a validation of its executive management's commitment to maintaining a strong security posture to guard its critical assets. However, many blunders may occur on the journey to developing an actionable and effective set of information security policies. The following is a checklist of questions to evaluate the potential for ROSI of policy controls:

- Are all policy items capable of being monitored and enforced using existing security controls or controls currently available in the technology marketplace?
- Does the policy contain aspirational items that may not be currently attainable by the organization or within a reasonable time frame, such as one to three years?
- Does the policy provide coverage for all mandatory regulatory requirements, such as governmental, industry-sector, and state data privacy laws?
- Do security policies address all issues identified in the current threat landscape?
- Do security policies consider risks created by emerging technologies, such as BYOD, cloud computing, virtualization, and social media?
- Is the tone and content of the information security policy in line with current and planned business and technology strategies of the organization?
- Is the information security policy complementary to the organization's unique culture?
- Does the information security policy address emerging technologies or is there a plan to address these issues in future policy revisions?
- Does the policy include provisions for addressing the security of legacy applications?
- How will the information security policies be distributed to the organization?
- Is there a strategy for revision control for the information security policy documents?
- Will the organization implement an information security policy review board? If so, what functions will it perform and how will its membership be determined?

Endnotes

1. Lloyd was sentenced to forty-one months in prison, but the case was later overturned on a technicality.
2. Old style IBM office typewriter popular in the 1960s and 1970s.

3. *Dirty Harry* is a 1971 crime movie starring Clint Eastwood. The movie's famous quote is spoken by Eastwood, "You've got to ask yourself one question: 'Do I feel lucky?'"
4. CardSystems Solutions was a credit card processing company that experienced a breach in 2005 of 40 million. The company had been storing unencrypted data that it was contractually obligated to purge. The company was acquired and ceased to exist as an independent company in 2008.
5. http://www.trackvia.com/blog/technology/gartner-idc-name-consumerization-of-it-among-top-2013-trends
6. COBOL is one of the oldest programming languages, released in 1959. It is an acronym for COmmon Business-Oriented Language. Today, it is found most often on mainframe application systems.

9

"Is This Necessary?"

Do We Need to Do Everything We Are Currently Doing?

When my sister-in-law moved from Mexico to Massachusetts, it was an unusually warm January day (60 degrees). I took her shopping to buy winter clothes. Her response to being inundated with winter gear was, "Is this necessary?" and the next more seasonable day (mid-30s), she got her answer. I do not think we ask the question, "Is this necessary?" enough. We continue to do something because we have always done it and autopilot takes over.

One way to reduce costs is to reduce the overall amount of work, if that work yields little security value. This is similar to zero-base budgeting. It starts by reviewing all security tasks, controls, solutions, and procedures to determine their contribution to the overall security posture.

Why Some Security Processes Endure beyond Their Expiration Date

Some security processes hang around for a variety of reasons and may outlast their original purpose. Usually, the "why" of a process is answered by "because we have always done it this way." This always reminds me of an old joke I read somewhere years ago. A husband asks his wife why she always cuts the ends off the ham and she responds, "because that's the way my mother did it." Then he asks his mother-in-law why she always cut the ends off the ham and she responds, "because that's the way my mother did it." Finally, he asks his wife's grandmother why she always cut the ends off the ham and she responds, "because I did not have a big enough pan." There are a number of reasons this may occur, including:

1. It has always been done this way (failure to question existing controls).
2. "Invented here" syndrome (proprietary ownership of controls).
3. "Zombie" controls.

It Has Always Been Done This Way (Failure to Question Existing Controls)

Often, security teams continue to do something because it has always been done. When a member of the group, usually a new addition to the team, inquires why something is done in a specific way, that individual may risk the ire of the team. This can be truer of teams with close relationships or teams that have been together for a long period. While maintaining strong team relationships is a good thing, there exists the potential for suppressing the questioning of existing processes and inhibiting innovation. This can limit the potential for maturation of the information security team. It can also create frustration for new team members who feel like their opinions fall on deaf ears. This can possibly create costly turnover from a continuing pattern of newer team members leaving the group. This can stifle innovative thinking even further in the team.

"Invented Here" Syndrome (Proprietary Ownership of Controls)

A team member that develops a control may fight to maintain its existence. This individual may convince the rest of the team of the criticality of the control. In some cases, this individual may intimidate the rest of the team from questioning the purpose or validity of a specific control.

Early in my career, I worked in an accounting function. I remember questioning an annual control function that required reconciling three reports against each other. The effort took three weeks in total and consumed three resources from three departments. There had never been any variances found between the three reports. After a little research, it was determined that all three reports used exactly the same data and were the same report with minor formatting differences. By eliminating this task, all three departments regained three weeks of effort to apply to other activities.

The individual in charge of this process complained about the termination of the control. Further research determined that this individual had advocated and created this control. He terrorized his coworkers to maintain it. Eventually, senior management moved this individual to another group for a variety of long-standing behavioral issues.

This is an example of a control with proprietary ownership, which should always undergo investigation for its effectiveness. The primary reason to question this category of controls is lack of vetting for cost- or risk-reduction effectiveness prior to implementation. A red flag is that the support for the control emanates from one or two individuals who remain solely responsible for it. Any questions regarding the control meet with aggressive resistance from the control "owner." Another possible symptom of proprietary ownership of a control is that the team does not use the information derived from the control.

"Zombie" Controls

Some security controls are seldom questioned regarding their effectiveness. Often, they were part of the original system or have existed for a long time. One characteristic of these controls is they run without any human intervention. I refer to these as "zombie" controls because they would continue, even if the security team failed to exist.

However, these controls' ability to continue to run does not necessarily mean they continue their effectiveness in risk reduction. The nature of risk changes as new technologies and new exploits evolve. However, security team members may not scrutinize these controls because of their long history and desire not to antagonize other team members.

In addition, there may be concerns regarding what could potentially turn up during a review of the system and its controls. If a deeper analysis finds issues regarding either the security of the system or its controls, the practitioner may be reticent to bring them to light. Sometimes, the "messenger" may have concerns regarding a reaction to opening a potentially serious problem.

Most information security practitioners who have had the experience of uncovering severe risk issues around an application or business process can attest to how uncomfortable it can be to bring these issues to executive management. This is often a complex situation. Resolving the issues makes the organization more secure. In the short term, the investigation and possible remediation means costly, often unbudgeted expenditures and some embarrassment for those involved. The result improves the organization by preventing the situation from much more devastating potential exploitation later. Many major security breaches might have been prevented by questioning of ineffective controls.

Team Stagnation and Lack of Control Innovation

Without question, the information security team stagnates and remains stuck indefinitely in the same level of maturation. Symptoms of team stagnation include overwhelming *team think* and might include the following:

- Reticence of team members to question existing processes or controls
- Extremely negative reactions to new ideas, especially those promoted by newer team members
- Limited relationships among security team members and other information security practitioners external to the group, even those from other organizational risk or technology teams
- Belief that internally developed solutions are superior to other control applications created by other groups or even commercial security vendors
- Failure to support or adopt new organizational security controls with the rationalization that they will fail or fade away over time
- Desire to maintain security control silos that are separate from the rest of the organization
- Us-against-them attitude that pervades team activities and interactions with other groups

Some security executives may perceive some of these behaviors as team loyalty. However, when viewed all together, they may represent a toxic type of *groupthink* that may lead to stagnation of the team. The information security team suffering from stagnation may fail to question or review whether current controls remain sufficient to manage the changing threat landscape faced by the organization. They may reject all external control alternatives without much evaluation of their potential for improving the security posture or reducing the total costs of security.

A good example was a team that developed a homegrown security solution that was ahead of its time in the functionality it provided. Other groups developed similar solutions with the net consequence of creating isolated silos of security data with no mechanism to view an aggregated picture of the organization's overall security posture. Eventually, an organizational solution was adopted with the capability to manage all the organizational information from a single viewpoint. The group continued to insist that its homegrown solution was superior to the integrated solution and still depended upon it for the majority of its tasks.

While innovation often may have its seeds within one group, then germinate and spread throughout the organization with the outcome being a stronger security posture for the organization, this requires an open and objective team attitude.

Another information security team in the organization looked both internally and externally for innovations in security technology. The team is an early adopter of new control technologies and actively seeks out vendor solutions. If commercial options fail to meet their specific requirements, they will develop sophisticated in-house solutions that they freely share with other teams. They have a reputation for providing objective feedback on the security solutions they have implemented to assist other teams in their purchasing and development decisions. This security team is highly influential in determining the information security strategy of the organization.

Avoiding Team Stagnation: Encourage and Support Questioning

The critical success factor in avoiding team stagnation is a frugal chief information security officer (CISO). The frugal CISO needs to create a culture that encourages questioning. In order to promote a learning organization, staff members need to feel free to question current processes in order to improve them and bring innovative thinking to the team. This is not as easy as it seems for teams already in the grasp of stagnation.

While some may view stagnation as a bad situation, the individuals in its grip may feel comfortable and secure because everything feels safe and familiar. If the information security team members feel that they have the best controls imaginable and the systems for which they are responsible are safe, it is not easy to shake that belief. Questioning has the potential to create change. Change is uncomfortable and difficult.

To evoke real change, the frugal CISO might want to adopt the leadership style of the late General George Patton to initiate such a paradigm shift in the information security team. General Patton was famous for his hands-on direct style, which included two basic leadership concepts:

1. Always lead from the front.
2. Lead by example.

One potential option is for the frugal CISO to initiate a series of control reviews. The objective of the control review is to offer the team an opportunity to determine what is currently going right and what controls might be refreshed to better manage the current threat environment and emerging technology risks, such as mobile devices and cloud computing. The overall goal is to optimize expenditures for security controls by identifying what works, what needs tweaking for new risks, and what controls need retirement.

The frugal CISO might lead from the front by facilitating the initial series of meetings and creating a series of teams to review and recommend changes in the current security controls portfolio. Membership on these teams should be considered an opportunity for team members. If possible, team members should not review controls for which they are responsible or developed to ensure complete objectivity.

Red Flags for Potentially Ineffective Controls

There are a number of red flags to identify possibly ineffective security controls. These controls may not be cost effective in performing their security control objectives. This can occur for a number of reasons.

1. The control was developed for a different operational environment than the one in which it is currently deployed.
2. Control results are not recorded or tracked.
3. Control variances or anomalies are not investigated.
4. The control is not utilized in the resolution of operational problems.
5. The control's results are not reviewed as part of the operational cycle by staff.
6. No staff member can effectively explain the purpose of the control or the results created by it.

7. The control is negatively affecting performance or effectiveness of the system(s) with which it is associated.
8. A cost–benefit analysis of the control was not undertaken prior to its creation or implementation.
9. The unit cost of running or managing the control exceeds the value of the asset(s) it protects.
10. The control has not been assessed for effectiveness for a period of five or more years against its security requirements as part of continuing due diligence activities.
11. The control may be affected by emerging technologies, such as wireless technologies or cloud computing.
12. There exists a potential mismatch between the control type and the target it is supposed to secure, such as a manual control for an automated process.
13. The control creates higher-than-average costs for maintenance, patching, or licensing fees.
14. The control can be easily defeated by casual users.
15. Multiple instances of control failures have been reported.
16. The control must be layered with another control to sufficiently secure assets, such as layering of multiple antimalware products on user desktops.
17. The control performs the same security function as a number of general IT controls.
18. A software-based control is no longer under vendor support or requires an expensive upgrade to continue in use.

Evaluating the Current Value of Existing Security Controls

One way to avoid the perpetuation of "zombie" controls is to maintain an inventory of all security mechanisms and their control objectives. Periodically, this inventory needs to be evaluated to determine the continued effectiveness and efficiency of each control.

The control sorting system has three possible outcomes for each control:

1. Keep (Continue to perform.)
2. Toss (Terminate, because it has no real security benefit.)
3. Replace (This is still a control objective, but the current mechanism is insufficient.)

By periodically reviewing controls, we can identify ineffective ones and target those controls for elimination or replacement. Some collateral benefits of this process include maintaining a current inventory of controls and identifying controls with the potential for reuse in other areas.

Performing a Security Controls Inventory

Performing regular self-assessments of all existing security controls is an important means of discovering inappropriate or ineffective security controls and their related procedures. The security controls inventory may be performed by the security team or by contractors, depending on the staff availability or budget. The objective of the control inventory is to ensure that all existing security controls offer adequate protection against threats and provide cost-effective security of organizational assets.

Appendix F contains a sample security control matrix based upon the fields listed below.

1. Control Name
2. General IT Control (Y/N)
3. Asset Being Protected
4. Vendor (H/W)
5. Vendor (S/W)
6. Support Agreement in Place
7. Preventive/Detective/Corrective/Hybrid Control
8. Location
9. Automated/Manual
10. Logs (Y/N)
11. Implemented Date or Year
12. Compliance Regulation Use
13. Protects Personally Identifiable Information (PII)
14. Protects Intellectual Property (IP)
15. Related Policy/Standard/Guideline/Procedure/Technical Directive
16. Contact Name and Information
17. Last Reviewed/Reviewer
18. Failures or Errors Reported (Text Comments)

19. Planned Replaced (Date/New Control Name)
20. Decommissioned Date

After completion of the initial security controls inventory, its input may become the basis for a continuous controls inventory under which existing controls receive periodic reassessments and addition of new controls. Decommissioned security controls will eventually drop off the active inventory onto a controls history inventory.

Depending on the information security team's resources, the controls inventory may exist in a simple spreadsheet format or be maintained in a database management system with a web front end for viewing and editing.

Finding the "Sweet Spot" for Controls

Without an effective control portfolio, an organization is more susceptible to security breaches than with adequate and effective controls. Just adding more controls will initially boost the organization's security posture significantly. However, at some point, each new control added is less incrementally effective in increasing the organization's overall security. Security controls, like many other forms of investment, demonstrate the *Law of Diminishing Returns*. The Law of Diminishing Returns states that resources added after a certain level of performance is achieved will be less effective in increasing performance and will eventually cause a decline in effectiveness. The information security team is spending more money, but getting no benefit from the additional expenditures. Most controls at some point exhibit the Law of Diminishing Returns, where continuing to add resources actually hinders an effort, such as adding too many people to a team decreases performance as the team members get in each other's way.

Maximize the Value of IT Controls

A way to get the "most bang for the buck" is to focus on a set of strong general IT controls that support most security control needs and compliance requirements, rather than implement security mechanisms in silos for specific compliance or security needs. A potential solution to expensive single-purpose controls might involve implementing broad control categories aimed at securing classes of information based upon an organization's data classification groups, such as highly confidential, personally identifiable (PI) information, or personal health information. This approach could provide coverage for up to 90% of the organization's data.

Special-Purpose Controls

The remaining controls inventory could target specific regulatory requirements that exist beyond these general IT controls, such as two-factor authentication required for remote access of some Payment Card Industry (PCI) environments. Some potential candidates for IT general controls include vulnerability management applications, encryption tools suites, and data-loss prevention applications. By buying multiple-purpose security controls that service multiple environments, it may be possible to purchase licenses using a volume discount pricing agreement or share costs across multiple business areas.

House of Logs

Maintaining security logging is vital to understanding what is going on in an organization's technical environment. Not all logs require daily reviews, and the sheer volume of data contained in even a day's worth of logs can be daunting. For many information security practitioners, reviewing logs is something to be avoided at all costs until a cyber incident is suspected. However, this approach can make log reviews overwhelming because the practitioner has limited familiarity with the logs, and often, the tools required to analyze them.

A dirty secret in many information security organizations is that a great many of the logs that we pay big bucks to create and maintain never see the light of day with the exception of showing them to an auditor to prove compliance with a regulatory requirement. The first time that many information security professionals get intimate with their logs is after an actual cyber incident.

The problem with this log strategy is that the information security practitioner may not be familiar with what is "normal" for their organization. Depending upon the configuration of a particular IT infrastructure, certain types of log messages, such as login or authentication errors, may be normal for the organization. Such factors as virtualization and cloud can radically alter the types of messages generated by the security monitoring system. For example, changing and then propagating password changes using some virtual private networks and other virtualized desktop solutions may create authentication errors that end up on security logs.

Some compliance-centric organizations purchase logging and monitoring solutions to satisfy the requirements of a particular compliance regulation. These organizations may not expend the resources or pay the vendor for additional consulting services to get any value beyond a simple checkmark on an audit questionnaire on a very pricy expenditure. Later, when a crisis arises, it can be difficult to impossible to get through the normal "noise" on the log files to use them for diagnostic purposes.

In order to optimize the value of creation and retention of log files, the following operational pratices are recommended.

Tips for Getting the Most Bang for the Buck from Logs

- Even if the information security staff does not do a full-on review daily, require some level of review, even a cursory review of specific risk items, to gain familiarity with the log format and tools.
- Ensure that appropriate rotation and retention of log files occurs.
- If feasible, use write once read many (WORM) storage technology and encryption to protect logs. Logs can be corrupted or lost from random hardware and software problems, which can damage the continuity of log files.
- Make sure that the log solution vendor assists you in determining the potential causes of log anomalies before you make the last payment, or include consulting services as a part of the purchase agreement. After they leave the organizational premises, the information security might find it more difficult to get answers to unexplained variances or unexpected error messages.
- Store log entries, using a common format, in a log-monitoring and reporting solution to produce standard reports and allow correlation of log files.
- Have the team members gain some practice using the log files before an actual incident occurs, so they will be familiar with

log formats, reporting capabilities, and other log management utilities. This could be included in mock cyber incident drills.

- In many organizations, responsibility for the firewall and its maintenance resides within the network organization, not the security team. However, it is crucial that the security team be familiar with the firewall logs. One way to accomplish this is to team one, preferably two, members of the security team with members of the firewall team to get familiar with the firewall console and viewing the logs. While it may be possible to load the firewall logs into a security log management solution, often the firewall console may be a more direct way to view this data or at least prepare extracts for analysis. The benefit for the firewall team is that the security team can perform tasks that previously were assigned to firewall engineers.

What Type of Control Is the Most Cost Effective?

When it comes to security controls and costs, the question that frequently comes up concerns the type of controls that provide the best value in terms of protection and value. Let's return to a quick review of the three basic types of security controls. *Preventive controls* thwart or limit the impact of an error, omission, or unauthorized use or intrusion. *Detective controls* identify and report an error, omission, or unauthorized use while it is occurring or after it has taken place. *Corrective controls* fix errors, omissions, or unauthorized use or intrusions after their detection. All three types of controls have their place in a comprehensive security strategy.

Preventive controls are generally considered the most cost effective because they diminish overall impact costs. However, no control is 100% effective, including preventive controls. Some exploits are multifactorial, so a single preventive control in isolation might fail to halt an attack using a two-pronged assault on the security perimeter. Preventive controls might fail to stop attacks perpetrated by collusion or other insider exploits. In addition, preventive controls, like the other control types, can only stop attack types for which they were designed. New exploits or novel attacks might not be prevented.

Therefore, the need to invest in myriad controls, including preventive, detective, and corrective controls, remains vital to implementing an effective and comprehensive control strategy. Controls do not exist in isolation. Controls are a combination of people, processes, and technology. While we might continue to search for the elusive *silver bullet* security control, it is not currently on the horizon, at least not yet.

Defense-in-Depth and Layered Security Controls

The distribution of security controls needs balance to manage the identified risks from the threat landscape. A *defense-in-depth* strategy requires the layering of controls to halt exploits that manage to successfully evade initial layers of the control infrastructure. Sometimes the first control fails, not because of a deficiency in the technology, but because of human intervention.

For example, an antimalware/antispam solution may correctly identify a possible phishing email and place it in a junk/spam/quarantine folder. However, most of these applications allow users to move the potential spam to their inbox in case of a false positive misidentification of a valid email. If the user opens a phishing email and downloads a Trojan program to their device, the primary control layer (email filter) was evaded and the second control layer, antimalware, should take over the task of defending the organization. To put it simply, with a defense-in-depth strategy, one control has the other one's back in terms of stopping attacks.

Human Aspect of Controls

Many technical controls fail because the control designer failed to factor human behavior into their design. Humans are more complicated than technology, and this should be considered in the design of security controls. There are three areas in which control failures can occur in relation to human interaction:

1. Controls creating user frustration and dissatisfaction
2. Controls creating misunderstanding leading to security failures
3. Humans bypassing security controls

Controls Creating User Frustration and Dissatisfaction

Often, we humans create control failures inadvertently, such as errors or misunderstanding their use. It is vital to consider usability, in addition to security, when evaluating potential controls, especially those that need to interact with end users.

Consider your own experiences with frustrating controls, such as entering the incorrect information in the wrong field on a form or using a different format for a phone number or Social Security Number. These errors are so common, we accept them as unavoidable and try to detect and fix problems before it is too late.

Awkward controls can create two different types of problems for the information security team. The first category of control problems centers on end-user satisfaction issues. Some organizations, in an effort to be secure, antagonize their customers. This is where security can appear clueless as to providing business alignment.

One good example was a local credit union that made the decision to use a *case-sensitive user ID*. Now, nowhere on its site does it mention this little security feature. It also has a nonworking password reset button on its login page. Apparently, it decided against offering this feature, but left the nonworking link next to the login box. It also failed to mention that passwords can only be reset using the phone during normal business hours.

Having worked on a helpdesk, I am sure that these security controls, and the lack of information related to them, increases both support costs and customer frustration significantly. The credit union spends liberally on customer events, but it does not understand that convenience is something we expect in our banking transactions.

Controls Creating Misunderstanding Leading to Security Failures

Awkward controls can create the potential for a security incident as well. If setting up the security features of a control is open to interpretation and errors, such as enabling network ports open or permitting dangerous traffic types, small mistakes have the potential for leaving the security perimeter vulnerable and unprotected. Human error is far more likely to cause serious security breaches than technical vulnerabilities.

The way to combat the human risk and frustration problems associated with security controls is through a combination of human factors engineering, use-case testing, and common sense. In the 1990s, software development organizations introduced human factors engineering to optimize dashboards, menus, and other application components with which the end user interacted directly. The objectives of human factors engineering testing were to minimize errors, decrease frustration, and reduce the cost of support. Use cases should mimic the way a regular user approaches security-related tasks, such as logging into the system, changing a password, and other common security-related functions. It looks to identify common errors that a user might make. While common sense often appears to be increasingly scarce, it is often the cost-effective way to reduce support costs, customer churn, and expenditures created by security control software rewrites.

For example, a software company released a product that virtually tripled its support costs and threatened its ability to migrate its customers to the next release level. The application was riddled with bugs. Attempting to resolve all the open bugs within a few version updates was not possible. Instead of trying to boil the ocean, the development team concentrated on the most common use cases (functions performed by virtually all uses on a regular basis). Support costs dropped by two-thirds in the months following that product update. The company did not lose a single customer.

Humans Bypassing Security Controls

Human ingenuity can bypass some of the best-designed security controls. This has been true since office workers discovered how to prop open the emergency exit doors to facilitate smoking breaks. Most bypassing of security controls by individuals does not have a malicious intent. The most common motivations for circumventing security controls is frustration or the belief that the control is inhibiting the productivity of the individual.

Several recent cyber breaches were the result of individuals either bypassing security control mechanisms, such as ignoring messages to scan USB drives, or ignoring the actions taken on their behalf by a security control. These individuals often opted to use their own decision-making process to accomplish their personal agenda, such as fulfilling their curiosity about the contents of a file or drive, to the detriment of their whole organization. No matter how draconian we try to make controls, if individuals perceive them as getting in the way of their productivity or needs, they will find a way of eluding those controls.

Controls are most effective when they mesh with the needs of the individuals using them. Another option is providing an acceptable and easy-to-use alternative to bypassing the control that still accomplishes the individual's objective(s).

For example, for individuals looking to access documents from their work computer to do tasks remotely, rather than having them send documents to third-party email or cloud-based *drop boxes,* offering them a web-based email or virtual desktop where they can access documents securely might inhibit risky behaviors. Another example would be providing standard encrypted USB drives to allow users to transport documents securely rather than using risky methods, such as third-party email with attachments or free drop box utilities.

The key is listening to what end users need to be productive and giving them a secure alternative. Otherwise, the information security team will find itself locked in a race with end users who will find creative workarounds to the increasingly rigorous controls.

Adding "People Literacy" to Security Controls

To improve the user experience with security controls and prevent cyber incidents resulting from poor human factor design, the frugal CISO looks to understand and optimize security controls to prevent these issues from occurring. This means adding human factor considerations to initial evaluations and subsequent reassessments of security controls used by both end users and the information security team.

The information security team also needs to acknowledge that while security controls can assist in promoting strong security, the controls cannot prevent all user-created security incidents. Users need to be made aware of their responsibility for securing the organization through continuing education about risk issues.

Understanding the Total Cost of Ownership of Controls

When it comes to total of ownership, not all controls are equal. It is important to understand not only the security benefits of the controls that the organization is considering acquiring, but all the costs

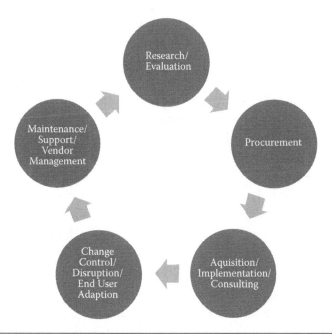

Figure 9.1 Total cost of a security control.

that will be associated with those controls over their operational life (Figure 9.1).

Too often, the focus is on the immediate costs, especially the purchase price or annual licensing fees, rather than the total expenditures required to effectively run the security control.

An often overlooked expenditure is the cost associated with identifying and evaluating security controls for future purchase. In pursuit of the latest and greatest security technologies, a significant amount of resources can be consumed. Some information security professionals may enjoy the "hunt" for new technologies too much, and waste considerable time and budget doing research for control acquisitions. These costs include travel expenses to attend conferences and trade shows where new security solutions are on display and demonstrated for potential buyers.

While security staff should consider a wide range of security solution options, it is more cost-effective and better time management to narrow the field of security controls to a few options based upon some established criteria. Established criteria narrow the focus to what the organization actually needs to close gaps in its security perimeter, complement existing security technologies and processes, and achieve regulatory compliance. More importantly, it narrows the pool of potential solutions from the search to reduce evaluation costs.

For example, if a solution includes a feature that is incompatible with an organization's culture, such as maintaining user activity histories, excluding that product from the evaluation saves the costs associated with its review. Some information security professionals worry that excluding some solutions based upon a specific feature might limit potential solutions from being considered. Their view is that just because a feature exists, the organization does not need to use it.

While on the surface this appears to be true, the devil is in the details when it comes to technology. Often, functionality cannot be easily disabled or subsequent updates to the product might revert the feature back to an enabled state. There is also the simple accounting rationale for not buying products with features for which the organization has no use. The organization would be paying for something it is not going to use, which is a waste of its budget.

Without any criteria for the identification of potential security solutions, information security staff may feel compelled to include the whole universe of potential solutions in their search. This could result in "analysis paralysis" or excessive product evaluation costs absorbed into core operational budget cost centers. The issue with the categories of costs associated with controls is that they may not be readily apparent and are hidden within other cost items and may not be easily quantified.

Other costs associated with security controls are the expenses involved in the procurement process. These are often absorbed into legal and general administration cost centers, but may end up charged back to the information security budget. The majority of security control acquisitions are simple and just require some basic contract administration to finalize the purchase. However, the procurement of sophisticated, high-technology, or complicated security controls, can require extensive and protracted contract negotiations requiring support from the legal team and procurement teams. These costs come out of someone's budget.

For example, a firm looking to implement bleeding-edge security control with a leading provider of this category of technology spent several hundred thousand dollars on an outside legal firm to negotiate the contract, in addition to the internal legal team and vendor management organization. The total for the procurement was close to half a million dollars. The costs associated with the procurement were charged back to a security project budget.

Implementation is the vital element in the success or failure of any security control. Implementation can represent one of the most significant cost areas. Some sophisticated technology controls may require consulting to customize and implement the security control within an organization's infrastructure. Some implementation assistance may be included within the purchase price. However, the included consulting services may not be sufficient for some security controls or organizations. For highly technical controls, additional implementation consulting services should be included as part of the total cost of the security control. These costs may fall under the capital expenditure budget as a component of the initial purchase. Insufficient implementation assistance can result in a failure to successfully optimize a security control and diminishes the return on security investment (ROSI) of the control's acquisition.

After implementation, the costs associated with the security control will continue. However, they convert to management and support costs. These costs fall under the security team's annual operating budget and may appear as staff hours or contractor hourly costs. The more complex and complicated the nature of the security controls, in general, the more expensive ongoing operation costs will be during the production life of the control.

In addition to these more easily tracked costs, both less-quantifiable and intangible costs must be considered as part of the control's total costs. These costs include disruptions in productivity created by change, assimilation, and ongoing management of a vendor over the course of the product/service life cycle.

One area of concern regarding the total cost of implementing new security controls is the cost associated with the control for the end user, such as productivity loss created by use of a two-factor authentication device. While not completely insignificant, these costs often represent the smallest expenditure across the entire user population, after a small adjustment period.

All these costs need to be factored into the total cost of a security control over its operational lifetime and can be summarized by the following formula:

Total Cost of a Security Control

= Product Research/Evaluation + Purchase Cost/Licenses Fees

+ Procurement Costs + Initial Implementation

+ Configuration + Support/Troubleshooting + End User Training

+ Cost of Change/Adjustment Disruption

Not all of these costs can be tracked and many are intangible. However, they must receive consideration when evaluating the impact of adding or replacing a security control by the information security team and organization as a whole.

Developing a Bespoke Security Controls Strategy

A security controls strategy is like a great business suit. It needs to be custom tailored to look and feel right to get the most use and value out of the expenditure. Sometimes a CISO coming from an effective information security team at another organization will attempt to re-create exactly the same security control strategy they used successfully before. They will even use the same security control products and services implemented in exactly the same manner. However, more often than not, the strategy is not nearly as effective as it was in their former organization. This can be especially bewildering if the new organization is using leading technology solutions coupled with best practices in information security.

Each organization is unique. It is the fusion of its history, culture, mission, vision, individuals, and organization functions. Its information security control strategy needs to consider its business sector(s), regulatory compliance requirements, past audit history, prior security incidents, and technical infrastructure. Each of these elements influences both the types of security controls and how they need to be implemented. The information security team itself has a significant influence on the security control strategy. The maturity level of the security team, the size of the team, and its amount of technical expertise will determine the types of controls it can effectively manage and support.

The last factor, and perhaps the most critical in developing an effective control strategy, is budget, the amount of money available for the acquisition of security controls.

An organization with limited budget availability is going to need to be very selective in the types of security controls it purchases and deploys. Often, organizations with tight budgets for security controls need to get it right the first time because there will be little budget available for do-overs. Organizations with generous budgets may have the opportunity to acquire and implement elaborate technical solutions and can take chances with implementing innovative control technologies. These organizations have enough budget available to fund proof-of-concept trials with new categories of security controls, such as biometric device readers.

There are two common strategies for developing security control architecture. Both have their roots in military defense tactics. The first and most common are *defense-in-depth* or layered defense strategies. It is the use of layered security controls to safeguard the information assets of an organization. It is based on the military tactic that it is harder for an enemy to defeat a complicated multilayered perimeter than to pierce a single barrier.

It is sometimes described as an onion because of the series of layers. If one control fails, another is behind it to take on its protective role. The defense-in-depth strategy diminishes the probability that a hacker's attacks will be successful. Even if the hacker makes it through the layers of protection, it may give the security team time to minimize the attack's severity. Recently, this strategy has come under fire as impractical or outdated as the perimeter becomes more porous.

Defense-in-breadth strategies are multidisciplinary controls with the objective to identify, manage, and lessen the risk of exploitable vulnerabilities at every stage of the application or infrastructure life from design to decommissioning. An example of this approach is secure development that aims to move away from bolt-on security as an afterthought to including security with every stage of the life cycle from design to application retirement.

Some recent white papers and blogs pit defense-in-depth and defense-in-breadth strategies against each other as competing cyber defense strategies. In actuality, they complement each other in terms of the defensive postures they offer. Defense-in-depth's combining of layers fortifies the perimeter to resist attacks, and at the very least, when using different categories of controls, slows the cyber attack and offers early warning of exploits in progress. Defense-in-breadth

252 THE FRUGAL CISO

attempts to close many gaps in the application or infrastructure life cycle. The result can be a security perimeter that is resistant and resilient to myriad exploits. It can be compared to constructing a facility with a series of inner walls and then reinforcing each internal wall. The resulting structure would be incredibly strong.

Using Maturity Level and Budgeting Availability to Develop a Security Control Strategy

A customized strategy should consider the organization itself and its information security item. Two important criteria in the development of a basic set of strategies for implementing and managing security controls is the information security team's level of maturity and resources available. The interaction of these two attributes offers guidance in the development of a strategy for security controls. The next three offer an example of a potential control strategies matrix based on these two vectors.

MATURITY LEVEL	LOW BUDGET	MODERATE BUDGET	HIGH BUDGET
Low (1 to 2)	• Focus on flexible, but simple general IT controls. • Use a homogenous control strategy to simplify operations and get best unit price. • Use specialized controls only when required to achieve regulatory compliance. • Avoid open source tools unless several members of the staff have expertise in their use. • Avoid or limit the use of complicated technological control tools.	• Focus on flexible, but simple general IT controls. • Use a homogenous control strategy to simplify operations and get best unit price. • Use specialized controls only when required to achieve regulatory compliance. • Avoid open source tools unless several members of the staff have expertise in their use. • Use of moderately complicated technological control tools.	• Focus on flexible general IT controls. • Use primarily homogenous control strategy to simplify operations and get best unit price. • Use specialized controls only when required to achieve regulatory compliance or appropriate to business sector. • Avoid open source tools unless several members of the staff have expertise in their use or consulting service can be procured to implement and document their use and maintenance.

Continued

MATURITY LEVEL	LOW BUDGET	MODERATE BUDGET	HIGH BUDGET
Low (1 to 2)	• Be selective in logging. Log only what is required and can realistically be reviewed in a timely manner. • Create comprehensive documentation and use guide for all controls as they are implemented, including usage checklists. • Maintain and revise all documentation as controls are upgraded or patched, as necessary. • Regularly reevaluate controls based upon new requirements or emerging risks, and availability of new control technologies.	• Introduce additional logging to supplement basic logging gradually. • Only collect and maintain logs that can realistically be reviewed in a timely manner. • Create comprehensive documentation and use guide for all controls as they are implemented, including usage checklists. • Maintain and revise all documentation as controls are upgraded or patched, as necessary. • Regularly reevaluate controls based upon new requirements or emerging risks, and availability of new control technologies.	• Use of complicated technological control tools is coupled initially with consulting services for successful implementation phase. • Introduce additional logging to supplement basic logging gradually. • Only collect and maintain logs that can realistically be reviewed in a timely manner. • Create comprehensive documentation and use guide for all controls as they are implemented, including usage checklists. • Maintain and revise all documentation as controls are upgraded or patched, as necessary. • Introduction of one or two heterogeneous controls where their impact will be most beneficial. • Regularly reevaluate controls based upon new requirements or emerging risks, and availability of new control technologies.

MATURITY LEVEL	LOW BUDGET	MODERATE BUDGET	HIGH BUDGET
Moderate (3 to 4)	• Focus on flexible, but simple general IT controls. • Use primarily a homogenous control strategy to simplify operations and to get best unit price.	• Maintain focus on general IT controls. • Use a primarily homogenous control strategy to get best unit price.	• Focus on flexible general IT controls. • Use primarily a homogenous control strategy to simplify operations and get best unit price.

Continued

MATURITY LEVEL	LOW BUDGET	MODERATE BUDGET	HIGH BUDGET
Moderate (3 to 4)	• Use specialized controls when required to achieve regulatory compliance. • Use open source tools if several members of the staff have expertise in their use. • Limit the use of complicated technological control tools to where their use will have the greatest benefit. • Be selective in logging. • Log only what can realistically be reviewed in a timely manner. • Create comprehensive documentation and use guide for all controls as they are implemented, including usage checklists. • Maintain and revise all documentation as controls are upgraded or patched, as necessary. • Regularly reevaluate controls based upon new requirements or emerging risks, and availability of new control technologies.	• Limit the use of specialized controls to achieve regulatory compliance or to manage high-priority risks. • Use open source tools if several members of the staff have expertise in their use. • Use complex technological control tools to where they will have the greatest benefit. • Be selective in logging, but gradually add new logs to support business or security needs. • Log only what can realistically be reviewed in a timely manner.	• Introduce heterogeneous controls in high-impact areas, such as vulnerability management. • Use specialized controls when required to achieve regulatory compliance or to manage high-priority risks or appropriate to business sector. • Avoid open source tools unless several members of the staff have expertise in their use or consulting service can be procured to implement and document their use and maintenance. • Use of complicated technological control tools is coupled initially with consulting services for successful implementation phase, but may involve the eventual inclusion of internal technical experts. • Introduce additional logging to supplement basic logging gradually. • Only collect and maintain logs that can realistically be reviewed in a timely manner. • Create comprehensive documentation and use guide for all controls as they are implemented, including usage checklists.

Continued

MATURITY LEVEL	LOW BUDGET	MODERATE BUDGET	HIGH BUDGET
Moderate (3 to 4)			• Maintain and revise all documentation as controls are upgraded or patched, as necessary. • Introduction of one or two heterogeneous controls where their impact will be most beneficial. • Regularly reevaluate controls based upon new requirements or emerging risks, and availability of new control technologies. • Consider adding a digital forensics function or retaining a firm that offers these services.

MATURITY LEVEL	LOW BUDGET	MODERATE BUDGET	HIGH BUDGET
High (5 to 6)	• Focus on flexible, but simple general IT controls. • Use a homogenous control strategy to simplify operations and to get best unit price. • Use specialized controls when required to achieve regulatory compliance. • Use open source tools if several members of the staff have expertise in their use.	• Maintain focus on general IT controls. • Use a homogenous control strategy to get the best unit price. • Use specialized controls only when required to achieve regulatory compliance. • Use open source tools if several members of the staff have expertise in their use.	• Focus on flexible general IT controls. • Use a combination of a homogenous control strategy supplemented by heterogeneous controls to maintain cost control, but build in resilience. • Use specialized controls only when required to achieve regulatory compliance or appropriate to business sector. • Avoid open source tools unless several members of the staff have expertise in their use or consulting service can be procured to implement and document their use and maintenance.

Continued

MATURITY LEVEL	LOW BUDGET	MODERATE BUDGET	HIGH BUDGET
High (5 to 6)	• Limit the use of complicated technological control tools to where their use will have the greatest benefit. • Be selective in logging. • Log only what is required and can realistically be reviewed in a timely manner. • Create comprehensive documentation and use guide for all controls as they are implemented, including usage checklists. • Maintain and revise all documentation as controls are upgraded or patched, as necessary. • Regularly reevaluate controls based upon new requirements or emerging risks, and availability of new control technologies.	• Use complex technological control tools where they will have the greatest benefit. • Be selective in logging, but gradually add new logs to support business or security needs. • Log only what is required and can realistically be reviewed in a timely manner. • Create comprehensive documentation and use guide for all controls as they are implemented, including usage checklists. • Maintain and revise all documentation as controls are upgraded or patched, as necessary. • Regularly reevaluate controls based upon new requirements or emerging risks, and availability of new control technologies.	• Use of complicated technological control tools includes the recruitment of internal technical experts. • Introduce additional logging to supplement basic logging gradually. • Only collect and maintain logs that can realistically be reviewed in a timely manner. • Create comprehensive documentation and use guide for all controls as they are implemented, including usage checklists. • Maintain and revise all documentation as controls are upgraded or patched, as necessary. • Regularly reevaluate controls based upon new requirements or emerging risks, and availability of new control technologies. • Consider certification of the information security function, such as ISO 27001. • Consider adding a digital forensics function or retaining a firm that offers these services. • Consider small proof-of-concept trials to evaluate emerging security technologies.

Using Open Source Security Controls

Open source has been a continuing trend in the technology world for more than a decade and thrived during the Great Recession, which was dominated by reduced, flat, or only marginally increased technology budgets. *Open source* refers to the code that is freely available to the public. Most organizations now not only permit the use of open source solutions, but also encourage them as part of a continuing strategy. Information security organizations were often one of the first groups in a technology department to adopt open source software and security controls. Many popular cyber security controls and tools began their life as open source software and eventually became commercial products that included such extras as support and more user-friendly interfaces. Many of these security tools continue to exist in both commercial and open source versions today.

There are some significant benefits to creating a security controls strategy that seeks to utilize open source whenever feasible. Of course, the most significant advantage is reduction in the cost associated with software purchases or licensing keys. This can be especially appealing to many organizations looking to reduce budgets or at least not grow them significantly.

However, open source is not necessarily the right solution for every organization. Open source security solutions can be as effective as their commercial competitors can. However, the support model is radically different than that used by commercial vendors. Because vendors either charge explicitly for support or build it into their pricing, the availability of support is uniform and predictable. Open source vendors may provide little to no technical support. The most common channels for open source support are open source community organizations that offer assistance through informal means and mutual assistance.

These user communities can serve as an alternative to getting support and advice on these products. The same is true when looking for a patch/fix for an identified vulnerability. Commercial vendors often have a regular patching cycle, such as the infamous *patch Tuesdays*, and may offer emergency fixes in a short time period for critical vulnerabilities. The releases of patches for open source products may not be as predictable, which could create issues in maintaining regulatory compliance.

When evaluating open source alternatives, it is vital to consider the total cost of the security controls versus just the purchase price or licensing fees. The total cost includes training, installation, maintenance, support, and reviews of any legal agreements associated with the solution. Research into the cost factors associated with commercial and open source solutions differ regarding the lifetime cost of both models. However, it is probably safe to assume that many lifetime costs, with the exception of purchasing and licensing fees, are similar between the two ownership models. One reason this is particularly true is that most of the cost of security controls may be attributable to support.

Another issue to consider is that commercial software vendors have a financial incentive to innovate to entice customers to purchase new versions and upgrade by offering new features, functionality, and added value. This drives additional research and development spending and further innovations. In addition, open source products may not deliver a complete solution, so multiple open source products may need to be combined or additional in-house custom code created. This will add to the maintenance and support cost of the open source solution. It will also contribute complexity, which is the enemy of strong security and stability.

The main drawback of open source security controls is their reliance on technical expertise for installation, configuration, and ongoing support. It would be difficult for the average security practitioner to troubleshoot any problems or even determine if the security control is working correctly.

A common scenario for the use of open source controls occurs when a security team is lucky enough to include a talented technical expert among its members. That individual uses both his or her considerable technical skills with a substantial dash of creativity to put together a strong portfolio of security controls that rival much bigger "world-class" security organizations. He or she might even develop some custom code to integrate disparate open source controls. Often, there is an absence of documentation regarding the use and troubleshooting of this highly customized security control solution.

Unfortunately, this talented individual moves on to a new opportunity. Often, there is no other member of the team waiting in the wings to assume that person's duties and the controls run unattended until eventually the security control portfolio is replaced at a significant cost that includes extricating the old open source controls and replacing them with commercial security controls, which can basically almost double the expense. The "lesson learned" is, do not depend solely on one subject matter expert (SME) to deploy open source controls. Effective use of open source controls requires strength in numbers in terms of support and expertise in their use.

When "Free" Controls Are Not Free

Sometimes, overly enthusiastic security team members find a security control at a bargain price and deploy to show how proactive they are. The problem crops up because "free" is not always free when you read the fine print of the user agreement. The devil is in the details, especially when it comes to end-user and licensing agreements. Many "free" security controls are actually trials or meant for deployment under some significant restrictions.

The most common restriction on free-use licenses is that they must be deployed for noncommercial use. This one appears to escape a fair number of smart people that install these licenses in a commercial enterprise. Another constraint is a restriction on the size of the organization deploying these controls. The "free" version limit is usually under 100 employees. The enterprises that offer free licenses are being good citizens of the information security community by providing security solutions to smaller or noncommercial organizations that might not have sufficient resources to purchase these controls to increase their security posture.

These "free" controls should not be deployed in environments that violate the end-user licensing agreements. A similar situation can occur when trial security controls are used in a production environment. Not only is this unethical, but it also opens up the organization to legal actions for copyright violations. If illegal implementations of security controls exist on systems, regulators or auditors can easily find them. This can taint the reviewers' attitudes toward how the organization conducts its operations.

Security Control Strategy: Homogenous versus Heterogeneous Controls

There is another strategic approach to deploying security controls. One is a homogenous control approach to selecting controls under which the same vendor control product is deployed across all platforms. For example, a homogenous deployment strategy could involve using one vulnerability scanner solution across all platforms to meet the compliance and security requirement of the organization. The benefits of the homogenous control strategy may include:

- Lower training costs for security staff
- Lower unit cost for each control due to volume discounts
- Developing substantial internal expertise in use and trouble-shooting the security control

However, there are risks associated with this security strategy. If there is vulnerability in the security, for example a potential buffer overflow condition or type of malware that cannot be detected, the exploit can quickly propagate and escalate. All the assets protected by these controls will be susceptible to the same exploits.

The other strategy is a heterogeneous control approach that intentionally selects security from a number of different vendors. The ideal heterogeneous control approach would look for diversity in all control categories used within the organization's architecture.

For example, a heterogeneous control strategy could involve using one vulnerability scanner that performs dynamic scans on web code and then running the same code through a statistic code analysis tool. The benefits of the heterogeneous control strategy may potentially identify different types of security risks from different perspectives rather than a single focus. In the vulnerability scanner example, a dynamic scanner makes a series of passes through the application that mimics the ways a hacker might use to find potential security holes. However, the very approach used by this category of scanner, a dynamic testing method, cannot cover 100% of an application's source code, and therefore not all the possible paths that an application might take or interactions between modules, leaving the potential for the existence of undiscovered vulnerabilities.

Static code analysis tools are designed to analyze source code or object code (compiled source code) to aid in identifying security flaws in the code itself. These tools can find many potential flaws in the inside code and provide complete coverage of the entire code base. The weakness of these static code analysis tools is the opposite of the dynamic scanners. Currently, these tools can automatically find a small percentage of web-application security flaws and they often generate a relatively high number of false positives.

A heterogeneous security control strategy offers one primary advantage, diversity. Diversity offers resilience against exploits. Using a completely homogenous control strategy could potentially make the infrastructure vulnerable to a single type of malware and cyber infections could cascade throughout a network like a brush fire in a dry forest. Nature's survival strategy has always depended on diversity to offer resilience from devastating infections. Where diversity was lacking, tragic consequences have often been the result.

A good example was the Irish potato blight. In the 1800s, the Irish population depended on one primary crop, potatoes, for much of their sustenance. Between 1845 and 1852, an agricultural blight hit the potato crop and resulted in the Great Famine, a period of mass starvation that killed an estimated one million people. It irrevocably changed the history of Ireland because it prompted a mass migration of one million or more people from Ireland to other nations. Nature itself seeks diversity as a strategy for survival; certain individuals' DNA, the human genetic code, made them resistant to the Black Death (aka bubonic plague) during the medieval period, which assured that some people would live to propagate the species.

While resilience is a principal benefit of a heterogeneous control strategy, there are also disadvantages. The disadvantages of a heterogeneous strategy may center on potentially higher costs for security controls.

- Higher training costs for security staff (staff must be competent in more than one security control within a category)
- Potentially higher unit cost for each control because controls are being purchased in small quantities
- Potential technical incompatibilities between controls
- Need to resolve any conflicts between the results emanating from each control process (if the controls conflict, which one is correct?)
- A heterogeneous control strategy adds complexity that translates into a greater probability of errors in configuration and operational tasks. This can potentially induce vulnerabilities. Remember, complexity is security's enemy.

While a heterogeneous control strategy offers resilience through the diversity it promotes, it also can create additional burdens in terms of cost and complexity. Heterogeneity in controls is a case where a little may go a long way, and its introduction needs to occur slowly and with sufficient prudence. A possible strategy for the heterogeneity in controls might involve introducing one or two heterogeneous controls where their impact will be most beneficial in improving the security posture of the organization, such as application security scanning and vulnerability management.

One mistaken use of heterogeneity in controls is the application of another control to support a control with a poor performance history, such as an antimalware control that has repeatedly failed to prevent or detect viruses. This might be a short-term solution, especially for a security control under an active licensing agreement. However, it doubles both the control cost and support costs. Controls with continued problems need reevaluation to determine their efficacy. The long-term solution is most likely replacing the control after the licensing agreement expires.

Critical Key Success Factor in Managing Controls: The Need to Document

Why Is Documentation So Important and Often Overlooked?

One commonly overlooked step in implementing security controls is the documentation of each security control and the processes that surround them. There are several reasons this may occur:

- Limited time and budget to create the documentation
- No resource with technical documentation skills on the information security team
- No one likes to do documentation
- Members of the team feel it is not necessary because they understand the process

Another insidious reason for the lack of documentation for security controls is the mistaken belief by some staff member(s) responsible for those controls that no documentation provides some level of job security/stability. It rarely does, and often it traps those staff members in the same position for years on end. On more than one occasion, I have assumed positions where the controls around critical applications and functions had no associated documentation at all.

For example, the security controls associated with an application that manages billions of dollars consisted of a bare-bones checklist without any explanation. All the individuals associated with the process had moved on, been demoted or transferred, or were unavailable for a variety of reasons. The new manager literally had to wing it until they could create the documentation to support these critical processes. The documentation included both a revised checklist and comprehensive operations guide. The documentation was tested using staff members unfamiliar with the daily process to ensure its understandability and usability. Fortunately, no major issues occurred during this transitional period. However, if a major problem had occurred, the outcome had the potential to be disastrous.

A year later, significant system corruption occurred. A similar event had never occurred previously, so there was no "playbook" for managing the event. However, using the control documentation for guidance, the team successfully managed the event without loss of a single processing day.

What Should Security Control Documentation Include?

Comprehensive documentation is a critical success factor in the implementation of all security controls. At the very least, it should include the following:

- The asset(s) the control protects
- The mechanism(s) the control uses to protect the asset(s)
- The tools or indicators used to determine if the security control is functioning
- Descriptions of log file formats and any internal codes used in the log entries
- Control vendor information (contract, support numbers, etc.)
- Description of how the security control works
- Steps for configuring and using the security control
- Team member(s) responsible for the security control and their contract information

- Checklist(s)
- Updates/fix processes

Documentation needs to be current to be effective because many technical controls undergo regular revisions and updates. After a few releases with appropriate revisions, a security control's documentation may be of little use in configuring, managing, or troubleshooting a control.

Checklists

Checklists are an excellent device to ensure the proper use of security controls. The aviation industry and NASA space program pioneered the introduction of checklists to assure that all appropriate steps were taken prior to takeoff of a flight or mission launch. With so much on the line, in terms of safety of human beings, these organizations needed a mechanism to minimize human errors.

The primary advantage of using checklists as documentation for the operations of security controls is reduction or elimination of human error. The control checklist describes a set of different tasks that a user must perform or verify in order to configure the security control properly and ensure its proper operation.

The typical checklist formats use the same basic strategy:

1. Read the checklist item.
2. Do the item, such as verifying the configuration setting or executing the checklist instruction.
3. Respond to the results of performing the action.
4. Take any corrective measures required based upon results of the action.

Checklists can be manual or automated, such as a tablet-based checklist app. A vast amount of research around the development of effective checklists exists. The NASA space program has published extensive research in this area, including studies performed to decrease human errors in the aviation checklists. This information is available on the Internet and may offer guidance in the development of checklist procedures.

Tips for Implementing Cost-Effective and Efficient Security Controls

1. The cost of a security control should not exceed the cost of the asset it protects.
2. The primary security control strategy should first focus on a strong portfolio of strong general IT controls. Supplement these general IT controls with specialized control mechanisms to support the needs of particular assets or compliance regulations, as necessary.
3. If you have multiple security controls that do the same function in a similar manner, ask why. There may be a valid reason for the redundancy, or the potential may exist to eliminate redundant controls and cost.
4. Look for similar controls located in isolated organization silos, such as different secure email solutions in different business groups, and evaluate the possibility of migrating to a common security solution. This could dramatically lower licensing costs per unit, training, and support expenditures.
5. Look to eliminate obsolete controls and control procedures. Just because the security team has always used a control, does not mean it should keep doing it when it adds no security value.
6. Try to avoid purchasing small volumes of similar controls to support a single security objective, such as multiple vulnerability management tools for Payment Card Industry Data Security Standard (PCI-DSS) compliance. Often, this occurs because of a piecemeal purchasing tactic that is trying to stay under a specific target amount or trying to please several security team members by following their recommendations.

   The overall cost of multiple similar control solutions is often greater than standardizing one solution. Each acquisition seems relatively cheap until they are aggregated. In addition, the lack of standardization increases the cost of analysis and training. One potential strategy to standardize security controls is to retire alternative solutions and switch over to a single solution across the organization as the different products' licensing agreements expire.

7. Look for security costs hidden in different cost centers, such as security controls like Secure Sockets Layer (SSL) certificates purchased under development budgets. Look to obtain standard contracts for commonly used security controls that the entire organization can use. This may reduce costs by getting lower prices per unit purchased.

8. Look for security controls purchased through inappropriate mechanisms, such as corporate credit cards. There are several control issues surrounding these practices. One is that it makes it difficult to track the actual expenditures for security controls. There may be no mechanism for tracking the location or use of these security controls. Even more concerning is that security controls, such as digital certificates, may not be deployed according to information security standards and guidelines.

> For example, sensitive critical files might undergo encryption using a digital certificate/public key, but the private key required for decryption might not be stored appropriately in a central key repository. If the key is subsequently lost or corrupted, this data is irretrievable. This can result not only in costs related to the lost data, but legal judgments, if this data is required in a lawsuit.

9. In selecting security controls, be realistic about the information security staff's ability to manage and support them. Unused security controls are one of the biggest budget wasters.

10. If your organization has the budget or can get a vendor to agree to it, try a *proof of concept* of any innovative security control before committing to any production implementation. During a proof of concept, the objective is to determine if the security control performs the necessary tasks effectively and efficiently, integrates well with the organization's technical infrastructure, and achieves the necessary level of performance based upon the organization's requirements.

11. Make sure the security control is a good fit for the organization's culture, as well as technology infrastructure. If a product contains a feature that runs contrary to the organization's belief system, they trying to "make it fit" will likely result in

higher costs. Sometimes what a product does *not* do can be equally as important as its features.

12. Determine if the proposed control achieves the *Principle of Psychological Acceptability* in terms of its impact on end users in that it is transparent or creates minimal barriers to use. Otherwise, users may find ways to evade the controls, which not only wastes the money spent on the acquisition of those controls, but also opens up the organization to cyber incidents and significant remediation expenditures.

13. Avoid the "keep up with the Jones" mentality when it comes to acquiring and deploying new controls. Just because something works well in another organization's environment does not necessarily mean it is the best control solution for your organization. All security controls should undergo a selection and assessment based upon criteria for a specific organization.

14. Do not try to "port" an old employer's security control strategy and controls portfolio to a new organization. Each organization is unique in terms of its attributes, even those in the same business sector and similar size. The frugal CISO takes some time to get to know and understand the new organization and understand its needs before making any drastic adjustments in its security controls strategy.

15. Periodically reassess the organization to determine the current effectiveness of its security controls. Controls can be evaluated on some rotating schedule based on the type of control, such as technical or procedural, value of assets it protects, or past assessments' recommendations for re-review.

16. Before deciding to discontinue support for commercial security controls and adopt an open source strategy, be sure that the staff is ready for the transition. Open source tools may not be as user friendly as the interfaces on commercial versions. It may come down to a trade-off between the purchasing cost/licensing cost of the control and increased staff expenditures.

17. One inexpensive way to test the *user literacy* of controls is to try them on actual users. Give the tool and minimal instructions to users and let them hack away at a task. Let's face it, that is what most real users do anyway. This technique is

cheap, simple, and works equally well on end users, technical staff, and customers. An array of inexpensive tools can be used to analyze the results, such as screen capture utilities, video cameras, and audio recorders.

18. Before committing to purchasing a security control, ask the security staff the following questions:

- What security objective is this security control going to be used to accomplish?
- Who is going to use it?
- How often is it going to be used?
- Does it produce logs or metrics that can be used for tracking?
- What is the total cost of acquiring and running this control?
- What new value or benefit is this control going to contribute to the organization's security posture?
- Is control replacing an existing or augmenting an existing control?
- What organizational assets is the proposed control going to protect?

If there are no immediate answers to these questions, then it is likely that sufficient evaluation of the proposed security control has not been completed and needs to be undertaken before further action is taken.

If a security control has a continued history of failure, such as an antimalware control that has repeatedly failed to prevent or detect viruses, it should be reevaluated for potential replacement. Another solution might be to augment the control with another similar control. This might be a short-term solution, especially for a security control under a licensing agreement. However, it doubles both control cost and support costs. The long-term solution is most likely replacing the control after the licensing agreement expires.

10

UNDERSTAND THE
BUDGETING CYCLE

What Is the Budget and Why Is It Important?

When individuals move from being individual contributors to management/executive positions, they often receive their first introduction to the budgeting process. Prior to this dose of cold hard reality, budget might have been a nebulous concept of a pool of money put there to be spent as management saw fit. Budget can take an almost mystical air in discussion. The frequent question, *"Is there enough money in the budget to cover <insert the expense>?"* can sound similar to "It's good—we do not have to the bank" from the film *I Remember Mama*, which meant that there were sufficient funds to cover expenses for the month.

One of the first signs that an information security team is maturing is that it gains control over its own budget. Often, in information security teams at lower maturity levels, the security budget is under the control of a larger organization. In some organizations, it remains that way, despite increasing competency and maturity of the information security team. If, or when, the information security organization gains independent control over its own budget, it begins the process of creating its own identity and destiny.

In order to be taken seriously by peers in other departments, the information security teams (or at least some team members) need to possess or develop budgetary, as well as financial, acumen. This may be difficult for some more technically focused individuals who may not have been exposed to financial or accounting courses during college. Team members with experience in project management may assume leadership roles in the budgeting process because of their experience in managing project budgets. This group may mentor other information security team members in budget basics.

The key to successful budgeting is establishing a direct alignment between the information security budget and business strategies. Unfortunately, some information security teams focus on projects that are significant to the team, but no one else in the organization. This is because these projects have no tie to specific business needs. These teams may run projects that, if they resulted in failure or success, no one else in the organization would care. This disconnect may create difficulties for the information security team in getting a sufficient budgetary allocation to run its daily operations and move forward with innovative projects to protect the organization's assets from would-be attackers.

Until the information security team learns to effectively develop and promote its budgetary needs along with the other departments, it may remain "budget lint" (what is left in the budget after every other department gets its allocations). Successful budget management is as much about organizational politics as it is about financial knowledge. It involves getting to know the key players, speaking the *right language* (*budgetese*[1]) to build rapport and create credibility, and understanding the basics of selling budgetary proposals by tying them to business requirements.

What Makes a Good Budget?

In addition to being a spending plan for the next year, the annual budget is a communication device for the department or organizations involved in its preparation. While it seems that budgets are solely used to allocate and track spending, they can reveal a great deal about an organization, its culture, and specifically its strategy. By analyzing budgets across a range of years, you can often detect modifications in business strategies, economic conditions, and technology trends; for example, decreases in travel/entertainment, personnel/salaries, and training may indicate organizational belt tightening during economic downturns.

A well-developed budget is characterized by these attributes:

1. Includes an executive summary that offers a concise description of activities and initiatives included in the budget proposal
2. Encompasses both long-term and short-term outlooks

3. Demonstrates alignment to organizational objectives and mission
4. Justifies budget decisions on their potential return or benefit
5. Effectively communicates with all stakeholders
6. Is easy to read and understand
7. Avoids jargon
8. Assumes a business perspective on all issues

By examining the information security budget proposal, the reader should understand the activities and projects that the information security team is proposing to embark on over the coming year, as well as their alignment with the business and its strategic focuses.

In these lean economic times, it is essential that every department, especially departments that do not produce revenue, visibly demonstrate a commitment to effective cost management and streamlining of operations. Finding a way to tie security initiatives to other organizational efforts to streamline or manage costs is another tactic for the information security team to align with this strategy.

For example, if the business is looking to reduce costs and increase worker choices by implementing a BYOD (bring your own device) policy, information security activities related to offering BYOD, while maintaining a strong security posture, should be highlighted.

A good budget justifies any requests for additional staffing with supporting metrics to explain why these additional resources are required in the performance of existing and new security activities. All requests for additional staffing should include a description of what benefits the position offers in supporting business activities.

What Is a Budget? (Traditional Approach)

At its simplest level, a budget is a plan. A budget is, in essence, a transformation of the organization's mission and objectives into an accounting format. The budgeting process lets the organization lay down priorities, recommit to its mission, and distribute resources where they can be used most effectively, and tracks performance against spending targets. A budget reflects the amount of money needed to perform planned activities in the coming year. This includes standard activities and any additional amounts necessary to run new projects or activities.

There are two basic categories of expenditures included in a budget. One is operating expenses, also called *OPEX*. Operating expenses are the costs associated with running a business, such as the daily costs of staffing and managing the security help desk. These costs may be relatively static because they assume a continuation of specific service levels. Generally, operational costs only need adjustments to compensate for inflation, cost trends, and any contractual obligations. The only way to reduce operating costs significantly is to stop providing a service, decrease service levels, reduce salaries, or obtain cheaper sources of services and products.

The second category of budget expenditures is capital expenditures (also called *CAPEX*). These expenditures provide future benefits to the organization. A capital expenditure occurs when the organization buys fixed assets or enhances the value of an existing fixed asset. Intangible assets, such as software, are recognizable under the capital expenditures category under most circumstances. Some capital expenditures are required to support current operating activities, such as replacing worn-out hardware. Other capital expenditures support future ventures and other planned activities.

In tough economic times, CAPEX requests may be delayed or eliminated from budgets to reduce costs and continue to fund current operational activities. See Table 10.1 for more information on determining the type of expenditure.

Table 10.1 CAPEX versus OPEX Budget Items

	CAPITAL EXPENDITURES (CAPEX)	OPERATING EXPENSES (OPEX)
What it is:	Funds used to create future value	The costs incurred in performing daily activities/functions
Way to remember:	Keep CAPEX	Consume OPEX
When it occurs:	When money is spent to purchase fixed assets or to extend the value of an existing asset	When money is spent to pay the expenses resulting from operational activities
Tax and accounting implications:	Assets are depreciated (tangible) and amortized (intangible) over a period of time	Operating expenses are recognized when they actually occur
Examples:	Equipment, such as hardware, real estate, furniture, and purchases of software	Salaries and benefits, telecommunications, utilities, rent, software licenses, service contracts, retainer fees, consulting firms

Zero-Based Budgeting

Zero-based budgeting is an alternative approach to budget planning that turns traditional budgeting methodology on its head. The traditional budgeting approach uses historical expenditures as a baseline for future spending needs, and then tacks on an incremental increase to each existing line item to build the spending model for the next year. Zero-based budgeting transforms the traditional budgeting method by starting each budget as a blank slate with no assumptions about spending based on history.

This approach requires managers to examine all budget items and justifying their inclusion in the proposed budget. This budgeting technique is radically different because it makes no (zero) assumptions around levels of service offered or types of expenditures to be made. Zero-based budgeting requires the entire budget proposal be reexamined in detail, starting from a zero base.

The primary benefit of zero-based budgeting is that it attempts to remove the tendency to continue to fund some efforts year after year that produce limited to minimal value. This can result in the final termination of zombie projects. *Zombie projects* are projects that initially received funding to achieve a specific set of objectives. Yet, after those objectives were achieved, the project continued to have its funding request renewed with little justification for its continued existence.

Many zombie projects originally started as capital expenditure projects in their early years. After completing the project's initial objectives, revisions and maintenance should have been included in the OPEX budget. However, this never occurred. If these projects continue as ongoing activities, their costs should be placed under operating expenses.

The disadvantage of zero-based budgeting is that it can be extremely time-consuming because it requires the justification of every budget line item, even those supporting core functions. The costs of preparing, reviewing, and approving the budgetary proposal can also escalate to a point where more is spent in budgetary activities associated with a line item than the amount requested for the line item.

Hybrid Budgeting

Some organizations use a hybrid approach to the budgeting process that incorporates some of the benefits of both the traditional and zero-based budgeting, while limiting the disadvantages associated with both methods. This is a hybrid budgeting methodology. Budget items associated with core operations, such as contractual obligations, life safety, and regulatory compliance, receive a traditional budgeting treatment. The justification for this approach is that the performance of these activities is vital to the ongoing existence of the organization. Therefore, additional justification for their continued funding is unnecessary.

Discretionary projects, projects funding renewals or extensions, or other noncore spending requests must be justified based on alignment with business activities or another compelling rationale for funding the effort. Funding of projects that have continued beyond their estimated completion date involve the highest level of scrutiny to receive ongoing funding, such as new regulatory requirements or support for new business areas. All other budget requests receive a moderate level of assessment based upon the provided justification for funding in the next budget cycle.

The primary benefit of the hybrid budgeting approach is that it reduces some of the costs and expense associated with zero-based budgeting by exempting core business activities, while still preserving scrutiny for projects and efforts that may not be cost-justifiable based upon the current needs and direction of the organization. This is a classic application of the Pareto principle, otherwise known as the 80-20 rule. The Pareto principle at it simplest level means that few things (20%) are vital and many (80%) are trivial or of lesser importance in the scheme of things.

Basic Principles of Budget Management

The basics of organizational budgeting are simple to learn and understand.

1. Treat budgetary funds like they are your own personal money.
2. The budget's top priorities and expenditures should reflect organizational priorities and strategies.
3. Budgeting tactics should seek out innovative ways to decrease operational expenditures to provide funds for continuous improvement.
4. All major projects, outside of providing or supporting core functionality and services, should have a business sponsor to assure they are supporting a business priority.

5. All budgetary expenditures should deliver business value.

6. Budgeting is a planning activity where the organization determines how and when it will spend funds allocated to operation functions.

7. Some projects, especially large and complex projects, may span multiple budget cycles. This needs to be reflected in the initial year's budgetary request and referenced in subsequent years' budgetary proposals.

8. Budget proposals need to separate out capital budget requests from operational budget items. Capital expenditures that require operational expenditures in subsequent year budgets should make this clear in the narrative accompanying these requests.

Financial Selling: Getting More Budget

Understanding the Budget "Game"

Probably the number one question among chief information security officers (CISOs) in regard to budgeting involves the most effective way to request an increase in the information security budget. Most organizational executives view the information security function as a *necessary evil* and not a revenue-producing cost center. These executives often hold greater sway with the budget review committee and can influence which projects receive funding and which department budgets get a bump up.

Traditionally, the default strategy for information security to obtain greater funding for initiatives or getting an increase in the overall budget has amounted to an overreliance on fear, uncertainty, and doubt (FUD). This tactic creates credibility problems, because after a decade of proverbial warnings, the cyber sky is not falling. A majority of executives understand more about cyber security issues than they did a decade ago. They are aware that the outcomes of many high-profile security breaches, while costly, rarely result in the catastrophic scenarios used by FUD aficionados.

No one likes to ask for additional budget to fund expansions of information security services or special initiatives. It is uncomfortable to say the least, and somewhat lonely. Any manager who has had to stand alone in front of a committee of their peers delivering a request for funding understands the difficulty of this task. What makes it more difficult for frugal CISOs and other information security executives is that many of their peers do not really understand what they do. Information security and risk management mean different things to different people based upon their experience and background. Many of the frugal CISO's peers may only be familiar with parts of the information security program with which they have had direct contact, such as security administration or antimalware installation.

The security controls necessary to create a strong security posture for the organization are often difficult to explain to executives from other departments or disciplines. By far the greatest obstacle in terms of obtaining additional funding for security initiatives remains the fact that executives may view providing this funding as possibly funding an activity that does not generate revenue.

A basic truth that you learn in your first economics class is that the pool of resources is finite. Any organization has a finite amount of funds to distribute in terms of budget. Since the beginning of the Great Recession in 2007, this finite pool of funds has remained flat or been shrinking in many organizations. The unspoken truth in budgeting is that for every department that gets their request for additional funds approved, another department or departments experiences a corresponding decrease in their budgets. The budgetary approval process is, in essence, a competition for funding. In order for frugal CISOs to succeed at the budget "game," they need to understand business, in addition to information security, to communicate effectively during the budgeting process.

Putting On Your Budget "Game Face"

According to the Urban Dictionary,[2] a *game face* is "a confident swagger you bring out when you are about to get ready to tackle something difficult, or when you are about to take on a challenge, or when you are getting ready to get down to hard business." Players in team sports need to suit up before taking the field. Information security professionals need to dress themselves, figuratively and literally, in a manner that creates a perception of them as businesspeople rather than "security geeks." Other organizational peers may perceive the members of the security team as somewhat paranoid and hypervigilant techno-geeks. More importantly, they see the team as living in its own silo, isolated from the core business functions, and having the sole objective of saying "no" to new business and technology opportunities.

Prior to the budgeting cycle, the frugal CISO needs to demonstrate engagement with the business. There are several ways to do this. One of the *most* effective is to provide proof that the information security team is committed to improving business efficiency to make the organization more competitive in its marketplace. The information security team can go about this objective by reviewing controls and eliminating or replacing controls that add overhead to business processes or limit expansion of business opportunities.

For example, the information security team can spearhead a project to provide single sign-on for users, instead of requiring users to log into multiple applications separately. In addition to the minutes saved each day per user, using a single password or other authentication method, such as a secure token, would create the potential for information security cost savings as well, such as fewer password resets because users would have fewer passwords, perhaps only one, to remember.

Other information security projects with the potential to create business efficiency and streamlining of processes include:

- Self-service security access request site
- Automated passwords resets
- Self-service Secure Sockets Layer (SSL) server certificate dashboard for system administrations and developers
- Self-service site to request or procure security-related items, such as encrypted external hard drives and USB flash drives
- Remote-access user site that offers information to staff about securing their home networks and devices
- Self-service BYOD security site (in conjunction with network-ing/telecommunications group)

Information security initiatives like these offer evidence of information security's strategic direction to support the business needs as its first priority. Peer departments need to view the information security team as a part of the organization's team, rather than an obstacle toward its progress. Showing that the information security team understands costs and creating efficiencies through stream-lining possesses will go a long way toward that goal. One effective

technique to couple with this transformation in strategic direction is
financial selling.

It is critical to avoid backsliding once the team has begun the process of building credibility with peer departments. If peers perceive any backsliding, such as the information security team appearing to be returning to its old ways, it will be likely to view future efforts in building credibility with some skepticism. Peers might feel that the information security team attempted to deceive them by displaying positive behavioral changes to get budgetary requests approved, but reverting to old ways after accomplishing this objective.

What Is Financial Selling?

I first came across the concept of financial selling when I did a brief stint in technology sales right out of college. The idea is that you justify a sale, based not only on the specific benefits of the purchase (such as increased processing efficiency), but on the fact that the investment would, over time, literally pay for itself in reduced costs. For example, an organization is using older software that is no longer covered under the vendor's service level agreement (SLA). In order to maintain the software, the organization may need to support the application on a costly time-and-materials basis. Often, the cost of purchasing a new application, and even the hardware to support it, may be cheaper than continuing with the current break–fix strategy.

The concept behind financial selling is to convince the buyer that a short-term increase in security spending can boost efficiencies and lower total cost overall and in the long term. Financial selling can assist the information security team in gaining financial credibility and will aid in getting support for future investment in other similar endeavors. This can be a "game changer" from a win–lose outcome to a win–win scenario. This strategy is a significant step up from FUD.

Rebranding Return on Security Investment

Return on security investment (ROSI) is not just a different flavor of ROI (return on investment), despite the similar name. However, most executives outside of information security probably consider it to be just that, and get confused because it cannot be viewed by the traditional financial metrics. Traditional ROI measures a direct financial return on investments in equipment, staff, software, or services. ROSI cannot be measured using this traditional approach and the frugal CISO needs to make that clear during the budget process. ROSI involves benefit, but not the standard measurement for the creation of benefit, such as increased revenue generation or expense reduction.

A more accurate paradigm for ROSI is a hybrid between insurance and a home alarm system. Information security investments in people, process, and technology can diminish the potential impact of cyber incidents when they occur. For example, an investment in a layered defense strategy that incorporates a traditional network firewall, intrusion detection system (IDS), and antimalware application can assist in identifying and possibly blocking a cyber attack on the organization. This can minimize the potential scale of a security breach.

Information security also can prevent attacks from occurring entirely by its presence by strengthening the organization's security posture. This is similar to the way home alarm systems work. Their presence discourages attackers, so they move on to easier targets. Insurance companies have long recognized the value of protective defenses because they offer discounts for the presence of monitored home alarm services. Many cyber liability insurers offer discounts for appropriate information security defenses.

By "rebranding" ROSI in this way, the frugal CISO is freed from trying to sell security budget requests based on the absence or occurrence of cyber security events. The frugal CISO can explain the concept of ROSI as the value of protecting critical assets from exploits and preserving the revenue-generation capabilities of those assets. By tying security budget requests to the business value of assets, the benefits of information security are clarified.

For example, if an organization makes an investment in purchasing and using an application vulnerability scanner, and it identifies a number of SQL injection flaws in its Internet transaction processing system, the ROSI of this investment might include the avoidance of data breach fines, legal costs, providing credit monitoring, and the protection of its customer database from possible competitors. In addition, cyber attackers might move on to another easier target because the site is not vulnerable to an easy exploit like SQL injection. This rebrands ROSI as the value associated with revenue preservation rather than as an operating cost. It moves the frugal CISO away from FUD and toward the business value provided by information security.

Getting to Know the Budget Gurus

In every organization there exist individuals with whom the frugal CISO should not only be causally acquainted, but with whom they should establish a strong relationship. Number one on this list should be the chief financial officer (CFO). This title may vary across organizations. If there is a director of budget, put that individual on the *Get to Know* list. These individuals can provide guidance on the budgeting cycle and tips to effectively manage the information security team's budgeting activities. Particularly, for those new to the budgeting process in general, there can be a lot to learn during their maiden attempt at creating a budget.

There are likely some unwritten *rules* or *cultural norms* related to budget preparation. For example, in one organization, it is *verboten* to use a red cover on a budget proposal because it is believed to symbolize red ink (*budgetary deficiencies*).

Even managers with extensive experience in the budgeting realm may need some guidance from the organization's budget gurus because each organization may have its own take on the budgeting process. It is always a good idea to get to know the individuals who can provide this information. Because of their close contact with the budget approval process and members of the budget committee, these key budget gurus can offer insight into different tactical approaches to get budget requests approved or ways to tie information security requests to existing strategic projects.

Budget and financial contacts may also be able to provide samples of the following:

- Budgets
- Budgetary requests and justifications
- Current year's forms
- Instructions or manuals on preparing budgets
- Budget cycle calendar with submission date(s)
- Meeting schedules for the budget review committee

Like any good relationship, it needs to be mutual. Budget staff wants departments to submit well-prepared budgets in a timely manner and with a minimal need for revisions. The frugal CISO needs to make sure that they communicate these objectives to the budget and financial staff, so they understand that the overall intention is to make their jobs easier.

Do not monopolize their time, if the information security team is looking to maintain a good working relationship with the budget group. The budget group is generally willing to provide the assistance a team needs to gain a solid understanding of participating in the budget process. However, do not expect them to actually prepare the information security budget proposal. That is the job of the frugal CISO or their designee. In order to maintain an effective relationship with the budget/financial services team, take the following advice:

1. Listen and do what they ask, such as use the right forms and complete all required paperwork.
2. Respect due dates for budget submissions.
3. Get the math right (use a spreadsheet or calculator and check figures).
4. Make reasonable and educated estimates for the approximate costs of each budget line item.
5. Avoid using SWAG (scientific wild-ass guess) as your primary cost estimation strategy. Sometimes, especially when doing initiatives using emerging technologies, this will be necessary to a small degree. However, this should not be the approach used for the majority of budget items.
6. Unless your organization requires zero-based budgeting, use the traditional (also called the *incremental*) approach to budget preparation. Ask finance, procurement, and payroll for historical data on which to base next year's cost estimates, then add an incremental percentage to these amounts. Then add in any net new planned expenses, such as planned hires or licensing fee upgrades.
7. Learn and use appropriate budget terminology. This will provide both increased credibility when discussing budget issues, but also avoid any potential misunderstanding during budget discussions.

8. Avoid excessive padding of budget line items. An experienced budget analysis will catch this and immediately request more accurate estimates for budget items. Some degree of padding is normal and expected, especially for new initiatives or functions. It is excessive padding, such as padding percentages above 20% that will draw the ire of the budget group. More importantly, they may prevent approval of budget requests.

9. Justifications for budget requests should be well thought out and well written. Always make sure to spell check all documents.

10. Show up at all meetings on time with hardcopies, just in case, of the information security team's budget proposal for the committee members.

11. Prepare an executive summary of the budget proposal that highlights the overarching strategy for information security, new projects, continuing initiatives, and ongoing supported security functions.

12. Become familiar with all the members of the budget committee, such as their names, background, and tasks on the committee. This may assist in the formation of a strong working relationship during discussions.

13. The frugal CISO should always personally express thanks to the budget group for their assistance.

The Budget Cycle

Budgeting activities occur on a cyclic basis. The budget cycle allows the various internal groups to develop and submit a spending plan for the upcoming period, usually a year. The budget cycle allows the organization to modify its spending to respond to changes in its environment, such as economic conditions, technology trends, or marketplace opportunities. It enforces discipline in the spending process by ensuring that each department/team determines its annual fiscal requirements to perform its required operations and any other projects it wants to undertake. It requires justification of all spending based on business needs.

By reviewing all proposed budget plans and their supporting justification as a whole, the budget committee can ensure that all parts of the organization are moving toward a set of common objectives rather than disjointed initiatives with limited connectivity to a central organization strategy. The budget cycle consists of five phases:

1. Budget planning, preparation, and submission activities
2. Approval
3. Execution
4. Audit and evaluation
5. Budget replanning

Budget Planning, Preparation, and Submission Activities

The budget planning stage usually starts about six and twelve months before the start of the next budget year. A common first step is the performance of a organizational needs assessment to determine what role(s) the information security team needs to consider assuming in the next budget cycle, including programming planning to support the team's objectives. During this period, the information security team needs to both assess its current operational activities and any other activities it plans to consider taking on in the next year.

The costs of both new and planned activities, include:

- Personnel costs (salaries, contractors) and benefits
- Outsourced or procedures services (such as consulting firms, Penetration Testing (pen-test) services, etc.)
- Annual software license fees
- New capital expenses, such as hardware, infrastructure upgrades, software purchases
- Travel and entertainment
- Training and certification
- Organizational service chargebacks, such as networks
- Miscellaneous, such as phones, mileage, reimbursement, subscriptions, etc.
- Physical space rents or maintenance costs
- Consumable materials, such as office supplies
- Supporting services, such as cleaning
- Indirect costs

In addition to the expenditures for current and expanded service offerings provided by the information security team, the proposed budget needs to include estimates for any new or continuing initiatives proposed for the next budget year, including:

- CAPEX (infrastructure, equipment, outright software purchases, etc.)
- Additional personnel required by proposed initiatives
- Organizational service chargebacks, such as networks
- Miscellaneous, such as phones, mileage, reimbursement, subscriptions, etc.
- Outsourced or procedures services (such as consulting firms, pen-test services, etc.)
- Annual software license fees associated with the project

After assessing the different activities and projects that it wants to consider undertaking, the information security team needs to do its first round of budget development. This step requires developing preliminary estimates for each budget item. After developing the first draft of the proposed information security team's budget, the budget request needs to be reviewed using the following questions:

1. Are all budget figures and total costs aligned with the fiscal realities of the organization, such as general economic conditions and the budgetary strategies of the organization?
2. Is the budget in line with past information security budgets and comparably sized non-revenue-producing departments?
3. Are mandatory compliance requirements or remediation of audit findings responsible for significant new funding requests?
4. Can you identify any budget items that can be reduced if the full funding request is not received *(Plan B)*?
5. Can project funding requests be prioritized in terms of criticality, such as maintaining regulatory compliance, remediating identified vulnerabilities, fixing audit findings, and injecting technological innovations into the information security program?
6. What budget items is the frugal CISO prepared to drop if budget levels must be reduced?
7. What budget items is the frugal CISO prepared to fight for in the event of reduced budget levels?

Before submitting the information security budget proposal, the team needs to develop alternative strategies in terms of how to approach budget negotiations. This means determining which budget items need to be preserved at any cost and which budget requests the team needs to be prepared to sacrifice or postpone until the next budget year. This means the team's budget negotiator needs to have the facts and justifications prepared to preserve each budget item. After finalizing the budget, it is ready for submission to the budget committee.

It is important that the members of the team responsible for submitting the budget know the proper procedure for the budget's submission, such as:

- Date the budget is due to the budget committee
- How and where to submit the budget (format, email box/ website, contact names)
- Expected next steps after submission
- Meeting schedule for budget negotiations or discussions

Approval

Prior to final approval of the budget, most organizations go through a series of negotiations with each department, team, or group submitting a budgetary proposal. At this step, the team's representative will engage in a series of discussions with members of the budget committee in regard to different budget line items. This process may be formal or informal, depending upon the organization, its fiscal practices, and culture.

Members of the budget committee will ask questions about the budget item, the estimated costs, and its funding priority as a component of the total budget. It is essential that the team representative have this information available and speak in the appropriate fiscal vernacular to maximize their credibility during this crucial stage in the budgetary process. As a result of these discussions with the budget committee, the information team may need to revise the budget and resubmit the budget with the required adjustments. Depending on the organization, there may be one or several iterations of budgetary revisions and resubmissions before the finalization of the budget.

During the budget negotiation stage, the frugal CISO should be prepared for some significant announcements emanating from the discussions, such as a request for across-the-board budget reductions.

Often, these announcements and new budgetary requirements result from end-of-year revenue changes or projections that can necessitate budget cuts or enhancements in order to meet revenue or other financial targets in the coming year.

As unpleasant as last-minute budget news can be, getting a requirement for budget revisions at a later point in the fiscal year is usually considerably more difficult to manage. Trying to make up a budget shortfall, for example at the six-month point, can result in a need for a reduction in force (RIF), project cancellations, or suspension of project activities, and other draconian measures. When getting bad budget news, early is always preferable. In addition to other budget contingency planning strategies, frugal CISOs and their teams need to develop tactical approaches to manage either specific percentage increases or decreases in overall organizational budgets.

Budget Execution

After the approval of the final budget, the information security team needs to transition into the budget execution stage. While theoretically the budget execution stage does not begin until after the finalization of the budget, the work required in executing the budget efficiently and cost effectively needs to start almost in parallel with the preparation of the budget itself. To prepare for the execution of the new budget, the information security team needs to do the following:

- Prepare requests for proposals (RFPs) or requests for quotations (RFQs) for any services or products that the team's proposed plans require.
- Draft contracts for insurance or retainers for service firms.
- Establish points of contact with agencies that supply temporary or contract staff that proposed plans will require.
- Draft agreements for renewals of any licenses or SLAs that will expire over the next fiscal year.

While no action can occur without budget approval, all the necessary pieces need to be ready after the finalization of the budget, otherwise many planned activities will experience delays created by these procurement activities.

Once the budget is in place, the fiscal management phase begins. This phase starts during the first month of the current fiscal year and terminates on the last day of the fiscal year. The primary objective of fiscal management activities is to ensure that internal funds are appropriately allocated and managed to cover all planned team expenses. This is similar to personal budget management. It is important for all teams, and especially managers, to understand their specific approval amounts for signing off on expenditures. If the group is not assigned a financial analyst to manage the cash flow, it is necessary to assign this responsibility to a team member. The key to successful budget execution is tracking to keep the budget *on plan* and performing any necessary course corrections before digging too big a hole to climb out of easily.

Unfortunately, contrary to most budget examples, funds are not allocated and spent in twelve equal increments. For example, some information security projects might expend larger budget amounts early on to make purchases that will benefit the initiative throughout its duration, or some costs may not be incurred until late in the project's life cycle. This is normal and expected, as long as the expenditures correspond to the project spending plan. However, if project expenditures are outside the normal variances, such as travel expenditures are double the expected amount, this discrepancy warrants investigation to see why the additional expenditures occurred. If the expenditure cannot be justified, steps need to occur to put the budget back on track.

Care should be taken to assure the appropriate accounting of financial transactions. This includes both actual expenditures and internal chargebacks. Solid budget accounting is crucial to cost control and expenditure containment. A frequent mistake by a budgetary novice is postponing budgetary reviews until after completion of the project or fiscal year. However, with budgetary power comes the responsibility[3] to manage the organization's assets effectively.

Audit and Evaluation

Solid accounting and variance investigation is crucial to the next step in the budget process, audit and evaluation. Like any plan, the proof of the pudding[4] is in the results. This is true of expected deliverables, as well as the ability to stay on budget. The ultimate goal of a budget and project is to succeed in achieving the promised deliverables and staying on (or under) the budget. In addition to end-of-the-year fiscal reporting, organizations may perform random budget audits to evaluate performance against budget (or look for fraud).

Most organizations start budget auditing activities within a few months after the preparation of the end-of-year financial statements. The audit data becomes input for the next future budget cycle. The following types of audit may be included in the post-budget-year assessments:

- Basic financial audit
- Performance audit
- Cost/financial analysis

There are several reasons to perform budget audits. The most obvious is detection of possible fraud. Over the last decade, many businesses and government entities have been rocked by budget scandals involving the misuse and potentially fraudulent use of budgetary funds. Some of the most recent budget scandals include the potential mishandling of government credit cards and excessive travel/entertainment expenses at the Internal Revenue Service (IRS).

For this reason, the Auditing Standards Board (ASB) of the AICPA (American Institute of Certified Public Accounts), created the SAS 99 standard. It directs auditors to exercise professional skepticism when considering the possibility that fraud could be present when performing engagements involving financial matters. In addition to looking for instances of fraud, budget audits evaluate whether funds are being expended in a manner consistent with organizational strategies and approved purposes. Audits compare actual expenses against approved budget line items to verify that the expenditure of funds was consistent with agreed-upon use.

Another focus area for budgetary audits is whether expenditures are being appropriately categorized as CAPEX or OPEX. One area of concern for a CFO is expenditures recorded as CAPEX when the funds were actually consumed for OPEX.

The primary reason that categorizing budgetary expenditures correctly is important is that the use of the CAPEX category implies that the organization will derive continuing value from the expenditure rather than just consuming the funds to maintain current operations. CAPEX budget should be reserved for long-term investments in equipment, plant, or property. Sometimes managers conceal poor budget/project management by paying operating expenses using CAPEX dollars. For example, the budget allocates CAPEX dollars for the customization of a vendor security solution. However, CAPEX dollars are used to cover shortfalls in operational areas, thus depleting the earmarked customization funds.

A continuing pattern of this budgeting tactic can result in failure to deliver on CAPEX-funded projects. It can also be an indicator of a failure to manage budgetary expenses effectively. Using funds allocated for a different purpose to cover operating deficiencies shows the inability to either adhere to the budget or estimate actual operational costs. In either case, the situation warrants further investigation and possible remediation to prevent recurrence. It also creates tax reporting issues for the organization. CAPEX assets appear on the balance sheet as *assets*. They undergo depreciation for taxation purposes. OPEX purchases are daily operations costs that are fully deducted when they are incurred.

The best strategy to manage the audit process is maintaining meticulous accounting records and backup documentation for all expenditures. This means monitoring to ensure the use of the appropriate cost centers to report budget expenditures. All substantial variances require prompt investigation. The responsibility to manage an independent budget requires that the information security team demonstrate maturity in the managing of its budget.

Budget Replanning

Budgeting, like risk management, is an iterative process. It never truly ends because while frugal CISOs are managing the current budget, they are planning for the next budget cycle. At certain points, activity may be occurring on up to three budgets:

1. Budget audit and assessment (past year's budget)
2. Fiscal management (current year's budget)
3. Budget planning (next year's budget)

Unless your organization requires a strict zero-based budgeting approach, a great deal of the work used in the preparation of the prior year's budget can be refactored into the preparation of the coming year's budget. Determining which budget item can be recycled for use in the next fiscal year's budget usually starts late in the current year's budget cycle. Since the information security team likely performs a standard set of activities, the current year's budget offers an excellent starting point for estimating budget items using an incremental increase based upon current inflation amounts.

If the information security team plans to increase its current level of service for some activities, such as decreasing turnaround time on some tasks, the projected budget item needs to reflect the costs of providing a higher service level, such as the cost of additional staff members and software licenses. For many teams, a substantial component of budget replanning involves funding for a variety of new and existing security projects and programs. Project and program budget planning can be more complicated for two reasons:

1. All the costs involved with running programs and projects may be difficult to estimate with complete accuracy because of the many unknown factors involved.
2. Budgets for some programs and projects may come from multiple funding sources, such as external grants or both departments' operating or project budgets.

A program is a group of related projects coordinated to provide advantages that could not be derived by running each project individually. Projects are efforts of fixed duration to accomplish a specific set of deliverables or objectives. A project is unique, with both a beginning and an end. A program, in a larger sense, is a group of related projects that are coordinated simultaneously to achieve a specific result. A project can exist outside the existence of a program. However, the inverse is not true. Programs are always composed of a series of interconnected projects. Programs may have no specific end date and continue indefinitely while its objectives remain relevant to the business's needs.

An information security team at a lower level of maturity continuum tends to use primarily projects. Information security teams at higher maturity levels often utilize projects run under a program structure. For example, an enterprisewide IT program to convert to cloud computing might include a project with the information security team to ensure the security of sensitive data stored in the cloud. Due to the continuing nature of programs, their budgets require replanning on an annual basis. Some projects, both stand-alone and as part of programs, require replanning if their duration extends beyond one fiscal year (see the next section, "Budgeting for Multiyear Projects").

Budgeting for Multiyear Projects

Some significant information security initiatives can literally take years to complete. This is common with a transformational shift in technology or strategy. This means that an initiative's funding request may span more than one budgetary cycle. Depending on the organization, this may be accomplished in different ways, for example, a project may receive one cost center that will follow it through to the completion of an initiative. In other organizations, different approaches may be taken, such as assigning a multiyear project a different cost center annually or using a master project cost center with subsidiary cost centers for every year that the project remains active.

If the project has distinct phases with specific funding requirements, the initial budget and subsequent budgets should reference this information. Project plans should also reference budgeting information to provide traceable expenditures. Budgets should be tied to annual deliverables, especially CAPEX, and personal expenditures, such as salaries and contractor hourly costs. It is important to maintain accountability and traceability to track performance to budget and potentially provide an audit trail later, if required by the internal audit or financial departments. This is especially important to the frugal CISO if their team or the organization as a whole receives federal funding related to programs or projects.

Avoiding Requesting Additional Funds for Nonbudgeted Expenses

The bane of most C-level and senior executives, as well as their financial teams, is the request for funds that did not appear in the current year's budget. Many executives regard these requests as inadequate or poor planning on the part of the executives or managers submitting them. Unfortunately, in information security, these types of requests may not be totally avoidable due to the dynamic nature of the environment.

Some information security–related events or incidents can crop up without much notice, such as unanticipated audit findings, an innovative species of malware infection, or a security breach. However, some expenses can be, at least partially, anticipated or planned.

Information security budgets need to include budget line items for management of security events and incidents. The budget justification for these line items should make it clear that managing and containing potential cyber incidents is an expected component of the function of the information security team. Therefore, it is vital, in terms of good budget management, to build these anticipated costs into the budget plan.

However, there will always be cyber security scenarios that even a seer could not predict. Often, this is because they involve the introduction of a new breed of malware and infection mechanism that had not previously been seen, such as the mass mailer attacks and blended threats of the early 2000s. Often, these events fall to a degree under the category of *Black Swan*[5] events. Black Swan events are unforeseen events of great enormity and effect. The best example of a Black Swan event was the 9/11 attack on the World Trade Center towers.

There are two budgeting strategies to avoid requesting additional budgetary allocations to manage these types of unanticipated events. The first one has been previously mentioned, which is to include a specific budget line item to meet the expenses of remediating smaller cyber security incidents, such as minor malware infection affecting a number of devices or tracking down lost devices.

Funding for more significant cyber issues, such as major security breaches and larger-scale malware infections, would be financed using a cyber insurance policy, included in a line item on the information security budget. There are a few remaining categories of potential unbudgeted expenses that can be difficult to effectively manage.

One of these categories may occur as the result of audits that require immediate remediation to resolve the finding. Depending on where in the annual budget cycle these findings are presented, it may not always be possible to postpone remediation until after the start of the next budget cycle. High-risk issues may require resolution prior to an opportunity to include them in the next budget.

Often, the risk issues may originate outside the information security team. However, it is often the information security team, and perhaps its budget, that is responsible for closing the audit finding. In these situations, the ideal is to get the responsible business areas to foot the costs of the necessary remediation, but this may not always be possible. In addition, if the situation arises from a regulatory audit, the cost of postponing remediation activities may result in an escalation of fines and other penalties that could potentially exceed remediation expenditures. The best strategy for managing these types of events is the development of a strong working relationship between the frugal CISO and other C-level executives, especially the chief executive officer (CEO) and chief information officer (CIO) of the organization. The frugal CISO needs to effectively communicate these issues with his C-level colleagues, and they need confidence in the frugal CISO's ability to manage these situations effectively and efficiently.

Another category of unanticipated expenses may occur as the result of a security breach. As the result of a security breach or attempted breach, planned cyber security initiatives may require expedited scheduling to prevent future incursions. These may be justifiable instances for requesting additional nonbudgeted funds. This is because the cost of detecting, containing, and correcting future attacks will generally be greater than any costs of moving up the implementation of control solutions, such as encrypting databases or hardening wireless networks.

Tips for Information Security Budgeting Success

Dealing with budgets can take many technically focused professionals out of their comfort zone. It can be laborious and frustrating. In addition, the need to "sell" information security to gain additional budget can be awkward, especially without FUD as a familiar crutch on which to lean. However, without appropriate funding, information security teams cannot mature and innovate.

1. Do not procrastinate in preparing budgets. Just like any document, the more time there is, the more time available to polish, the stronger the final product.
2. Develop a relationship with your assigned budget or financial analyst. Take your analyst for coffee (or lunch) on a regular basis.
3. Avoid FUD as a justification for increased budgetary allocations. It is not nearly as effective as it used to be, and most

boards of directors and senior executives rarely respond to this tired strategy anymore.

4. Identify the "budget whisperer" (individual with financial prowess) on the information security team and assign them to lead budget efforts. Make sure this individual receives recognition for his or her efforts and that his or her performance review reflects his or her contributions.

5. Continuously track spending against spending plans to identify (and potentially correct) many substantial variances.

6. Create a matrix that maps information security projects and spending to organizational strategies.

7. Always expect to be audited.

8. Identify and initiate discussions with potential sponsors for future security initiatives, such as federated identities or BYOI (bring your own identity) with ecommerce teams.

9. Continuously promote information security capabilities to enhance business initiative with organizational peers, senior executives, and C-level officers, not just at budget time.

10. Practice solid program and project accounting to avoid issues during financial audits.

11. Encourage your team to perfect their ability to estimate program and project costs and avoid SWAG as a default cost prediction strategy. This will increase the team's credibility in budget preparation and management with the budget committee and senior executives.

12. To reduce cost or provide funds for innovative initiatives, look for existing projects that have continued past their original completion date. After all, projects by definition have a start and finish date. Projects that have existed beyond their estimated completion may have evolved into a service offering. They should be funded appropriately as a core service. The project might also be a candidate for retirement or absorbed into another functional area.

13. Have the team explore different strategies for streamlining tasks, such as combining redundant activities or mitigating tasks to another more appropriate team outside of the security area.

14. Look for potential revenue enhancement activities, such as charging back costs to another internal group, for providing services, such as external security reviews.
15. Ask the team to do an in-depth analysis of the costs of providing information security services using a total cost basis using financial reporting and observation. This information can become input to justify the expansion of service level or requesting additional resources.
16. At the budget committee meeting, come prepared with metrics to support the request for additional funding.
17. Avoid any appearance of lavish spending (think of the IRS and AIG conference scandals), unless this is the organization's normal practice. Donuts and pizza may be OK occasionally, but avoid lavish dinners or expensive tchotchkes as event loot may not be appropriate.
18. Demonstrate *tone from the top* in careful and effective spending of corporate budget.
19. Do not sacrifice training as an easy budget reducer. Eliminating the training is often a reflexive action when budgets are flat or reduced. The cost savings achieved is short term, but the impact of diminished training can create a long-term impact on the course of the team's maturation. Training does not have to be expensive, require conferences, or travel. Encourage the team to look for inexpensive training and development options available locally or via the Internet. Provide recognition for team members who develop internal training courses for their colleagues. If your organization offers tuition reimbursement, make sure that members know about the benefit.
20. Encourage team members to attend other internal groups' functions and act as ambassadors for information security services.
21. Look to eliminate or reduce redundant information security offerings, such as multiple secure email or antimalware suites.
22. Look to standardize a suite of security solutions to take advantage of volume purchasing discounts.
23. Whenever possible, look to incorporate public domain security solutions, such as encryption tools or encrypted password solutions. However, to ensure the potential success of public

domain security, allocate resources toward their implementation. Otherwise, the net result may not be cost savings, but increased complexity and confusion. Implementation is often inexpensive, such as providing well-written instructions for end users.

24. If members of the information security team need to travel on a frequent basis, analyze previous travel and expense reports to determine any ways to reduce costs, such as traveling on specific days or using hotel discount programs. This information can create guidance for more cost-effective travel.

25. The frugal CISO should meet with the CFO (or equivalent position) at least on a quarterly basis to discuss fiscal issues and budget projections.

26. If large unanticipated expenses look possible, such as remediation of audit findings or new regulatory requirements, notify the CFO, CIO, or CEO as soon as possible to allow for the potential reallocation of budgets to cover these costs, if they come to fruition. This provides the finance department with more time to explore possible funding strategies.

27. Evaluate if it is more cost effective to outsource a specialized information security function, such as digital forensics or penetration testing, or create an internal team with the required competencies. Often, retainer contracts or hourly fees may be less than maintaining the requisite competencies and technology in-house.

28. Consider the use of cyber insurance to cover Black Swan events or major security breaches that cost more than a specific expenditure threshold.

29. Identify potential places where the application of security controls and solutions can potentially contribute to lowering of overall costs. If the costs of fixing software flaws associated with security vulnerabilities and maintaining "bolt-on" security continues to escalate, the addition of a secure development training initiative by the information security team might assist in the identification of potential software flaws earlier, when they are cheaper to fix, or preventing them from occurring at all.

30. Tell team members that the information security team's budget should be treated as if it were their own paycheck.

Endnotes

1. Author's own term for using appropriate budget terminology.
2. "Game face," Urban Dictionary, http://www.urbandictionary.com/define. php?term=game+face.
3. Transformative use of quote from Franklin D. Roosevelt's last speech (1945): "Today we have learned in the agony of war that great power involves great responsibility." A variation of this quote was used in the *Spiderman* saga.
4. "The proof of the pudding" is just a shortened version of the phrase "the proof of the pudding is in the eating." The verb is another word for *test*.
5. Black Swan theory was developed by Nassim Nicholas Taleb and discussed in his popular 2007 book, *The Black Swan* (New York: Random House), which discussed the role of high-profile, unanticipated, and uncommon events on society and history, such as the 9/11 attacks.

11

USING THE GOLDILOCKS PRINCIPLE

Getting It Just Right

The frugal chief information security officer (CISO) endeavors to size and scope his or her organization's information security program to fit *just right* by using the *Goldilocks Principle*. This avoids the common mistake of underbuilding or overbuilding an information security program. The Goldilocks Principle says that something must fall within certain margins rather than going to opposite ends of a spectrum of options. To build a long-term sustainable program, the best place to be is *just right* where the amount of resources devoted to efforts is commensurate with the risk landscape of the organization it serves.

You Can't Go Home Again

One common error occurs when a CISO or information security manager attempts to re-create the program at their prior employer rather than developing a program based on their new organization's risk profile. I call this approach the "if it doesn't fit, I will make it fit" syndrome. Even if the executive manages to create a perfect copy of his or her former program, it rarely lives up to his or her memory of it.

The primary issue is that the former employer's risk landscape may differ considerably from that of the current employer, creating a mismatch between risks and control costs. A common symptom of this desire to re-create a prior employer's information security program is the purchasing of the same security products used at the former company, even when this security function already exists in the new environment.

A number of reasons exist for why *cloning* attempts might not succeed. One is that it is impossible to re-create the staff that was responsible for the old program exactly. When we analyze winning sports teams, such as Super Bowl or World Series winning teams, it is often the perfect combination of attributes, especially team membership, rather just sheer raw talent. Teams may be successful because the strengths and weakness of the various team members complement each other perfectly.

If one member of the team were taken out of the equation, the team might not operate as well. This has certainly proved to be the case with other types of groups, such as winning sports teams. When one player leaves the organization, sometimes not even a *major player*, the overall performance suffers and sometimes never completely recovers to its former level of success. Sometimes, it can take years for the winning *right combination* of players to emerge again to allow the team to achieve a comparable level of success.

Many leaders have experienced similar phenomena during their careers. Some leaders are wildly successful in one position and achieve superior results across all their initiatives. However, when they move or receive a promotion to another organization, they never quite attain the same level of success as in their former position. The cynics often attribute this inability to realize the same level of success that they previously enjoyed to the Peter Principle.[2] However, while strong leadership is an important component of superior performance and outcomes, it is not enough to guarantee success in every situation.

Often, the composition of the team will play a significant role in outcomes. Not all teams need to be composed of "stars"; in fact, that can actually hamper team performance. Achieving optimal performance requires having both a diversity and balance of skills and personal attributes among team members.

Even if a new CISO manages to recruit a number of members of their former team, it can be difficult to re-create that *je ne sais quoi* (French for "something special") behind its success. Attempts to re-create old teams more often result in failures for the CISO attempting them. The recruiting of old staff into key positions on a new information security team might backfire because the existing team might resent their new peers. Former "stars" might not be as successful in a different organizational culture and another team makeup. The new team might resent the hiring of old team members into key slots and resist assimilating them into the team. Another typical attempt at re-creating is by purchasing the same security solutions or implementing the same best practices.

It is crucial for the CISO to understand the reason why we tend to try, to some degree or another, to re-create our old environments. As human beings, we gravitate toward what is familiar, even when we espouse a desire for change. Usually, once we admit that to ourselves, it is easier to move on and create a new information security program specific to the organization and its unique needs.

Do We Need to Be *World Class* or *Best in Breed*?

Not every organization needs a world-class risk management program. While *reach* goals are admirable, devoting too many resources to unnecessary objectives can be costly and divert focus from the immediate information security needs of the organization. The risk management program needs to support compliance and identified risks for the organization it services. Overarchitecting a security program can waste resources by implementing unnecessary or inappropriate controls. The scope and resource intensity of a specific organization's information security activities should reflect the risks identified in the current IT risk assessments and audit reports. Controls should be added as required based on newly identified risk issues and threats associated with emerging technology trends.

The question that every frugal CISO needs to be able to answer to appropriately secure assets from potential threat agents is, "How much security is enough?" The response is often to meet all identified compliance requirements plus best practices.

Best practices represent the most efficient or effective way to accomplish an objective based upon the opinions or recommendations of a subject matter expert or some other authority, such as a governing body. While best practices generally dictate the recommended course of action, they are predicated upon specific circumstances. Best practices are situational in nature, and therefore their implementation is not always prudent. Best practices are not always cost effective.

One key concept that I learned during my MBA studies is that the amount of resources are finite. In the last couple of years, resources have become increasingly scarce, especially for activities that are perceived as having no direct contribution to revenue generation. Therefore, from a cost and risk management perspective, it becomes important to devote available resources to the most significant areas of risk.

Are Best Practices Really Always "Best"?

Frederick the Great said, "In trying to defend everything he defended nothing." Implementing controls around best practices is often an attempt to protect *everything* rather than taking a bespoke approach, which evaluates the specific risks and targets the preponderance of controls around those threats. The effective implementation of best practices is dependent upon the maturity stage of the organization's information security program. Certain best practices are dependent upon the information security team's maturity stage for effective implementation. Some practices require a very high level of maturity to be effective.

For instance, noncompulsory information security certifications, like ISO 27001, have a strategic focus and are best adopted by an Information Security (IS) organization that has achieved at least the midpoint stage of maturity, equivalent to the Nolan Model's Control stage, in which security evolves from a project to a program approach. The best reason for not adopting ISO 27001 at an earlier maturity stage is that this certification evaluation is targeted at the program level and the process itself requires significant resources to manage successfully. Some information security practitioners substitute the *recommended practice* for *best practice* to reduce the perspective that *best* is appropriate for all organizations.

In reality, best practices seek to offer the most security possible for information assets balanced against responsible budget management and information access. Best practices are meant to provide guidelines and not dictate particular methods, materials, or practices. They are discretionary and can be modified or customized to meet the needs of a specific organization's needs.

Best Practices

Best practices are tactics that have proved to be effective in a number of organizations and consistently produced superior outcomes. Often, industry leaders, innovative organizations, or enterprises with an established reputation for promoting effective management techniques establish best practices. Over time, the practices spread to other organizations and may be documented in media or discussed at conferences. They become used as benchmarks for other organizations to emulate. However, best practices may become obsolete because technology or other innovation may create new best practices to replace existing ones. Best practices are not always cost effective.

After a best practice catches fire, it can assume a life of its own. A best practice may be adopted by organizations to avoid compulsory compliance requirements or to impress auditors. The use of best practices by an organization can become a kind of status symbol among some CISOs and information security practitioners to impress peers. Often, the justification for the implementation of the best practice is solely that it is a *best practice.*

Before implementing any best practice, the potential benefits and costs associated with them need to be examined by asking some questions, such as:

- What is the total cost of implementing this best practice?
- What risks is this best practice designed to protect against and are metrics available on its performance in reducing these threats?
- Is this best practice required or strongly recommended by any compliance regulators?
- Has this best practice been used in similarly sized organizations or other organizations in the same business sector?
- Do any disadvantages exist in relation to the use of this best practice?
- Do any existing security controls defend against the same risks?

Keys to Success in Implementing Best Practices

If an organization makes the decision to go forward in the implementation of a best practice, there are some keys to increasing the opportunity to optimize its benefit.

Is It Feasible?

The first step in determining whether a best practice is appropriate for the organization is to determine the feasibility of using it within the environment in which it will be applied. The overarching question in regard to the deployment environment focuses around having the resources to support the best practice. There are a couple of ways to analyze the feasibility without a full-scale implementation.

One option is to make some estimates based upon projected averages. For example, if the best practice is to perform a user access review on a quarterly basis, use the average time to perform an individual review process multiplied by the number of accounts to determine a realistic estimate of the resources necessary to implement the practice. The disadvantage of this approach is that not all implementation variables may be considered in the estimates.

Another way is to run a *proof-of-concept* pilot using the best practice. The disadvantage of this approach is that it is more expensive because it entails putting in place some of the resources and processes required to implement the best practice. The benefit of the proof-of-concept pilot is that it will identify some variables that the initial analysis might not have considered. For example, there could be some cultural resistance to the best practice or it might create a performance impact on downstream processes. It is better and cheaper to discard a proof-of-concept pilot than move forward with a complete implementation that would ultimately not succeed and create great budget losses.

Another disadvantage of the proof-of-concept pilot is that even if it is successful, it may not be possible to expand the pilot implementation into a full-scale production environment *as is*, so a new implementation may be required. This will increase the cost of implementing the best practice.

Regardless of the method used to determine feasibility, it is important to understand how a best practice might be assimilated into a specific organization. In addition, it may assist in identifying any factors that might increase the opportunity for success, such as ways to reduce cultural resistance, in the implementation of the best practice under consideration for adoption.

Make It Your Own

While some organizations try the "if it doesn't fit, I'll make it fit" approach to implementing a best practice by putting it into operation in the same manner as other enterprises, customization offers a better chance for success. When customizing a best practice for another organization, it is important to identify and preserve the fundamental components of the practice, while providing adequate flexibility to adapt it to the specific conditions of the environment. A strong best practice is adaptablely most organizations, while still providing its benefits.

Get Real

Have realistic expectations about the benefits that will be derived from implementing a best practice. Best practices, like security tools, are not "silver bullets" that make all security risks evaporate. The rewards of best practices may not be proportionate to their total costs of implementation and support.

Consider People, Process, and Technology

People, process, and technology are the Golden Triangle of all successful implementations. Alignment of the Golden Triangle is essential to ensuring that any change will work. People act as the catalyst for implementing change. They must be committed to making it work, and ready to do what is necessary to fix the problems that may occur along the way.

Start by identifying key steps (from end to end) that are required by the best practice and drill down to capture the details and various exceptions that will need to be managed. Utilize technologies to ensure that the best practice is consistently applied and that no side channels are available to bypass the process.

For example, if the best practice requires that all production changes go through a formal change control that includes an information security review, there should be no way to implement a change without this sign-off, such as the use of an emergency fix.

Determining the Efficiency of Best Practices for an Organization

Best practices are like shoes, in that the fit varies. The appropriate fit is dependent upon a number of factors that are specific to an organization at a specific point in time, and its unique risk landscape.

Some factors that influence the efficiency of a best practice include:

- Size of overall organization
- Resources available to the information security team, such as staff, budget, and technology
- Support from across the organization, especially at the executive/board level
- Inherent risks of business model
- Infrastructure complexity
- Value of assets
- Regulatory environment
- Risk tolerance/appetite of executive management

Each best practice requires a risk assessment to weigh its protective benefits against any possible disadvantages, such as cost or a clash with organizational culture. Most importantly from the frugal CISO perspective, there needs to be proper justification beyond a control is a best practice for its implementation.

From the frugal CISO's perspective, the most important question is, "Why we are doing this?" It is fine to justify implementing a best practice by stating that from an audit and compliance viewpoint, it is expected of an organization of a certain size or operating within a specific business sector, and that the absence of the best practice might draw unwanted attention. However, this should not be the reason behind the majority of best practice implementations.

Smart Operating Practices

While many best practices are only appropriate in an organization demonstrating specific attributes, such as the maturity stage of the information security team and overall development level of the organization, *smart practices* are, in general, universally applicable to most organizations. Smart practices offer a defense against the wide variety of security threats, both internal and external to the organization.

Smart practices are more generic in their application versus best practices, whose applicability will vary with the context in which they are practiced. Smart practices allow an organization to gain benefits at a very low cost of entry. Smart practices usually involve tactical approaches to reducing multiple risk categories, increasing the effectiveness of security operations, or reducing the cost of security.

Thirty Nearly Universal Smart Practices for Information Security

1. Encrypt all data at rest and in transit on all platforms. Encryption protects sensitive data from unauthorized access and prevents data exposures created by device loss and theft.

2. Implement data-loss prevention (DLP) solutions beyond compliance requirements. Do not just look to identify only financial account numbers or government-issued identification numbers, but also look to utilize the full value of the investments by looking for other types of potential high-value data that may be at risk. Use DLP to monitor, identify, and prevent the flow of data into and out of the organization IT infrastructure, such as the use of unapproved encryption to transmit potentially sensitive data out of the organization.

3. Place limits on the appropriate use of removable storage and storage devices, such as USB flash drives, external hard disks, and CD/DVD media. Unencrypted and uncontrolled removable media has been associated with a number of security breaches and data thefts.

4. Require all media to be scanned prior to use. Use policy and configuration management to disable the *autoplay* feature (launches a program when media is connected to the device) for all removable media.

5. Maintain security patches.

6. Continue to educate users and promote security awareness. A knowledgeable user will be less likely to take risks with the organization's assets.

7. Do not forget the importance of physical security measures. Once an attacker is inside a facility, the number of exploits grows exponentially.

8. Make use of strong encryption keys. Due to increases in processing speed, 2048-bit encryption key should be the minimum baseline used for all symmetric keys.

9. Use the frugal information security principle of spend where it is most impactful (SWIIMI). MBA 101 tells us to make investments where you get the most bang for the buck, also called return on investment (ROI). There is a finite amount of resources available within any organization.

10. Make strong, simple, and cost-effective policies the foundation of the information security program. Avoid aspirational policies and concentrate on basic risk reduction, rather than avoiding potential Black Swan exploits.

11. Create a bespoke information security program that is specific to your organization's risk landscape, culture, and needs. Do not try to emulate other information security programs.

12. Concentrate on strong general IT controls first, to provide a blanket of protection over the majority of risks, and then add specialized security, as necessary.

13. Do not reflexively eliminate training and education as a way of reducing the budget. People are the few assets that appreciate in value rather than depreciate.

14. The frugal CISO sets a tone from the top that demonstrates that rules apply to everyone. Be the team member you want others to emulate.

15. Actively network and communicate with the business to seek out opportunities to tie security into enterprise strategies.

16. Just say no to FUD (fear, uncertainty, and doubt) as a budget justification.

17. Look before you leap when attempting to decrease technical security costs by using open source security tools. Open source security tools are usually free or available for a small fee and are software that is available to the public and maintained by a volunteer community. While an open source approach may, on the surface, appear to reduce costs, it is important to look at the total cost of ownership, of which purchase or license price is only one component. To create a comprehensive security solution may require combining several open source tools. Using open source tools requires expertise for configuration, implementation, and support. Make sure this is available in your organization if electing to go with this strategy.

18. Always require a complete set of needs and requirements *before* moving forward with a search for vendor security solutions. This will allow the evaluation team to compare the potential products and services against a common set of objective criteria rather than being swayed by a particular solution. It also prevents purchasing a solution with features the organization does not need or will not use.

19. Make sure that all members of the information security team have a professional development plan in place to extend their value to the organization. A static skill set may weaken quickly in a dynamic environment like information security and technology.

20. Implement a vendor risk review process to provide due diligence on vendors and outsourcers managing, storing, and processing the organization's sensitive and proprietary information. As the security perimeter moves away from a centralized strategy, it becomes critical to ensure that organizational data remains secure wherever it exists.

21. Implement a secure development strategy to ensure the security is *baked in* instead *of bolted on*. While this strategy may require an investment in tools, such as vulnerability scanners, code reviews, training, and time, it can result in substantial cost savings in preventing security breaches and expensive remediation of security flaws.

22. Only log what you plan to review on a regular basis or will need in the event of incident remediation. Creating logs that are not used or reviewed increases both costs and risks.

23. A reduction in risk and security costs is possible by decreasing the amount of data that requires protection. Work with your peers in records and information management (RIM) to reduce redundant data and ensure the destruction of data beyond its retention date.[3] At least one major security breach was made significantly worse by the presence of personally identifiable information (PII) that was kept past its retention date.

24. Avoid an overreliance on acquiring the latest "silver bullet" solutions and concentrate on putting the people and process around the tools already in the technology arsenal. A mediocre solution that is well implemented generally works better than the latest technology toy without appropriate people and process in its implementation.

25. Treat the information security staff fairly and with the appropriate level of respect. Staff turnover is expensive and time-consuming. Frequent staff turnovers and loss of experienced information security professionals affect the overall performance of the team.

26. An easy and inexpensive way to reduce security costs is to make sure that individuals only have the access rights and

privileges that they need for their current position. On average, most individuals receive 35% more access than required to perform their duties.[4] By just removing the unnecessary access, security could be increased by the same percentage with little additional effort.

27. Work with the RIM staff to remove any redundant or obsolete files from organizational systems. Extra or unnecessary files create additional risks and costs to protect them from unauthorized users.

28. Do a security review of your organization for any potential porosity in the organization's security perimeter. Perimeter porosity exposes more attack surface, such as wireless networks, mobile devices, and Internet-facing applications, which cyber criminals can use as attack vectors. Invest your team's resources in these areas as a priority.

29. Learn from the misfortune of others. Review recent cyber breaches for their possible causes and ask whether a similar breach could have occurred in your organization just as easily. Then take steps to mitigate the possibility of a similar attack in the future.

30. Do not be an island. Take the time to attend functions and get to know your information security peers in other organizations. This is a valuable use of your time. Humans learn by sharing knowledge.

Endnotes

1. *You Can't Go Home Again* is the title of a novel by Thomas Wolfe, published in 1940.
2. The Peter Principle is a theory created by the late Dr. Laurence J. Peter in the 1960s and described in his book of the same name. Simply stated, it espouses that in a hierarchically structured organization, individuals tend to be promoted up to their level of incompetence, or as Dr. Peter went on to explain in simpler terms, "The cream rises until it sours."
3. Assumes that the data has no legal obligation for continued retention, such as being subject to a legal hold.
4. Eric Cole and Sandra Ring, *Insider Threat: Protecting the Enterprise from Sabotage, Spying and Theft* (Boston: Syngress, 2006).

12

THE HYBRID (FRUGAL) CISO

**Traits for Evolving, Enabling, and Transforming
Information Security Organizations**

The frugal chief information security officer (CISO) is distinguished by possessing proficiency across business, technical, and financial domains, while exhibiting agility and flexibility in his or her decision-making capabilities. The frugal CISO embodies the concept of the *hybrid professional*. In 2007, Diane Morello, vice president of Gartner and a Gartner Fellow, described the concept of the hybrid professional: the "intersection of business models and IT requires people with varied experience, professional versatility, multidiscipline knowledge and technology understanding."[1]

Frugal CISOs possess a diverse set of qualities and is adaptable in choosing to utilize them depending upon the specific circumstances in which they are operating. Being able to adapt to a variety of environments and circumstances is fundamental to information security that is dynamic and constantly under pressure to securely manage new technical innovations.

Not Afraid *Not* to be the Smartest Person in the Room

Some CISOs, or managers in general, are not comfortable with hiring staff that is smarter, more talented, or better educated than them. There may be a number of reasons for this. Some managers may worry that hiring talented staff may overshadow them or be difficult to manage.

Another common issue centers on insecurity or lack of confidence. Some executives, while they appear outwardly confident, suffer from a degree of the *Impostor Syndrome* or *Imposter Phenomenon*. This psychological syndrome is characterized by a belief that not all of an individual's success comes from their actual ability, but because of luck or fooling others.[3] This condition occurs with some extremely successful professionals that outwardly appear extremely confident.

The frugal CISO seeks out great talent. That means individuals who may be smarter, more educated, or more talented than themselves.

Starbucks CEO Howard Schultz considers this as a key characteristic of his personal achievements and the phenomenal success of Starbucks by saying, "Early on I realized that I had to hire people smarter and more qualified than I was in a number of different fields, and I had to let go of a lot of decision making. I can't tell you how hard that is. But if you've imprinted your values on the people around you, you can dare to trust them to make the right moves."

The frugal CISO seeks to hire the best possible staff as a key element of strengthening the organization's secure posture.

Open to the Ideas of Others

The frugal CISO needs to be open to the ideas of others. It is in perspectives and ideas of other people that we often can conceive the solution to a vexing issue. This is the reason the frugal CISO needs to maintain a diverse network of individuals to call upon when facing a difficult issue. This network should be both internal as well as external. Albert Einstein said, "The significant problems we face cannot be solved at the same level of thinking we were at when we created them."[4] The frugal CISO exemplifies the spirit of collaboration by involving both their team and stakeholders in evaluating an issue with the objective of optimizing a solution.

The frugal CISO ensures that team members and other stakeholders feel comfortable expressing their opinions without fear of reprisal or ridicule.

Flexible and Proficient across a Variety of Domains

It is impossible for the frugal CISO to be equally proficient in all areas. And even if this were possible, the time and resources required for maintaining a high level of competency across multiple domains would be neither cost nor time efficient. However, a basic working knowledge can be acquired by other spending time with different domain practitioners and online resources.

Sometimes a CISO or other senior-level executive may defer asking a question for fear of looking stupid. This is shortsighted because individuals only learn and gain proficiency by asking questions. Humans learn this way. In addition, when someone asks a question, we know they are interested and often the individual enjoys sharing their knowledge of the subject.

Rolls with the Punches

The frugal CISO is resilient and tenacious when faced with a challenging situation. The hard reality for the frugal CISO is that the question is not if a cyber security incident will occur, but when. The frugal CISO needs to be ready to roll up his or her sleeves and work through the problem until it is both contained and resolved. By taking this approach, the organization can return to normalcy as quickly as possible and limit potential costs resulting from the event.

Rolling with the punches means avoiding the blame game and learning from each misadventure, both big and small, so that efficient and cost-effective control can be put in place to avoid a reoccurrence of a similar event. Resilient individuals are a little like the Energizer Bunny™. They can take criticism, stress, and frustration without breaking down.

Problem Solver

Frugal CISOs are, at their core, proficient problem solvers. The dynamic nature of information security means that the frugal CISO will face new twists on issues that require fresh solutions. Problems are becoming increasingly multifactorial and require solutions that not only resolve the issue, but also optimize their outcomes. The frugal CISO looks at each problem that arises and looks to turn it around to become an opportunity.

The frugal CISO understands that throwing money at a problem does not necessarily resolve it. Often, throwing money at a problem seeks to resolve symptoms of the problem rather than its root cause. The problem solver looks to discover the root cause, because a problem's final resolution requires its resolution, otherwise the problem may resurface with a new variation of the problem.

A good example is *bolt-on security* used on application architectures. Bolt-on security fixes a symptom, code flaws, or bugs. While the immediate problem is fixed, at least temporarily, insecure code may reemerge as a different vulnerability elsewhere. Bolt-on security creates an iterative cycle of identifying and remediating software vulnerability, which is often increasingly expensive because the issues are discovered late in the software development cycle where the unit cost to fix a software flaw is the highest. The frugal CISO might look to identify the root cause of the problem, not as multiple instances of software vulnerability, but instead as a failure to introduce security into the software development life cycle with a solution of implementing a secure development training program for the organization. This solution looks to resolve the problem's root cause, increase the overall security posture of the organization, and reduce development costs by eliminating expensive fixes in production.

Lateral Thinker

A lateral thinker can look beyond the surface of the issue and explores assumptions around to it to determine their validity. By removing constraints, it is often easier to view the problem in a different light.

Lateral thinking[5] is a problem-solving technique that uses creativity and nonlinear thinking to develop innovative strategies that standard deductive reasoning might not achieve. The common business adage for this way of intellectual strategy is "think outside the box." A frugal CISO can literally use thinking to predict possible problems and trends, as well as identify opportunities for the information security team that had not previously been considered.

Business Acumen

The frugal CISO needs considerable business acumen to demonstrate credibility with their colleagues across the organization. Some CISOs may gain experience across a number of business areas prior to assuming the CISO position or acquiring an MBA that offers exposure to a range of business domains during the course of study. Experience in a number of business functions assists the CISO in developing a holistic view of the organization.

It also may offer a perspective on achieving a balance between performance efficiency and security. A strong collateral benefit of acquisition of business knowledge is learning the vernacular of various business areas that enhances the CISO's communication effectiveness with these groups.

Comfortable with Finance and Budgeting

To quote the lyrics of the song "Money" from the musical *Cabaret*,[6] "Money makes the world go round." All security activities and projects require budget. The frugal CISO needs to be well versed in both operational budget management and the budgeting process. The ability to present a solid business justification to a budget committee and receive funding is a critical expertise that distinguishes the frugal CISO.

The frugal CISO is actively involved in exploring financing options and budget strategies to provide funding to allow for maturation and innovation of the information security team. The frugal CISO needs to be conversant in financial terminology to communicate effectively with the chief financial officer (CFO), comptroller, and other financial staff.

If the frugal CISO's background has provided limited exposure to either budgeting or finance, they make it their mission to resolve this limitation by taking classes, reading books, consulting the Internet, or developing a relationship with their peers in finance.

Plays Nice with Others

Frugal CISOs get along with their peers and foster a spirit of cooperation. On occasion, some CISOs may view their role as Czars of Security and may use intimidation or bullying tactics to achieve their objectives. My personal yardstick for determining when an individual's bad behaviors have gone too far is when even "nice people" dislike them or avoid them. Often, the behaviors may take on an air of corporate bullying. Some CISOs mistakenly view these types of behaviors as being tough. The reality is that it repels business leaders from reaching out to information security.

A frugal CISO makes a concerted effort to reach out to business and technical leaders to gain their buy-in and involvement in security initiatives. They seek out opportunities to build bonds. They are nice to everyone, regardless of their place on the organization chart.

This strategy pays substantial dividends on investment. I started out with a career in technical sales. One of the most successful account managers always had the various consultants check in with all the stakeholders at every level on projects when they visited a site. She believed it creates ownership and has an important element in a project's outcome. The frugal CISO looks to build ownership at every opportunity. The frugal CISO does not encourage factions and actively discourages attempts to create dissent within the team or overall organization. There is zero tolerance for toxic behaviors by team members.

Realistic

Frugal CISOs have both eyes open when they look at their information security team objectively. They try to see the security team from two perspectives. First, the frugal CISO needs to gain an internal view of the inner workings of the team in terms of both its strengths and challenges. Often, there is a kind of *blind spot* that some leaders develop in respect to the effectiveness of their team or specific team members. A blind spot may originate from feelings of team loyalty or a wish to remain ignorant of issues. A CISO with a blind spot is doing a disservice to the team because it prevents them from identifying areas for improvement and opportunities for team maturation.

The frugal CISO practices "trust but verify"[7] when it comes to team practices. It is important to have backup metrics or other forms of verification to support compliance with both internal and external requirements. The frugal CISO wants to know how the rest of the organization perceives the information security team and its activities, such as:

- What is the general feeling regarding the information security team, such as helpful, supportive, or dislike?
- What experiences have departments had in their interactions with the information security team?

- What would other departments like to change about the information security team?

The frugal CISO seeks out a diversity of opinions and viewpoints to develop a realistic picture of the team and its actions. The objective is to identify opportunities for improvements in the functioning of the team, reinforcing strengths, and discontinuing negative behaviors.

Outreach

Security shouldn't be conducted in a silo. All IT staff—and employees—need to understand how important security is and how the decisions they make on a daily basis affect the organization's security. Whether it involves secure technical implementations or talking to users about a new security practice, the decisions that IT departments make have an effect on the company. Security is a serious issue and we all need to be vigilant. A positive attitude and proactive approach are just two ways to keep security at the forefront of everyone's daily activities.

One of the key frugal CISO traits is the drive toward promoting inclusiveness by going outside the traditional boundaries and communicating security threats in a manner that is clear to all business stakeholders. This means the strength to address any potential conflicts and offer resolutions guided by business requirements.

Proactive Agent of Change

I first came across the term *proactive agent of change* in a textbook while completing a graduate degree in information management systems. It struck a chord and always remained with me as a behavior to pursue. The concept of a proactive agent of change transcends any profession. It involves the willingness to make a paradigm shift. A paradigm is a shared set of assumptions and constraints an individual or organization must stay within to succeed.

A *paradigm shift* is a radical modification from one way of thinking to another. A paradigm shift is a key element of transformation and innovation. However, it does not just happen by itself, but must be driven by proactive agents of change. An example of some recent paradigm shifts are the move from enterprise-owned data centers to cloud computing and from corporate-owned or corporate-controlled devices to BYOD (bring your own device).

The frugal CISO needs to both deal with external paradigm shifts that influence information security and initiate internal paradigm shifts to move their organizations forward. Initiating a paradigm shift is not for the weak or faint of heart.

The frugal CISO needs to have the courage to ask the question "why" when others will not, and be prepared to take appropriate action when necessary. The proactive agent of change will generally encounter resistance because change is always painful for those involved. Some organizational cultures are particularly resistant to change. However, without change, there can be no growth.

Often, the most difficult group for the frugal CISO to attempt to transform is the information security team itself. This is especially the case with teams that may have isolated themselves from the rest of the organization and developed a tendency toward *groupthink*. In groupthink, a team strives to avoid conflict at any cost and avoids any critical evaluation of its own ideas or alternate course of actions. The consequence of groupthink is stagnation and isolation from external influencers.

Even when the frugal CISO can initiate innovations, some members of the team may attempt to undo their efforts because they believe the old way is better. Often, the underlying agenda of these individuals has more to do with maintaining their own power within the team. In order to sustain the changes, the frugal CISO must not allow backsliding to occur because even relatively small concessions can signal a lack of commitment on their part. Lasting change requires vigilance and nurturing to survive and flourish.

Strong Leader

Leadership requires the ability to inspire individuals to accomplish goals. The frugal CISO requires strong familiarity with leadership techniques and extraordinary communications skills.

Many frugal CISOs begin their careers in technology-focused positions and may not have early exposure to leadership skills. While some individuals are often referred to as *born leaders*, leadership skills can be acquired like any other expertise. Many great leaders are made rather than born. These leaders are products of their creation and effort rather than some genetic traits and become stronger leaders because of the process required to get there. There is a Chinese proverb, "The toughest steel is forged in the hottest fire," which describes this phenomenon.

The appropriate leadership style is contextual in nature and must take into consideration the leader, organizational maturity, required tasks, and other situational factors. Good leaders are flexible and proficient in the use of situational leadership that applies the appropriate leadership style depending on the context in which it is practiced. They *lead from the front*[8] with the appropriate style for the situation and groups involved.

Accepts Shades of Gray

The frugal CISO realizes that information security is both an art and a science. It is impossible to separate security risks from business and people issues. This means that the solutions may not be black or white in their nature, but fall within a gray area. This might be difficult for some technical professionals to accept. Accepting ambiguity is critical for the frugal CISO because security needs to accommodate people and process as critical components.

The frugal CISO needs to balance security requirements against business needs. Sometimes the frugal CISO needs to sacrifice some security for business realities. Often, it is this ability to accept that many security decisions will fall within the *gray zone*. The gray zone is the best solution possible based upon the constraints of the situation. This requires a pragmatic and balanced perspective on security, for example, not requiring expensive and performance-sapping controls in lower risk areas. CISOs and information security professionals who cannot accept ambiguity in security solutions will find themselves pushed into obsolescence.

Excellent Manager

Many managers fail, not because they do not have business or do not interact effectively with executive management, but they are not good managers of their own staff. Some senior managers develop a type of myopia when it comes to dealing with members of their team.

They may fail to recognize the impact that their behaviors have on their team and the consequences that this might potentially create on their own career aspirations. Senior levels of management often get to their lofty level because they maintain a sensitivity to what is going on at all levels of the organization. It is especially critical that the frugal CISO treat not only those above them, but those below them on the organization hierarchy, with dignity and the appropriate level of respect.

Howard Schultz, CEO of Starbucks, stated in an interview, "Our mission statement about treating people with respect and dignity is not just words but a creed we live by every day."

Not treating staff well can derail a career and create financial impact on the organization. Unhappy staff tends to leave and are generally less productive. A staff member's negative attitude may affect how they interact with others, both internal and external to the organization.

These consequences have negative financial impact on the information security team. They also may not go unnoticed by those above them. My personal take on an ancient Chinese proverb is that *the manager rots from the neck down.*[9] Usually, this situation may go on for a long time until some trigger unleashes suppressed problems.

Being an excellent manager is critical to having an efficient and effective information security team. The frugal CISO is always on the lookout for potential staff issues and takes action to resolve them immediately. The frugal CISO is vigilant in spotting potential red flags of staff problems:

- Lack of communication between managers and their staff
- Formation of cliques or factions in the team
- Hushed conversations
- Increased staff turnover and absences

Most problems can be resolved if they are acted upon quickly and decisively. The frugal CISO's key to excellence in management centers around open communications.

Bridge Builder

The frugal CISO looks to move away from information security being the Department of "No" with a penchant for answering queries with *not* and *prohibited*. A paradigm shift has occurred over the five years that requires information security to become consumer and business friendly. Examples of paradigm shifts include BYOD programs and the acceptance of social media at the enterprise level. The frugal CISO will rebrand information security as a business enabler that manages risks to allow organizations to innovate.

This means constructing bridges both internally and externally. Effective, open communication channels will yield a secure environment and the attainment of the organization's mission.

Strong Ethical Core

Unfortunately, over the last two decades, the business environment has undergone substantial turmoil created by ethical failures. One only has to look at the top news stories of the last decade to see a lack of ethics, such as the Madoff Ponzi scheme and continuing insider trading scandals. The ensuing fallout created mistrust of our financial markets, significant losses of capital, and a burden of compliance regulations.

In a world where taking a shortcut to wealth and success may be appealing, the frugal CISO must embody ethics values. This is especially important given his or her role as a protector of the security posture of the organization. If the frugal CISO appeared to be susceptible to compromise, it is likely that all information security would become suspect.

This means the frugal CISO needs to observe the letter and spirit of any ethics policy or code of the organization. If the CISO feels free to flex the ethics rules, then other members of the information security team might do likewise. Ethical conduct is the core of the frugal CISO role, whether dealing with vendors, regulatory agencies, internal compliance groups, or peers. The frugal CISO needs to hold his or her team to the same standard of ethical conduct, both in their business dealings and in behaviors related to the workplace.

Less than ethical conduct on the part of anyone in the organization can result in expensive legal actions and fines. It is also crucial that the frugal CISO set the *tone from the top* in holding others accountable for observing the organization's ethics policy or ethical code of conduct.

The Frugal CISO 2.0: Critical Success Factors

There is no ideal frugal CISO. It is a combination of skills, experience, attitudes, and personality traits. It is the individual that is the "right fit" for a specific organization environment at a certain time. However, two key success factors stand out above all others in what will define both the current and next generation of frugal CISO—the desire to continually renew skills and embrace changes. Without these traits, the frugal CISO or any individual security practitioner will limit future career options and success.

One of my brother's favorite sayings is "one year of experience repeated twenty times" to describe a syndrome where an individual fails to evolve along with technological and societal transformations. The frugal CISO needs to be ready to manage the security of the *next big thing* and what will eventually replace that innovation. The frugal CISO needs to be able to navigate the cyclic variations in budget that result from economic highs and lows.

The frugal CISO redefines the problem to make it an opportunity for success. The frugal CISO has the courage to work toward innovation by erasing past practices and restarting the search for security solutions without past assumptions. The frugal CISO has the courage to reject long-held beliefs and forge a cost-effective path toward a strong security posture.

Endnotes

1. "Gartner Warns of a Looming IT Talent Shortage," Press Release, Gartner, February 7, 2008. http://www.gartner.com/it/page.jsp?id=600009.
2. A twist on the title of the 2005 documentary film *Enron: The Smartest Guys in the Room*, based on the best-selling 2003 book of the same name by Bethany McLean and Peter Elkind.
3. Pauline Rose Clance, "Impostor Phenomenon," http://paulineroseclance.com/impostor_phenomenon.html.
4. Albert Einstein Site Online, http://www.alberteinsteinsite.com/quotes/.
5. The term *lateral thinking* was coined by Edward de Bono in 1967.
6. *Cabaret* is a musical set in Berlin in 1931. It was first produced on Broadway in 1966 and was made into a film in 1972.
7. President Reagan's favorite Russian saying was *"doveryai, no proveryai"* which translates to "trust, but verify."
8. Leadership style first associated with General George Patton.
9. The actual Chinese proverb is "The fish rots from the head down."

13

FRUGALITY AS A CONTINUING STRATEGY FOR INFORMATION SECURITY MANAGEMENT

Frugality and the Future

Unfortunately, economies will likely continue to trend in boom and bust cycles. There is nothing that can be done to prevent this. However, we can chose not to mirror economic cycles in our fiscal strategy. We all love a budget flush with cash, but this situation rarely lasts more than a few years at best as cycles of bubbles and recessions in the economy repeat, and then dread the fallout of severe budget reductions. The Great Recession starting in 2007 has also taught us that down cycles in the economy can last for years rather than bouncing back quickly once signs of economic recovery appear on the horizon. Businesses are also less likely to respond quickly to improving economic conditions in terms of both increased budgets and hiring.

Extreme budgetary shifts can affect both the effectiveness and motivation of the team in the long term. We should approach the information security budgeting by looking at the cost of providing essential services first and then plan for adding additional functionality to support one of six objectives:

- Achieve compliance with emerging external or internal requirements
- Support controls for emerging threats in the risk landscape
- Update, extend, or enhance information security to grow with business plans (alignment)
- Invest in training to expand value of staff
- Fund initiatives designed to evolve the overall maturity level of the information security organization
- Resolve open audit issues

Achieve Compliance with Emerging External or Internal Requirements

When the information security team has some additional funds available in its budget, it could represent an opportune time to spend the necessary funds to achieve compliance with known compliance requirements coming down the road. Often, the regulatory requirements have a lag between the announcement of compliance guidelines and the mandatory implementation date. This time lag may stretch from months to years. Typically, an organization may delay beginning the implementation until close to the mandatory compliance date. However, if budget is available, it might be possible to implement the requirements early. This offers double benefits. The organization gets extra time to work the kinks out of the compliance mandates. It may allow for a slower and more cost-efficient implementation, such as having members of the information security team perform some of the tasks versus using outside contract staff. The overall ROSI (return on security investment) may increase because the improvement in the security posture achieved by implementing new security measures is available earlier.

In addition, full compliance with internal policies and procedures might be possible in situations where full compliance of all policies depends on further investments in information security technologies. Some organizations may issue aspirational security policies in order to create reach goals for the organization. Aspirational policy items may not be attainable by the organization at the current time. The issue that may make policy aspirational may involve cost of implementation. For example, implementing full disk encryption across the enterprise may be aspirational initially, but additional budget availability may make it possible to achieve compliance and increase the organization's security posture.

Support Controls for Emerging Threats in the Risk Landscape

The one constant about information security and technology is that it remains in a constant state of flux. Often, the experienced frugal chief information security officer (CISO) can see the challenges with emerging technologies and new categories of threats coming down the road before they become visible on many professionals' radars. This provides the frugal CISO and his or her team with the luxury of ample lead time to manage new technology and risks to take action before issues arise. Many security costs involve the need to remediate technologies implemented without protective controls. It is often more expensive to add security protection after the fact than to implement the same control from the start. A similar situation occurs with emerging risks. Remediating security risk is frequently more costly than putting controls in place earlier.

Update, Extend, or Enhance Information Security
to Grow with Business Plans (Alignment)

Information security needs to remain in lockstep with business strategies. The frugal CISO stays current on business strategies and initiatives in order to anticipate the information security needs of the organization. The frugal CISO seeks to get ahead of the technology and business curves. For example, if the frugal CISO detects a strong interest in the business toward outsourcing noncore functions to cloud vendors, the information security team might elect to beef up the vendor risk review function to include a specific type of review geared toward cloud vendors or similar types of outsourcers. The frugal CISO needs to demonstrate a proactive instead of a reactive attitude.

Invest in Training to Expand the Value of Staff

The only investment that an organization can make that does not depreciate with time is in its human capital. Often, when budget reductions occur, the first place that managers look to cut is expenditures in staff and training. Training can be perceived as a boondoggle[1] that often seems to focus on expensive conferences. Training is necessary to maintain staff proficiencies.

If the information security staff lacks the skills or experience to perform a task, often it may become necessary to hire contract staff or an external firm to perform the functions, which can increase costs. Training increases the motivation of the individual team members. Professionals like to acquire new proficiencies because it increases their sense of self-esteem and efficacy. It builds loyalty to the organization and its leaders.

While it is true that some team members will seek out and pay for their own training, many will not or cannot do this. In addition, team members who are solely responsible for their own professional development and its associates might be more likely to jump ship for another employer, if the opportunity arises.

Training offers other benefits, such as preparing for succession planning by ensuring that an appropriately trained staff member is available to move into a position if another staff member leaves or receives a promotion.

Not all training needs to be costly or involve travel expenses. Many local chapters of many information security organizations, such as Information Systems Audit Control Association (ISACA), Information Systems Security Association (ISSA), or Internet Systems Consortium (ISC)[2] offer free or inexpensive training within driving distance of many security practitioners. There are an increasing number of Internet-based classes and webinars available. Another option is to encourage staff to utilize any tuition reimbursement options that the organization might have available.

A low-cost option is to have team members provide training classes to their peers. For example, in one organization a senior information security practitioner led an exam preparation review for the Certified Information Systems Auditor (CISA) and Certified Information Systems Security Professional (CISSP). Team members could also offer "brown bag" sessions in their areas of expertise. Consider building a lending library of books and self-study courses that all team members could use, inviting speakers to address the information security team, and putting together an internal training event in which different team members offer presentations.

When sufficient budget is available, it is important to begin offering training opportunities to all team members, to some degree, based upon their individual plans, positions, and upcoming assignments. The budget should include a mixture of both more expensive and inexpensive training options. It is preferable to offer each team some type of paid training, whenever possible, in the budget. It may be more budget-friendly to offer an on-site training class when there is sufficient interest among a number of team members.

Fund Initiatives Designed to Evolve the Overall Maturity Level
of the Information Security Organization

Organizations need to continue to evolve in order to thrive. If your information security team still has some distance to go in achieving its optimal maturity level, any potential slack in the budget might be put to effective use in moving the team along to the next stage. As part of the process of assessing the information security team's current maturation level, the steps necessary to progress to the next stage need to be determined. These steps should include both short- and long-term activities to address identified gaps in a cost-effective way. Most efforts to advance the maturity of the team involve the Golden Triangle (people, process, and technology).

Often reaching the next stage of maturation involves potentially extending some additional security services to the organization. For example, the information security team might consider bringing currently outsourced services, such as digital forensics or vendor risk assessments, in-house if there is enough demand for them by the organization. The frugal CISO should only seek to broaden services when it will contribute to the overall value and effectiveness of the information security team to their specific organization. Other items that might prove effective in driving the maturation of the information security function within an organization include:

1. Phasing in use of advanced cyber security tools, such as intrusion detection/prevention systems
2. Undergoing security accreditation, such ISO 27001
3. Providing advanced technical skills training to staff

Resolve Open Audit Issues

Many organizations may have open audit issues that remain after the remediation of higher-priority audit concerns. These items might fall under the category of residual risk or low-priority risks that are included on an audit report. Usually, these items may remain unresolved due to costs involved in their remediation. These items may continue to be included in subsequent audit reports on an annual basis.

Some audit items may increase in priority over time because of changes in the threat landscape or modifications to business strategies.

On occasion, auditors may increase the item's risk severity to force a resolution. During more generous budget cycles, there is often an opportunity to finally resolve these open audit issues. It is important to justify the remediation of open audit items by tying them into other business/security initiatives or based upon the emerging/current threat landscape. Many security breaches have originated from unresolved audit findings whose realization resulted in significant consequences and remediation costs.

Managing the Budget Merry-Go-Round

Depending upon the available funding for a specific budget cycle, not all of these five objectives may receive support. However, they should exist on a *wish list* for when financial support becomes available. While most of us have heard, at some point in our career, that we should treat budget funds as if they were our own money, this sage advice is sometimes ignored during a generous budget cycle.

Spending tends to expand to consume the funds available. If other groups spend lavishly on nonessential items, we might feel compelled to follow suit to motivate our teams.

However, the flip side of the scenario can get ugly when budgets are reduced. Rather than spending extra funds on nice-to-have items, invest in areas such as training, security tool upgrades, or risk assessments that will provide lasting value and assist in maintaining a strong security posture during restrictive budgeting cycles.

Be Prepared for Every Budget Eventuality

Most of us are familiar with Aesop's fable, "The Ant and the Grasshopper." The Ant works away all summer storing food for the winter and the Grasshopper plays away because he does not believe that the salad days will end. In the winter, the Ant has food, while the Grasshopper dies from starvation. The moral of the story is, "It is best to prepare for the days of necessity."

The frugal CISO manages budgetary resources so that expenditures during strong economic cycles continue to pay benefits during leaner times and maintains continuity in security posture. A collateral benefit of this approach is that it avoids the creation of excessive stress and frustration of information security staff attempting to maintain the security program with inadequate resources and tools.

Endnotes

1. A *boondoggle* is an unnecessary or wasteful use of money.
2. Internet Systems Consortium (ISC) is a nonprofit dedicated to developing and maintaining production quality open source reference implementations of core Internet Protocols, www.isc.org/. (Last accessed 4/7/2014.)

Index

A

Absenteeism, 104
Acceptable use policies, 197–198
Access audits, 34
Acknowledgments of ratification, 203
Additional funds, requests for,
        291–293
AICPA. *See* American Institute of
        Certified Public Accounts
AIIM. *See* Association for
        Information and Image
        Management
Akamai Technologies, 102
Alcohol, self-medicating with, 104
Alignment, 19, 22, 25, 244, 270–271,
        274, 305, 323, 325
American Institute of Certified
        Public Accounts, 288
Analysis paralysis, 14, 88, 101, 248
Another organization, information
        security policy of, 198–199
Antimalware, 11, 97, 152, 154, 184,
        237, 243, 262, 268, 276,
        279, 295

Anxiety about unknown, 88
API tools. *See* Application
        programming interface
Application complexity, 41–43
Application Detail Template, 41
Application inventory, 40–41
*Application Inventory Summary
        Template*, 41
Application portfolio, 39–41
Application programming interface
        tools, 59
Application Risk Assessment
        Questionnaire, 147–149
Applications
    complexity, 41–43
    hacking, 44
    information classification scheme,
        47–48
    information protection
        classification, 44–45
    inventory, 40–41
    legacy third-party, 50–53
    policy management, 216–218
    portfolio, 39–41
    risk levels, 48–49